The Crux of Theology

The Crux of Theology

Luther's Teachings and Our Work for Freedom, Justice, and Peace

Edited by

Allen G. Jorgenson
Kristen E. Kvam

LEXINGTON BOOKS/FORTRESS ACADEMIC
Lanham • Boulder • New York • London

Published by Lexington Books/Fortress Academic

Lexington Books is an imprint of The Rowman & Littlefield Publishing Group, Inc.
4501 Forbes Boulevard, Suite 200, Lanham, Maryland 20706
www.rowman.com
86-90 Paul Street, London EC2A 4NE, United Kingdom

British Library Cataloguing in Publication Information Available

Library of Congress Cataloging-in-Publication Data

Names: Kvam, Kristen E., editor. | Jorgenson, Allen G., editor.
Title: The Crux of theology : Luther's teachings and our work for freedom, justice, and
    peace / edited by Allen G. Jorgenson and Kristen E. Kvam.
Description: Lanham : Lexington Books/Fortress Academic, [2022] | Includes index. |
    Summary: "The Crux of Theology puts Luther's teachings concerning the cross in
    dialogue with the preamble of the United Declaration's Declaration of Human Rights,
    which advances a vision of the common good wherein freedom, justice and peace are
    enjoyed by all. Using diverse voices, it reframes theological loci and raises critical
    contextual questions"—Provided by publisher.
Identifiers: LCCN 2022010173 (print) | LCCN 2022010174 (ebook) |
    ISBN 9781978712515 (cloth) | ISBN 9781978712539 (paper) | ISBN
    9781978712522 (epub)
Subjects: LCSH: Luther, Martin, 1483–1546. | Theology of the cross. | United Nations.
    General Assembly. Universal Declaration of Human Rights. | Human rights—
    Religious aspects—Christianity.
Classification: LCC BR333.5.C72 C78 2022 (print) | LCC BR333.5.C72 (ebook) | DDC
    230/.41—dc23/eng/20220316
LC record available at https://lccn.loc.gov/2022010173
LC ebook record available at https://lccn.loc.gov/2022010174

Contents

Introduction

The Crux of the Matter

Kristen E. Kvam

This volume's title, *The Crux of Theology*, carries a word play—a double entendre. Those who have studied the theology of Martin Luther may recognize the allusion to Luther's so-called "theology of the cross." This reference to the central place a distinctive theology of the cross holds in Lutheran theologies, as will be discussed below, is fully intended. Yet the title holds another meaning when seen from the vantage point of a common use of the term "crux" in such phrases as "the crux of the matter." In such uses, "crux" points to what is crucial when exploring an unresolved question or even a puzzle. In this sense, the title can be seen as raising significant questions about Christian theology. For example, to what extent do the work and witness of theology remain crucial in the contemporary world? Further, if Christian theology has a crucial place, what convictions, topics, and teachings are central to its work and witness?

The essays in this volume take up both senses of "crux." The juxtaposition of two anniversaries formed the occasion for the work that lies behind this volume. The seventieth anniversary of the Declaration of Human Rights by the United Nations aligned with the five hundredth anniversary of the 1518 Heidelberg Disputation in 2018. The overlap of these two significant events inspired a call for papers that would explore ways these two occasions could speak to one another. Most of the essays in this volume grow out of presentations at a conference for the program unit Martin Luther and Global Lutheran Traditions, a program unit of the American Academy of Religion, a professional guild for professors of religious studies.[1]

The Universal Declaration of Human Rights (UDHR) has served as the most authoritative and most global statement of the rights to which all human persons are entitled.[2] While the Charter of the United Nations mentioned "human rights" several times, the Charter did not dwell on what such rights were. It was the task of the UDHR to enumerate them. In so doing, the UDHR was the first international document designed and developed to specify and describe the features of rights belonging to each and all human persons. The Declaration begins with a Preamble whose first point asserts that "foundation of freedom, justice, and peace in the world" is grounded in the "recognition of the inherent dignity and of the equal and inalienable rights of all members of the human family."[3] Thirty Articles follow, beginning with Article 1's assertion: "All human beings are born free and equal in dignity and rights. They are endowed with reason and conscience and should act towards one another in a spirit of brotherhood."[4] In the thirty Articles, UDHR articulates positive rights that should be granted to each human person as well as negative rights in terms of ways human persons ought not be viewed or treated. It thereby creates ways for understanding and promoting human rights around the globe.

The genesis of the Heidelberg Disputation contrasts sharply with the origins of the UDHR.[5] Rather than thirty Articles developed by persons from around the world collaborating in groups, the Heidelberg Disputation consists of 40 Theses written by one Augustinian monk, Martin Luther. Rather than the international community, the initial audience of Luther's Theses was a regional gathering of German Augustinians in Heidelberg, Germany (and hence the name of the document) in April of 1518. Six months earlier, in October of 1517, Luther had written and distributed his Ninety-Five Theses (or "Disputation on the Power and Efficacy of Indulgences"), thereby igniting theological, academic, and ecclesial firestorms that may have started in universities and towns but eventually spread across Western Christendom.[6] Luther was asked to help his confreres and others understand the fires that had started at the University of Wittenberg by writing theses that demonstrated new ways of understanding such Christian teachings as grace, sin, and free will.

Luther's particular "theology of the cross" was a central feature of his new approach to theology and its understanding of God's grace. Through the theses of the Heidelberg Disputation, Luther explained his theological stance by points that alternate between negation and affirmation. Thesis 21 contains both moves within it: "A theologian of glory calls evil good and good evil. A theologian of the cross calls a thing what it actually is."[7] What Luther intended by this sharp contrast was set forth in the surrounding theses. They show Luther's stringent criticisms of Christian theologies that undermine God's grace by allowing room for human efforts to initiate or contribute to right relationships between God and human beings. They also show that Luther's view of the theology of the cross was not only about teachings concerning atonement, justification, and salvation. Instead, Luther contended that a theology of the cross encompasses understanding God's self-revelation in ways that align with the pain and scandal of the cross. As Luther wrote in Thesis 20: "The person deserves to be called a theologian, however, who understands the visible and the 'backside' of God [Exod. 33:23] seen through suffering and the cross." Luther thereby redirected attention from perceiving God's character and activity through human understanding and the ways of the world to God's revelation of God's character through ways that human understanding might deem to be beneath or even contrary to divine ways of acting and being. On the basis of this redirection, Luther scholar Robert Kolb has asserted that the Heidelberg Disputation constitutes "a paradigm shift within Western Christianity in the understanding of God's revelation of [God's] self, God's way of dealing with evil, and what it means to be human."[8]

The essays in this volume set features Luther's theology of the cross into conversation with the Universal Declaration of Human Rights' attention to the necessity of recognizing human rights as the path to a world marked by greater "freedom, justice, and peace." Because the essays engage in such conversations, they offer exemplary contributions to the field of Constructive Christian Theology. The Workgroup on Constructive Theology has described the hallmarks of their particular approach to Christian Theology as:

> Theology is a kind of thinking that reflects directly on the meaning of these stories of God on behalf of the world *as it is today*. It is concerned with the many ways that Christians and others have tried to express their faith as they search for better ways to live together on this earth. It is an academic discipline in part, but more importantly, theology is what everyday people do when they try to make sense of the teachings that come from their religious traditions, especially when they try to think through the practical applications of their beliefs.[9]

Some theologians—including those of Lutheran persuasions—may be cautious about the work of constructive theology. It is hoped that the essays in this volume will illuminate how contemporary Lutheran theologians can analyze injustice and advance justice in local and global contexts, with both faithfulness and relevance.

The organization of the volume involves six chapters that analyze facets of social and climate justice with each one proposing resources within the Lutheran tradition that illuminate and reframe the issues. These chapters are set into pairs, and each pair is followed by a responding essay that extends the conversation by forging alliances and exploring areas for further consideration and development. The volume closes with a programmatic concluding chapter which sets the volume within a trajectory of Luther studies and calls for an additional trajectory. Each and all of the essays offer critical and constructive proposals through which theologians who are in conversation with Luther might better advance the crux of theology both in terms of addressing crucial theological themes as well as in terms of demonstrating the significance of Christian theology as a resource for informing thought and shaping action.

In the first pairing of essays, Caryn Riswold argues that Christian claims for religious freedom function regularly as a cover for discriminating against persons who are marginalized because of white privilege. An effective corrective to such discrimination, she contends, requires that claims of religious freedom be contextualized as belonging to the spiritual realm and then further contextualized by attending to the requisite service for those who inhabit privileged positions and identities. A more robust understanding of Luther's theological anthropology and ethic is finally informed by an intersectional understanding of Christian freedom that understands the interlocking nature of systems of oppression and freedom.

In the second essay of this pairing, Mary Elise Lowe offers a constructive proposal for a Lutheran account of conscience that draws Luther's understanding of conscience into conversation with current psychological research and moral thinking. Using the Evangelical Lutheran Church in America's 2009 decision about human sexuality as a test case, Lowe contends that the appeals made to conscience at that time involved preserving space for persons who not only opposed the ordination and marriage of LGBTQIA+ persons but also sought to exclude queer persons from their congregations. Thus, a contemporary appeal to conscience cannot proceed ahistorically—imagining a free, disembodied, rational, autonomous subject. Instead, Lowe argues for the importance of framing conscience and conscience-bound beliefs as constrained and embodied, highlighting ways that such a position resonates with many of Luther's commitments regarding conscience, including his conviction that serving all neighbors has greater importance than protecting private, conscience-bound beliefs of individual persons.

Anthony Bateza responds to the first pair of essays by a careful consideration of the obligations of freedom. He notes that he shares with Riswold and Lowe the concern to address ideas and practices concerning conscience, domination, oppression, and the normative burdens of neighbor love. He, however, works with a different approach to these ideas and actions because "we have different views of what love looks like, what it demands, and who counts as my neighbor." Drawing on Iris Marion Young's distinction between domination and oppression and Elinor Mason's typology on blameworthiness, Bateza calls for greater conceptual clarity into the values and beliefs of one's opponents as well as enhanced articulations of the dynamics and intersections of power.

The second pair of essays continue to investigate human rights and racism. Marit Trelstad approaches this theme by a close examination of Namibian Lutheran contributions to their nation's struggle for freedom from apartheid.

She uses this case study to explore how a contextual and relational awareness in Lutheran theology might advance social responsibility in service of the gospel. She describes how North American and European Lutheran theological categories often served to further the privilege of white Lutherans in Namibia. By contrast, Namibian Lutheran methods that highlighted scriptural authority and a homegrown "biblical theology" ultimately backed the social and political liberation of black Lutherans from apartheid in Namibia. Trelstad argues that this liberative and contextual use of Lutheran categories demonstrate that a responsible Lutheran theology is a nonuniversal process of interrogating Lutheran theological categories from within particular contexts and assessing them according to their effect on persons who are the most vulnerable to harm in that context.

Benjamin Taylor, in the second essay of the second pairing, analyzes ways that both Luther's critique of idolatry and his *theologia crucis* offer powerful analytic tools for exposing contemporary devotion in North America to the idols of greed and whiteness as well as to attend to and examining current ideological systems of domination, be they based on race, class, or gender identity. Taylor's uses these theological tools to examine, recognize, and transform relations of these idols of environmental racism. His constructive move includes pointing out the importance of love and awe toward God's good creation. Taylor uses these theological tools along with tools from critical theories including ideas from Walter Benjamin and Jacques Lacan as well as such critical race theorists as Kalpana Seshadri-Crooks, bell hooks, and George Yancy.

Mary Philip, a.k.a. Joy, responds to the pair of essays by Trelstad and Taylor by widening the aperture in several ways. Noting the importance of their foci on colonialism and racism, Philip asks about idols of Luther and early modern Christianity and also about the current surging of what she terms "pandemic racism." She also turns to other resources from Luther's theology, notably his understanding of Christian freedom and his doctrine of the so-called "two kingdoms." Across her response, Philip exemplifies her alertness to Chimamanda Adichie's warning about "the danger of a single story" by bringing to the page resources from science and biology as well as from India, her homeland. In regard to the former, she calls for a new way to understand being human as *"Spiritulia carnalia."* With regard to the latter, she highlights concepts and practices from the Kama Sutra and the words and teachings of a Dalit woman named Tharamama.

The third set of pairings consist of essays by Robert Overy-Brown and Terra Schwerin Rowe, with a responding essay by Allen G. Jorgenson. Overy-Brown's essay offers an extended examination of human freedom that is attentive to central features of Luther's accounts of human freedom as set forth in The Freedom of a Christian (1520) and The Bondage of the

Will (1525).[10] Overy-Brown then explores ways that Luther's accounts have been read (and even misread) by a number of interpreters including Soren Kierkegaard, Karl Marx, and Immanuel Kant as well as Mark C. Taylor, Juergen Moltmann, John Caputo, and Slavoj Žižek. Along the way, Overy-Brown contends that Luther's account is best understood as endorsing a heteronomous and paradoxical account of human freedom rather than an autonomous and singular one. Overy-Brown urges a return to this more expansive view in order to ground discussions of freedom in everyday life as well as to offer a theological understanding of the importance of human participation in public life.

Terra Schwerin Rowe sets the ground for her constructive work by first exploring historical and conceptual entanglements of the theology of the cross with "the modern extractive imaginary." Taking seriously the co-emergence of modern mining and the Reformation, she thinks theologically about extraction and, conversely, examines extractive impulses of Christian theology. In light of these historical/conceptual entanglements, she highlights how reading sites of extraction as localities where a theology of the cross can be brought to bear proves more complicated and troubled than may be readily apparent. Instead, a "scandalous" theology of the cross—which emerges more as Holy Saturday vigil—is proposed. Such a cross against cross theology attends to ways that sites of human and mineralogical extraction remain traumas that do not stay in the past but continue to haunt the present in the form of environmental racism and socio-environmental injustice.

Allen G. Jorgenson, in his response essay to the third set of paired essays, sets the themes and concerns from these essays into conversation with a close reading of the structure and wording of The Heidelberg Disputation's argument and with themes and voices of Indigenous persons on Turtle Island. Noting that "I do theology on stolen land," Jorgenson urges that Settlers listen to insights offered by Indigenous wisdom, particularly to insights concerning the significance and nature of balance. Jorgenson explores how Luther's theology of creation might inform Luther's theology of the cross to the end that "calling a thing what it is" involves using the lens of suffering and the cross to listen to created things for what they say about God. In our contemporary context, such listening cannot be extricated from the task of challenging the destructive ethic marking the era of the Anthropocene with a more robust understanding of God's love for creation.

Christine Helmer's afterword offers a departing summation and challenge that befits the volume's attention to Luther studies, Christian theology, and the things that make for "freedom, justice, and peace." Describing ways that Luther studies have portrayed relations between theology and politics, Helmer situates the themes addressed by the essays of this volume within this field. She then asks how theologians, who engage universal concerns such as human rights and environmental concerns even while they recognize the distinctive features in these for diverse communities, might employ language particular to theology in service of the task of the church. Further, she urges that a theological privileging of critical reason—with its diagnostic and political aspects—be complemented by a recovery of theology's contemplative dimension. In other words, she asks: how might contemporary progressive Lutheran theology with its focus on the *vita activa* benefit from the *vita contemplativa* in attending to the crux of theology?

The anniversaries that inspired the occasion for the initial presentation of these papers have passed, as anniversaries do. The importance of the issues and topics, however, have not passed; indeed, arguments could be made that the themes and methods as well as the audience and conversation partners that they engage are as crucial and significant for Christian theology now as they were a few years ago. Employing Luther's distinctive *theologia crucis* to name conflicts threatening freedom, justice, and peace, the authors of these essays highlight how these crucial matters are manipulated for the benefit of certain actors and at the cost of others. Luther signaled his own understanding of these matters when, near the conclusion of the 95 Theses, he wrote:

> 92. And thus, away with all those prophets who say to Christ's people, "Peace, peace," and there is no peace!
> 93. May it go well for all those prophets who say to Christ's people, "Cross, cross," and there is no cross![11]

Luther's *theologia crucis* urges theologians to "call a thing what it is," including the recognition that God is hidden in what seems to be opposite to common notions of God being revealed in power and majesty. The "prophets" whose writings constitute this volume examine wide ranging topics related to justice, freedom, and peace; they also engage with wide ranging discussion partners, explore several geographic locales, and employ a variety of theological methods. In so doing, they illumine ways that Reformation themes are misused and misapplied as well as offer constructive proposals for ways Luther's *theologia crucis* can contribute to constructing Christian theologies that are theologically sound and publicly accountable.

NOTES

1. While most of the essays grow out of presentations made to the Martin Luther and Global Lutheran Traditions session at the 2018 Annual Meeting of the American Academy of Religion, two essays grow of presentations made to this AAR program

8 *Kristen E. Kvam*

unit in 2019. The responding essays as well as the afterword are works written for this volume.

2. "Universal Declaration of Human Rights," in *Human Rights: The International Bill of Human Rights* (New York: United Nations, 1988), 4–9.

3. Ibid., 4.

4. Hansa Mehta of India is credited for the wording for Article 1's first sentence, including the change to this wording from "All men are born free and equal." See "Women Who Shaped the Declaration, " United Nations, accessed April 2, 2021, https://www.un.org/sites/un2.un.org/files/women_who_shaped_the_udhr.pdf.

5. Martin Luther, "The Heidelberg Disputation (1520)," in *The Annotated Luther, Volume 1, The Roots of Reform*, ed. Timothy J. Wengert, trans. Harold J. Grimm (Minneapolis, MN: Fortress Press, 2015), 80–88. See also Dennis Bielfeldt's "Introduction" to "The Heidelberg Disputation" on pages 67–80 of TAL 1, and Luther's "Proofs of the Thesis Debated in the Chapter at Heidelberg, May, AD 1518," on pages 88–120 of "The Heidelberg Disputation."

6. Martin Luther, "[The 95 Theses or] Disputation for Clarifying the Power of Indulgences (1517)," in *The Annotated Luther, Volume 1, The Roots of Reform*, ed. and trans. Timothy J. Wengert (Minneapolis, MN: Fortress Press, 2015), 13–46.

7. TAL 1, p. 84. This thesis carries echoes of the theses that conclude "The 95 Theses" including Thesis 92 and Thesis 93. Ibid., 46.

8. Robert Kolb, "Luther on the Theology of the Cross," *Lutheran Quarterly* 16, no.4 (2002): 443–66, as quoted by Dennis Bielfeldt in TAL 1, 67.

9. The Workgroup on Constructive Theology, "Introduction," in *Awake to the Moment: An Introduction to Theology*, ed. Laurel G. Schneider and Stephen G. Ray Jr. (Louisville: Westminster John Knox, 2016), 1.

10. Martin Luther. "The Freedom of a Christian (1520)," in *The Annotated Luther, Volume 1, The Roots of Reform,* ed. Timothy J. Wengert, trans. W.A. Lambert and Harold Grimm (Minneapolis: Fortress, 2015), 467–538. Martin Luther, "The Bondage of the Will (1525)," in *The Annotated Luther, Volume 2 Word and Faith*, ed. Kirsi I. Stjerna, trans. Philip S. Watson, Benjamin Drewery, and Volker Leppin (Minneapolis: Fortress Press, 2015), 153–257.

11. TAL 1, 46.

BIBLIOGRAPHY

Kolb, Robert. "Luther on the Theology of the Cross." *Lutheran Quarterly* 16, no.4 (2002): 443–66.

Luther, Martin. "The Bondage of the Will (1525)." In *The Annotated Luther, Volume 2 Word and Faith*, edited by Kirsi I. Stjerna, translated by Philip S. Watson, Benjamin Drewery, and Volker Leppin, 153–258. Minneapolis, MN: Fortress Press, 2015.

———. "The Freedom of a Christian (1520)." In *The Annotated Luther, Volume 1, The Roots of Reform*, edited by Timothy J. Wengert, translated by W.A. Lambert and Harold Grimm, 467–538. Minneapolis, MN: Fortress, 2015.

———. "The Heidelberg Disputation. " In *The Annotated Luther, Volume 1, The Roots of Reform,* edited by Timothy J. Wengert, translated by Harold J. Grimm, 67–120. Minneapolis, MN: Fortress Press, 2015.

———. "[The 95 Theses or] Disputation for Clarifying the Power of Indulgences (1517)." In *The Annotated Luther, Volume 1, The Roots of Reform*, edited and translated by Timothy J. Wengert, 13–46. Minneapolis, MN: Fortress Press, 2015.

"Universal Declaration of Human Rights." In *Human Rights: The International Bill of Human Rights*. New York: United Nations, 1988.

"Women Who Shaped the Declaration." United Nations. Accessed April 2, 2021. https://www.un.org/sites/un2.un.org/files/women_who_shaped_the_udhr.pdf.

The Workgroup on Constructive Theology. "Introduction." In *Awake to the Moment: An Introduction to Theology*. Edited by Laurel G. Schneider and Stephen G. Ray Jr. Louisville, KY: Westminster John Knox, 2016.

Chapter 1

Already Freed, Christians Should Serve (Cake)

Religious Freedom Claims and Christian Privilege

Caryn D. Riswold

In 1948, the Universal Declaration of Human Rights recognized "the inherent dignity and the equal and inalienable rights of all members of the human family [as] the foundation of freedom, justice and peace."[1] That this statement came on the ash-heap of a world war and the cooling fires of genocide, and in the face of worldwide fracture, makes it both confessional and defiant. It is confessional insofar as it recognizes a global failure to protect freedom and dignity of entire populations of people, and it is defiant insofar as people were searching for common ground on which to stand together as forces worked to pull them even further apart.

Today in the United States, some Christians are using claims of religious freedom to infringe upon the rights and dignity of other members of the human family, pulling a community apart. This twisted use of freedom is showing up in court cases and in the political landscape on issues particularly related to gender and racial justice. After discussing some of these examples, I will suggest that one of the things enabling such claims is white Christian privilege. Naming and confronting this reality is foundational to overcoming its effects.

An effective corrective requires contextualizing claims of religious freedom as belonging to the spiritual realm, as well as doubling down on the requirements of service as essential for those inhabiting privileged positions and identities. Martin Luther's theology is of particular use in this work.

Christians in the United States must stop abusing claims of religious freedom as cover for perpetrating discrimination on marginalized persons. In order to do this, we need a more robust and intersectional understanding of Christian privilege as part of the frayed fabric of this society. This requires understanding the interlocking nature of systems of privilege and oppression. Ultimately, we find corrective in a more robust understanding of a Lutheran theological anthropology.

POLITICAL CONTEXT

Failure to understand Christian privilege has brought about claims by white Christian persons and business owners that their rights are being infringed upon, when in fact they are using the unearned privilege of a culturally dominant religious identity to harm others. Two recent U.S. Supreme Court decisions demonstrate this.

In 2014, the Court ruled in *Burwell v. Hobby Lobby* that "the requirement that the two companies [Hobby Lobby and Conestoga Wood Specialties] provide contraception coverage imposed a substantial burden on their religious liberty."[2] The requirement at issue was a federal mandate that requires contraceptive coverage as part of preventative medical services that are part of employer-provided health insurance. This became law as part of the Patient Protection and Affordable Care Act in 2010. Notable for our discussion of religious freedom here, Justice Ruth Bader Ginsburg indicates in her dissent in the *Hobby Lobby* case that "the court had for the first time extended religious-freedom protections to 'the commercial, profit-making world.'"[3] The owners of Hobby Lobby, the Green family, had effectively cashed in their Christian privilege in order to deny comprehensive healthcare services to their female employees in the name of the business owners' personal religious freedom.

As part of the 2018 Supreme Court case *Masterpiece Cakeshop v. Colorado Civil Rights Commission*, the owner of a Colorado bakery argued that it violated his religious beliefs to make a wedding cake for a gay couple who sought his services. Because Jack Phillips "believes that marriage should be limited to opposite-sex couples, he told [Charlie] Craig and [David] Mullins that he would not design a custom cake for their same-sex wedding celebration."[4] The Supreme Court decision as written by Justice Kennedy focused on the process by which the case had gotten to the country's highest court. Kennedy argued that "the [Colorado] Civil Rights Commission's ruling against the baker, Jack Phillips, had been infected by religious animus. He cited what he said were 'inappropriate and dismissive comments' from one commissioner in saying that the panel had acted inappropriately and that its decision should be overturned."[5] In a concurring opinion, however, Justice Clarence Thomas finds broader protections for Phillips' and similar claims. He argues that "Mr. Phillips's cakes are artistic expression worthy of First Amendment protection, [and] requiring him to endorse marriages at odds with his faith violated his constitutional rights."[6] Thus, significant constitutional grounds are identified by Justice Thomas and others to use the banner of religious freedom in order to deny gay and lesbian couples access to public retail services as they plan to celebrate their marriages. As is the case with Supreme Court decisions, such a ruling could set a precedent for any business owner to deny services to a customer if they identify a religious difference.

These two cases, and other recent events like one involving a county clerk in Kentucky refusing to issue marriage licenses to same-sex couples[7] and another with a pizza restaurant in Indiana publicly stating that they would refuse to cater same-sex weddings under the state's religious freedom law,[8] illuminate what is at stake when privileged persons and institutions fail to recognize the power that they already have, when at the same time they use it to marginalize others. The theme of gender and sexuality runs through these cases, highlighting that it continues to be a flashpoint of political as well as religious conflict among Christians in the twenty-first century.

A significant reason that the Green family, Jack Phillips, Kim Davis in Kentucky, Memories Pizza in Indiana, and others have been able to prevail in their misuses of freedom claims is that they are white Christians in a society defined by Christian privilege. Naming and wrestling with this reality, as well as fully understanding the interlocking nature of systems of privilege and oppression, can help avoid such abuses in the future.

CHRISTIAN PRIVILEGE

Definitions and descriptions of Christian privilege have largely emerged out of multicultural education studies in recent years, while robust engagement with the concept and its implications in theological and religious studies have been later in emerging. In the same way that unpacking the invisible knapsack of white privilege, to use Peggy McIntosh's analogy,[9] has necessarily been the work of white people, shining a light on Christian privilege must become the work of Christian people and scholars of religion. Jacqueline Bussie employs the concept in relationship to religious pluralism and church-related higher education in a recent book, defining Christian privilege this way:

> a (conscious or unconscious) inequitable prioritization and favoring of the needs, perspectives, and education of Christian students to the detriment or marginalization of the needs of those who do not self-identify as Christian.[10]

Whether it's in the context of religion in higher education or the role of religion in politics, connecting the concept of Christian privilege to its real impacts in communal life is increasingly important. Naming it can it have a comprehensive impact on the study and practice of religion and the use of religious freedom claims like those we have seen in the legal and political realms. Using the above definition more broadly, we can see that favoring the needs and perspectives of Christians "to the detriment or marginalization" of those who aren't Christian goes against the supposed purpose of religious freedom in a democratic society.

This phenomenon needs to be named first because privilege "consists of unquestioned assumptions and unasked questions, of things that 'everyone knows' and upon which 'everyone' is presumed to agree."[11] It functions in much the same way whether we are speaking of racial or religious or other forms of privilege: Privilege allows its bearers to not notice it or even believe it exists while simultaneously enjoying its protection and advantages. Referencing McIntosh's work a generation earlier, Robin DiAngelo describes white privilege as "a sociological concept referring to advantages that are taken for granted by whites and that cannot be similarly enjoyed by people of color in the same context (government, community, workplace, schools, etc.)."[12] DiAngelo's book *White Fragility* focuses on unpacking the many reasons why white people are so resistant to talking about whiteness, racism, and their role in the system.

Similar to this resistance to talking about race, one can hear Christian people in the United States insisting that they are the ones being oppressed because of their religion. Vice President Mike Pence made a series of such claims in his speech at Liberty University's 2019 commencement, saying at one point that "Throughout most of American history, it's been pretty easy to call yourself Christian. But things are different now . . . . We live in a time when the freedom of religion is under assault."[13] In an essay in *The Washington Post*, historian John Fea points out that Pence and his audience could benefit from a little historical and global contextualizing of the ways that Christians in places like Syria, Nigeria, and Sri Lanka are actually persecuted by terrorist organizations like Boko Haram. The "assault" that Pence speaks of includes the legal cases detailed above, as well as an episode when his wife was criticized for accepting a position teaching at a Christian school that opposes same-sex marriage. Fea notes that "these challenges pale in comparison with what those who name the name of Jesus are facing worldwide."[14] When it comes to Christians in the United States, Christian privilege is real whether they admit it or not.

Christine Clark points out that "all Christians benefit from Christian privilege regardless of the way they express themselves as Christians in the same way that all White people benefit from White privilege."[15] One of the reasons that it remains hard for its beneficiaries to name Christian privilege, aside from the political motivations behind Pence's message to and from conservative evangelicals in the United States, is captured by Tricia Seifert: "Those within the spiritual norm gain a level of privilege that is often unconscious."[16] The ability to not think about one's race or one's religious identity in various social and political contexts is only one aspect of privilege, though it is a foundational one.

Clark and her co-authors construct a list of examples of Christian privilege that mirror Peggy McIntosh's classic 1989 list of examples of white privilege. They are largely mundane things like the fact that as a Christian, I know that state and federal holidays coincide with my religious calendar, I can safely share my religious holiday greeting with strangers, I can probably talk about my beliefs in public without being accused of spreading propaganda, and I can assume an authority figure will share my religion.[17] A Christian person in the United States can more or less presume these things and many others to be true; while my neighbor who is Muslim, Buddhist, or anything other than Christian cannot. I would add to this list that because of Christian privilege, I can claim that my religious beliefs are under assault when they are not, and I will be believed and defended.

Nelson makes the important point that Christian identity does not always confer privileges that Clark and others name, "unless combined with other identities."[18] In the current political context in the U.S., white racial identity is the blinding and determinative factor in these quests for even more power. The compounded effects of privilege conferred from both whiteness and a certain type of Christian religiosity enables some individuals and families to believe that they are being persecuted and that their freedom is under attack when in fact the inverse is true.

Whiteness may be as determinative as Christianity, if not more so, in these and other cases. The once popular and still lingering doubts about President Barack Obama's Christian faith serves as an illustration of white privilege when paired with commentary by some conservative evangelical Christian religious leaders concerning his 2012 opponent for the presidency, Mitt Romney. Despite the fact that Romney, a leader in the Church of Jesus Christ of Latter-day Saints, was considered "not Christian" by some, he was still the preferred candidate over the black and self-described born-again Christian Obama. Baptist pastor Robert Jeffress described Mormonism as a cult, but said that "Obama embraces nonbiblical principles while Romney embraces biblical principles like the sanctity of life and the sanctity of marriage."[19] Whiteness intersects with Christian identity in this case, seeming to overpower the integrity of other aspects of identity, enabling a person to support a candidate they believe is in a cult rather than one who shares their Christian faith.

In short, whiteness protects some Christians' privilege in this society, while casting suspicion on others. Under the guise of freedom, some white Christians exercise power in order to impose their beliefs on others using the political mechanisms ideally meant to ensure a level playing field and ensure the rights of the minority. This is a twisted use of freedom that produces its exact opposite. It is an invitation to fully explore the intersections of identities as well as construct a better understanding of religious freedom that resists the interlocking and compounding effects of privileged statuses.

SYSTEMS OF PRIVILEGE AND OPPRESSION

This discussion of Christian privilege is already connected with discussions of other systems of domination because they are interlocking and they intersect. We see this not only in the racialization of religion, but also in institutions like religion, law, and media.

Kimberlé Crenshaw, who coined the term intersectionality in 1989, describes this concept as "a lens through which you can see where power comes and collides, where it interlocks and intersects."[20] This emphasis on the source of power and where it collides with other sources is essential. Many individuals have some aspect of their identity from which they can draw power, whether it be their race, gender, religion, physical ability, or other things. For some people, it flows into other aspects of identity from which they also draw power. Christian people who are also white and heterosexual see themselves and their interests supported by the dominant culture, so they believe themselves to be "the norm." However, Christians who are black live with the fear of a white supremacist terror attack like the one perpetrated on Emanuel AME Church in Charleston, South Carolina, in 2015. And women, whose gender may be a structural vulnerability, can trade on whiteness, if they have it, in order to access power. This last example helps explain the historical alliance that allowed white women to gain the right to vote as well as access to the voting booth that was denied to women of color until the 1964 Voting Rights Act.[21] It also sheds light on the fact that the majority of white women in the United States voted for Donald Trump in 2016 even after his history of racism and abuse of women was well-documented and public.[22] Analysis in this case suggests that in addition to race, age and education are significant factors intersecting with gender when it comes to accessing power.

In her description of the "matrix of domination," Patricia Hill Collins points out that "people experience and resist oppression on three levels, the level of personal biography; the group or community level of the cultural context created by race, class, and gender; and the systemic level of social institutions."[23] Not only is a person's identity itself multifaceted and dynamically situated at the intersection of multiple forces, some of which are more determinative at times than others, but the cultural context that informs how we experience and understand ourselves is itself is shaped by systems of power and their streams of influence. Untangling all of this is impossible, so understanding it and having the mental agility to see multiple factors and common denominators of power and domination is critical. When introducing Christian identity into this matrix, we can see how it too functions on these three levels: an individual has her personal experience of the faith, a community level where the cultural context informs what that personal experience means, and a systemic level where religiosity influences social and political institutions. Collins notes that in 1989, bell hooks described the politic of domination as follows:

> The ideological ground that they [oppressions based on race, class, gender, and other axes of identity] share, which is a belief in domination, and a belief in the notions of superior and inferior, which are components of all those systems. For me it's like a house, they share the foundation, but the foundation is the ideological beliefs around which notions of domination are constructed.[24]

In all of these cases, the foundation is power and the ability to exert it over others. Once a person does not have access to power in relation to one aspect of her identity, she may seek out another path by which she can dominate others.

Returning to the specific example of Christian privilege, when we locate it in a house built on the foundation of power, as yet another example of the politics of domination, the error starts to become apparent. The heart of the Christian religion is not about human power and domination; in fact, the complete opposite is arguably true. Throughout the history of the tradition, whenever the religion has become allied with other sources of power (from the Roman Empire to the medieval political church to the all-male and often self-protective Roman Catholic priesthood today), it has needed to be called back from the abuses it produced. And so today, contemporary political players are using their Christian identity as a source of power and domination. The case against this version of Christianity itself, as well as a constructive understanding of theological freedom, comes from Martin Luther.

THEOLOGIANS OF GLORY, THEOLOGIANS OF THE CROSS

In *The Heidelberg Disputation*, Luther argues that "because human beings misused the knowledge of God through works, God wished again to be recognized in suffering"[25] and a theologian of the cross is one who comprehends this. It is precisely because of human misuse of what they do know about God that the divine sees fit to interrupt human wisdom. That we see such conflation of God's power with human ability over many generations and several empires demonstrates that the tendency is a deeply seated human flaw. Luther argued that "a theologian of the cross calls the thing what it actually is,"[26] because he understood that we human beings are uniquely capable of deluding ourselves that things are as we would expect or wish them to be, rather than what they actually are. For him, this meant that the divine appears not where we want or might safely expect. Instead, God is in the places that challenge our assumptions and constructs. In this way, coming to terms with Christian privilege and calling it what it is, even realizing that it exists, challenges one way of being religious with others in the world who may or may not share our particular commitments.

For Luther, it is the scandal of the cross that revealed the paradoxical nature of God. It is the event where we find life in death, birth in blood, freedom in bondage, and divine in human. A theologian of glory fails to recognize the confounding paradox embedded in all of this, and believes himself to be secure in his knowledge of God, to have a triumph of his own will, power over others, goodness in all things, and affirmation from the divine. This person sees the cross as a tool for conquest rather than an invitation to authenticity. By contrast, and more consistent with the biblical narrative for Luther, a theologian of the cross wrestles on the riverbank, questions the appearances of things, weeps in her grief, feeds the hungry, and seeks understanding. She sees the cross as a strike against evil in a world that is unable to withstand the full embodiment of the divine will, and at the same time she sees the cross as the instrument of execution, which is the very embodiment of that evil itself.

Luther also challenges claims to human wisdom when he says "that wisdom which sees the invisible things of God in works as perceived by human beings is completely puffed up, blinded, and hardened."[27] One who is "puffed up, blinded, and hardened" is unable to be surprised by grace and humbled at the cross or the tomb. Such is the danger of a certainty that is rarely warranted in human life. Furthermore, he points out that "the desire for glory is not satisfied by the acquisition of glory, nor is the desire to rule satisfied by power and authority."[28] Glory is like power in that it always needs more and more and more. The remedy, he says, "does not lie in satisfying" the desire, "but in extinguishing it."[29] This is how "without the theology of the cross a person misuses the best in the worst manner."[30] The gospel and a theology of the cross could embody the best of God's work in the world, and yet when it is misused it becomes the worst iteration possible. In this way, the ostensibly Christian political actors of the twenty-first century are theologians of glory who call evil good and good evil: They call oppression an obligation, and service a sin.

If we couple this insight with bell hooks' analysis of the politics of domination, we can see that when power is the foundation rather than a deeper Christian understanding of human community and a theology of the cross, twisted misuse of freedom emerges. Those who call denial of services to others "good" in the name of their Christian freedom fail to understand that freedom in any distinctive way apart from a freedom to dominate. This is because what is being sought is glory, triumph, and certainty, in contrast to service, humility, and incarnational living of even one of the acts of mercy detailed in in Matthew 25. A politic of domination has no room for feeding the hungry, visiting the imprisoned, sheltering the homeless or giving water to the thirsty. This is why a final turn to Luther's paradoxical theological anthropology offers a way to understand and live out religious freedom in a way that is more consistent with the gospel that Christians purport to embody and defend.

THE PARADOX OF CHRISTIAN FREEDOM

Because Luther's understanding of being human was nuanced, his understanding of religious freedom was more sophisticated than current political rhetoric would suggest it can be. We do well to revisit his claims in context of the present religious exemption claims by Christians in a Christian-dominated legal and political system. In short, these people are blinded by their Christian privilege, which allows them to completely invert the meaning of Christian freedom and in fact do evil. They rely solely on the first half of Luther's well-known pair of claims, that "A Christian is lord of all, completely free of everything," forgetting the second, that "A Christian is a servant, completely attentive to the needs of all"[31]

Luther's anthropology must be understood in context of his theological landscape. He routinely speaks of the Christian as existing at the intersection of four relational directions.[32] Primarily, the human exists in relationship with God, *coram Deo*. This means that a person owes their existence and life to God as creator and sustainer. The human also exists in relationship with other people, *coram hominibus*, a key aspect of his claims about freedom. In addition, this relationship among humans takes place in relationship to the world itself, *coram mundo*. This is the physical and cultural context that informs such relations among humans as well as the God-human relationship. Finally, and throughout all of this, a human person exists in relationship with herself, *coram meipso*. There is an interiority to human life in relationship with God and others in the world that provides important room for discussion about spirituality, vocation, and personal character. These four relational elements of human life for Luther contextualize his understanding of freedom as well as the call to serve one's neighbor.

In his 1520 treatise on *The Freedom of a Christian*, Luther explains thoroughly that an individual person has two natures: an inner, spiritual nature, and an outer, bodily nature. Understanding the dimensions and role of each is important.

With regard to the inner spiritual nature of a human being, Luther argued for absolute freedom from having to earn salvation; nothing that a Christian could do, say, buy or become could earn a ticket to heaven. This is because, for him, Christians are already saved by the power of God's grace: "when soul has the word, it is rich and needs nothing else, because the word of God is the word of life, truth, light, peace . . . and every imaginable blessing."[33] Faith is the only thing that can receive this word and confer its benefits upon the human soul, and thus the person is freed from having to obsess over salvific works like saying the right prayer or visiting the proper shrine. "The Christian is free from all things and is over all things,"[34] Luther insists, while pointing out that "this does not establish that Christians possess and exercise some sort of secular power over everything."[35] This qualifying statement about freedom and power is essential and particularly relevant to current debates about the extent of Christians' ability to exercise power in the public and political realm. Freedom in this case is very specific to the inner, spiritual person as concerns her salvation. It is not a sweeping claim about power in relationship to other people or the world.

This necessarily leads to the other essential aspect of being Christian in the world, what Luther refers to as the outer person. As a "servant of all,"[36] or as "attentive to the needs of all,"[37] the Christian is freed to serve his or her neighbor. Freed from having to be concerned with his or her own salvation, he or she could therefore focus on self-control so that the outer person "may obey and be conformed to the inner person and faith."[38] Luther describes extensively the need to discipline the body as the first form of subjection, concerned as he was about controlling desires. He uses the Latin word "*mortificatio*" in this discussion,[39] reflecting a medieval Augustinian view of the body and its sometimes-impediment to Christian spiritual discipline. Also important to him was situating the role of religious activities like fasting and vigils. He didn't seek to eliminate them from religious life and practice; rather, he insisted on their limited role as tools for "suppressing the body's wantonness and desire."[40] Disciplining the body was in service of the soul, rather than action meriting salvation and righteousness.

Subjecting and conforming the body to the soul has an ultimate purpose: It is so that the Christian "can serve others more genuinely and more freely."[41] This is the part of a person's life wherein she interacts with others (*coram hominibus*) in the world (*coram mundo*) through work, community and politics. As Luther said, the Christian must "speak, act, and live with other human beings, just as Christ was 'made in human likeness and found in human form.'"[42] The purpose is to be God in the world with and for other people just as Jesus was. "For this reason, in all of one's works a person should in this context be shaped by and contemplate this thought alone: to serve and benefit others in everything that may be done, having nothing else in view except the need and advantage of the neighbor."[43] Notice how completely contrary to contemporary Christian claims to use religious freedom this statement is. Luther argues that whatever a person does in life, the service and benefit of the neighbor should be her only concern. This is what it means to live out the gospel; this is what it looks like for a Christian to truly understand freedom conferred by the grace of God. She considers nothing "except the need and advantage of the neighbor." Nothing. Especially not her own salvation and righteousness, because that is already taken care of.

This attention to the neighbor and service to others is something the Reformer understood or hoped that Christians would undertake joyfully. Serving one's neighbor is how one lives as a faithful servant of God in the world. Attending to the needs of others entails all the things that we do as members of a community, including paying taxes that support public schools, safe roads and clean drinking water. It means running businesses fairly by following laws regarding hiring, pay, and public access. It includes states providing social services for the most vulnerable among us. It also means enforcing and abiding by laws that protect us from the harmful actions of others, like discrimination on the basis of race, gender, religion and sexual orientation.

CONCLUSION

What we find happening in some forms of twenty-first-century American Christianity, as a consequence of unexamined Christian privilege, is the toxic combination of the tendencies of a theologian of glory, as well as a failure to fully inhabit the call to serve the neighbor. It is grounded in an understanding of freedom as power to do as one wishes and exert oneself over others, rather than an understanding of freedom as a gift already given that empowers a person to put her own self-interests aside for the sake of a neighbor's benefit. It emerges as a result of intersecting privileges that enable distortion of core aspects of the gospel in favor of domination and triumph of human claims to certainty.

As Peggy McIntosh questioned thirty years ago in her pivotal exploration of white privilege: "What will we do with such knowledge? . . . [will we] use any of our arbitrarily awarded power to try to reconstruct power systems on a broader base."[44] I think that we are called to do what Luther understood to be the purpose of Christian freedom: something for someone else. It is thus, and perhaps ironically, a five hundred-year-old set of Christian theological treatises that have a more robust and effective understanding of Christian freedom than do twenty-first-century political actors. It's more complicated and arguably more difficult, evidence that it is perhaps exactly what is needed.

In 1948, there was a global effort to recognize that "the inherent dignity and . . . equal and inalienable rights of all members of the human family [is] the foundation of freedom, justice and peace." This can be heard as an international geopolitical riff on a theological anthropology animated by grace, where humans are empowered to work less for their own certain glory and more for the ever-changing needs of others. They are called to use their arbitrarily awarded power to expand its benefits to others and reject the unequal distribution of its advantages.

Will we fall back on our tendencies to glory and certainty? Will we actually serve our neighbors, especially when to do so challenges our assumptions? Will we give up social power conferred by interlocking aspects of our human existence? Because this is what is required, and this is what is in fact possible. Christians are already freed, and in the United States they don't need to go to the U.S. Supreme Court to prove it.

NOTES

1. "Universal Declaration of Human Rights," United Nations, 1948, accessed January 20, 2021, https://www.un.org/en/universal-declaration-human-rights/.

2. Adam Liptak, "Supreme Court Rejects Contraceptives Mandate for Some Corporations," *The New York Times*, June 30, 2014, accessed January 20, 2021, https://www.nytimes.com/2014/07/01/us/hobby-lobby-case-supreme-court-contraception.html.

3. Liptak, "Supreme Court Rejects."

4. Amy Howe, "Argument Preview: Wedding Cakes v. Religious Beliefs?," *SCOTUSblog*, November 28, 2017, accessed January 20, 2021, https://www.scotusblog.com/2017/11/argument-preview-wedding-cakes-v-religious-beliefs/.

5. Adam Liptak, "In Narrow Decision, Supreme Court Sides with Baker Who Turned Away Gay Couple," *The New York Times*, June 4, 2018, accessed January 20 2021, https://www.nytimes.com/2018/06/04/us/politics/supreme-court-sides-with-baker-who-turned-away-gay-couple.html.

6. Liptak, "In Narrow Decision."

7. See Alan Blinder and Richard Perez-Pena, "Kentucky Clerk Denies Same-sex Marriage Licenses, Defying Court," *The New York Times*, September 1, 2015,

accessed January 20, 2021, https://www.nytimes.com/2015/09/02/us/same-sex-marriage-kentucky-kim-davis.html.

8. See Justin Mack, "Indiana Pizzeria that Backed RFRA and Declined to Cater Same-sex Weddings Closes for Good," *IndyStar*, April 23, 2018, accessed January 20, 2021, https://www.indystar.com/story/news/2018/04/23/indiana-pizzeria-backed-rfra-and-declined-cater-same-sex-weddings-closes-good/542975002/.

9. Peggy McIntosh, "White Privilege: Unpacking the Invisible Knapsack," *Peace and Freedom Magazine* (July/August 1989).

10. Jacqueline Bussie, "Church-Related Colleges in a Multi-Faith World," in *Hearing Vocation Differently: Meaning, Purpose, and Identity in the Multi-Faith Academy*, ed. David S. Cunningham (Oxford University Press, 2019), 245.

11. Jason Erik Nelson, "Deconstructing Academic Writing: Continuing a Conversation on Christian Privilege," *Multicultural Education* 17, no. 4 (Summer 2010): 38.

12. Robin DiAngelo, *White Fragility: Why It's So Hard for White People to Talk About Racism* (Boston: Beacon Press, 2018), 24.

13. Allyson Chiu, "Mike Pence's Advice to Christian College Grads: Be Prepared to be 'Shunned or Ridiculed for Defending the Teachings of the Bible,'" *The Washington Post*, May 13, 2019, accessed January 20, 2021, https://www.washingtonpost.com/nation/2019/05/13/mike-pences-advice-christian-college-grads-prepare-be-shunned-or-ridiculed-defending-teachings-bible/?utm_term=.a56c6fb2f02b.

14. John Fea, "Dear Vice President Pence: The Real Persecution of Christians Isn't Here in America," *The Washington Post*, May 13, 2019, accessed January 20, 2021, https://www.washingtonpost.com/religion/2019/05/13/dear-mike-pence-real-persecution-christians-isnt-here-america/?utm_term=.e06cb7ff4986.

15. Christine Clark, Mark Brimhall Vargas, Lewis Schlosser, and Craig Alimo, "It's Not Just 'Secret Santa' in December: Addressing Educational and Workplace Climate Issues Linked to Christian Privilege." *Multicultural Education* 10, n. 2 (Winter 2002): 54.

16. Tricia Seifert, "Understanding Christian Privilege: Managing the Tensions of Spiritual Plurality." *About Campus* 12, no. 2 (May-June 2007): 11.

17. Clark et al. "Its Not Just 'Secret Santa.'"

18. Nelson, "Deconstructing."

19. Charles Matesian, "Jeffress: A Mormon is Better than Obama," *Politico*, April 18, 2012, accessed January 20, 2021, https://www.politico.com/blogs/charlie-mahtesian/2012/04/jeffress-a-mormon-is-better-than-obama-120885

20. "Kimberlé Crensaw on Intersectionality, More than Two Decades Later," Columbia Law School, June 8, 2017, accessed January 20, 2021, https://www.law.columbia.edu/pt-br/news/2017/06/kimberle-crenshaw-intersectionality.

21. DiAngelo, *White Fragility*, 21.

22. Matthew Yglesias, "Trump's Enduring Political Strength With White Women, Explained," *Vox.com*, July 25, 2018, accessed January 20, 2021, https://www.vox.com/2018/7/25/17607232/trump-white-women.

23. Patricia Hill Collins, *Black Feminist Thought: Knowledge, Consciousness, and the Politics of Empowerment* (New York: Routledge, 1991): 227.

24. bell hooks, *Talking Back: Thinking Feminist, Thinking Black* (Boston: South End Press, 1989): 175.

25. Martin Luther, "The Heidelberg Disputation (1518)," in *The Annotated Luther: The Roots of Reform. Volume 1*, edited by Timothy J. Wengert, trans. Harold Grimm. (Minneapolis: Fortress, 2015), 99.

26. TAL 1, 99.

27. TAL 1, 100.

28. TAL 1, 100.

29. TAL 1, 101.

30. TAL 1, 101.

31. Martin Luther, *The Freedom of a Christian: Luther Study Edition*, trans. Mark Tranvik (Minneapolis: Fortress, 2008), 50.

32. For further discussion of the "coram" aspect of Luther's theological anthropology, building on Gerhard Ebeling's work, see Caryn D. Riswold, *Coram Deo: Human Life in the Vision of God* (Eugene, Ore.: Wipf and Stock, 2006): 84–85, and Caryn D. Riswold, "Coram Mundo: A Lutheran Feminist Theological Anthropology of Hope," *Dialog* 48, no. 2 (Summer 2009): 126–33.

33. Martin Luther, "The Freedom of a Christian (1520)," in *The Annotated Luther: The Roots of Reform. Volume 1*, 491.

34. TAL 1, 507.

35. TAL 1, 505.

36. TAL 1, 488.

37. Martin Luther, *The Freedom of a Christian: Luther Study Edition*, 50.

38. TAL 1, 511.

39. TAL 1, 512.

40. TAL 1, 512.

41. TAL 1, 520.

42. TAL 1, 520.

43. TAL 1, 520.

44. McIntosh, "Unpacking," 5.

BIBLIOGRAPHY

Blinder, Alan and Richard Perez-Pena. "Kentucky Clerk Denies Same-sex Marriage Licenses, Defying Court." *The New York Times*, September 1, 2015. https://www.nytimes.com/2015/09/02/us/same-sex-marriage-kentucky-kim-davis.html.

Bussie, Jacqueline. "Church-Related Colleges in a Multi-Faith World." In *Hearing Vocation Differently: Meaning, Purpose, and Identity in the Multi-Faith Academy*, edited by David S. Cunningham, 239–59. Oxford: Oxford University Press, 2019.

Chiu, Allyson. "Mike Pence's Advice to Christian College Grads: Be Prepared to be 'Shunned or Ridiculed for Defending the Teachings of the Bible.'" *The Washington Post*, May 13, 2019. https://www.washingtonpost.com/nation/2019/05/13/mike-pences-advice-christian-college-grads-prepare-be-shunned-or-ridiculed-defending-teachings-bible/?utm_term=.a56c6fb2f02b

Clark, Christine, Mark Brimhall Vargas, Lewis Schlosser, and Craig Alimo. "It's Not Just 'Secret Santa' in December: Addressing Educational and Workplace Climate Issues Linked to Christian Privilege." *Multicultural Education* 10, no. 2 (Winter 2002): 53–58.

Collins, Patricia Hill. *Black Feminist Thought: Knowledge, Consciousness, and the Politics of Empowerment.* New York: Routledge, 1991.

Columbia Law School. "Kimberlé Crensaw on Intersectionality, More than Two Decades Later." June 2017. https://www.law.columbia.edu/pt-br/news/2017/06/kimberle-crenshaw-intersectionality.

DiAngelo, Robin. *White Fragility: Why It's So Hard for White People to Talk About Racism.* Boston: Beacon Press, 2018.

Fea, John. "Dear Vice President Pence: The Real Persecution of Christians Isn't Here in America." *The Washington Post*, May 13, 2019. https://www.washingtonpost.com/religion/2019/05/13/dear-mike-pence-real-persecution-christians-isnt-here-america/?utm_term=.e06cb7ff4986.

hooks, bell. *Talking Back: Thinking Feminist, Thinking Black.* Boston: South End Press, 1989.

Howe, Amy. "Argument Preview: Wedding Cakes v. Religious Beliefs?" SCOTUSblog, November 28, 2017. https://www.scotusblog.com/2017/11/argument-preview-wedding-cakes-v-religious-beliefs/.

Liptak, Adam. "Supreme Court Rejects Contraceptives Mandate for Some Corporations." *The New York Times*, June 30, 2014. https://www.nytimes.com/2014/07/01/us/hobby-lobby-case-supreme-court-contraception.html.

Liptak, Adam. "In Narrow Decision, Supreme Court Sides with Baker Who Turned Away Gay Couple." *The New York Times*, June 4, 2018. https://www.nytimes.com/2018/06/04/us/politics/supreme-court-sides-with-baker-who-turned-away-gay-couple.html.

Luther, Martin. "The Freedom of a Christian (1520)." In *The Annotated Luther: The Roots of Reform. Volume 1*, edited by Timothy J. Wengert, translated by W.A. Lambert and Harold Grimm, 467–538. Minneapolis: Fortress, 2015.

————*The Freedom of a Christian: Luther Study Edition*, translated by Mark Tranvik. Minneapolis: Fortress, 2008.

————. "The Heidelberg Disputation (1518)." In *The Annotated Luther: The Roots of Reform. Volume 1*, edited by Timothy J. Wengert, translated by Harold Grimm, 67–120. Minneapolis: Fortress, 2015.

Mack, Justin. "Indiana Pizzeria that Backed RFRA and Declined to Cater Same-sex Weddings Closes for Good." *IndyStar*, April 23, 2018. https://www.indystar.com/story/news/2018/04/23/indiana-pizzeria-backed-rfra-and-declined-cater-same-sex-weddings-closes-good/542975002/.

Mahtesian, Charles. "Jeffress: A Mormon is Better than Obama." *Politico*, April 18, 2012. https://www.politico.com/blogs/charlie-mahtesian/2012/04/jeffress-a-mormon-is-better-than-obama-120885.

McIntosh, Peggy. "White Privilege: Unpacking the Invisible Knapsack." *Peace and Freedom Magazine* (July/August 1989): 10–12.

Nelson, Jason Erik. "Deconstructing Academic Writing: Continuing a Conversation on Christian Privilege." *Multicultural Education* 17, no. 4 (Summer 2010): 38–43.

Riswold, Caryn D. *Coram Deo: Human Life in the Vision of God.* Eugene, OR: Wipf and Stock, 2006.

———. "Coram Mundo: A Lutheran Feminist Theological Anthropology of Hope." *Dialog* 48, no. 2 (Summer 2009): 126–33.

Seifert, Tricia. "Understanding Christian Privilege: Managing the Tensions of Spiritual Plurality." *About Campus* 12, no 2 (May-June 2007): 10–17.

United Nations. "Universal Declaration of Human Rights." 1948. https://www.un.org/en/universal-declaration-human-rights/.

Yglesias, Matthew. "Trump's Enduring Political Strength with White Women, Explained." Vox.com, July 25. https://www.vox.com/2018/7/25/17607232/trump-white-women.

Chapter 2

A Lutheran View of Conscience

Bound and Free, Constrained and Embodied

Mary Elise Lowe

THE CONTEXT OF LUTHERAN DEBATES CONCERNING CONSCIENCE

In 2009, the Evangelical Lutheran Church in America (ELCA) debated[1] and approved a social statement relating to marriage, ordination, biological sex, gender, and sexual relations entitled "Human Sexuality: Gift and Trust" (HSGT).[2] This document and subsequent policy change allowed ELCA congregations, clergy, and bishops to ordain noncelibate gay and lesbian pastors in committed relationships, and it allowed congregations (and their clergy) to hold marriage ceremonies for couples in "publicly accountable lifelong, monogamous same-gender relationships."[3] The ELCA appealed to "bound conscience" and "conscience-bound beliefs" as a way to allow persons with progressive as well as conservative views (regarding biological sex, gender, and sexual relations) to remain in the ELCA.[4] Claims regarding conscience, Martin Luther's understanding of conscience, and the conscience-bound beliefs of individual Lutherans were central to the social statement, and scholarly articles debating a "Lutheran" view of conscience abounded.[5] Some clergy and congregations chose to ordain and perform marriages for LGBTQIA+ persons,[6] while others elected to continue the pre-2009 ELCA policy and deny these rites.[7] Following HSGT, individuals and congregations on both sides of the issue appealed to their conscience-bound beliefs. HSGT states,

> In our Christian freedom, we therefore seek responsible actions that serve others and do so with humility and deep respect for the conscience-bound beliefs of others. We understand that, in this discernment about ethics and church practice, faithful people can and will come to different conclusions about the meaning of Scripture and about what constitutes responsible action. We further believe that this church, on the basis of "the bound conscience," will include these different understandings and practices within its life as it seeks to live out its mission and ministry in the world.[8]

Today, there is little agreement among ELCA Lutherans about whether HSGT was successful in maintaining unity in the ELCA. While many LGBTQIA+ Lutherans felt welcomed by the ELCA's new policy, numerous congregations and individuals left the denomination.[9] Now eleven years later, of approximately 9,100 ELCA congregations, only about 9 percent are Reconciling in Christ congregations that publicly welcome queer persons.[10] From my perspective as a Lutheran theologian who happens to be queer,[11] there are two fundamental problems with the way the ELCA understands and employs the concept of conscience in debates about biological sex, gender, and sexuality in relationship to marriage and ordination.[12] First, when HSGT states that all views of conscience are to be respected equally, the ELCA fails to recognize that many LGBTQIA+ persons suffer from discrimination and life-denying violence on a daily basis. In the United States, forty percent of homeless youth identify as LGBTQ.[13] Half of LGBTQ employees remain closeted at work.[14] And by the first half of 2019, at least eleven African American transgender women were murdered in the United States.[15] Statistics like these reveal the harsh truth that most LGBTQIA+ persons possess much less power, safety, and privilege than many straight persons. LGBTQIA+ persons are our neighbors, yet many ELCA congregations continue to ignore the needs of these neighbors. Respecting the conscience-bound beliefs of all Lutherans—especially of those Lutherans who view LGBTQIA+ persons as sinful and disordered—contributes to the ongoing violence done to LGBTQIA+ persons in the church and the broader culture.

My second criticism is that the view of conscience in HSGT (as well as those currently held by progressive and conservative Lutherans) is ahistorical and not based upon contemporary findings regarding conscience, moral judgement, discourse, and embodiment.[16] A Lutheran view of conscience must be informed by these insights if it is to be persuasive, reason-informed, and lead to justice for the neighbor. Luther himself appealed to reason when defending his reforming theology, saying "Unless I am convinced by the testimony of Scriptures or by clear reason . . . . I am bound by the Scriptures I have quoted and my conscience is captive to the Word of God. I cannot and I will not retract anything, since it is neither safe nor right to go against conscience."[17] Yet almost none of the current Lutheran models of conscience surveyed utilize contemporary findings from the neurosciences, philosophy, or psychology to clarify and support their understanding of conscience. Nor do any employ the theoretical insight that the individual—who exercises their conscience when making moral judgments—always exists within myriad discourses about religion, biological sex, gender, sexual relations, and race, and so on. I contend that utilizing one's conscience—making judgments— can no longer be ahistorically viewed as the activity of a free, disembodied, rational, autonomous subject. Rather, as I show, contemporary psychological and philosophical findings demonstrate that exercising one's conscience and making moral decisions are unified activities of a fully embodied individual who exists within complex discourses.

A contemporary Lutheran view of conscience must view conscience as bound and free (following Luther), and as constrained by discourses and fully embodied (following contemporary reason). As I demonstrate, framing conscience and conscience-bound beliefs as constrained and embodied actually resonates with many of Luther's commitments regarding conscience. And this reformed and reason-infused model of conscience may empower Lutherans to view serving all of their neighbors as more important than protecting their private, conscience-bound beliefs. Before offering my constructive proposal, I present an exposition of Luther's understanding of conscience, followed by a brief summary of how the ELCA invoked conscience in its 2009 social statement. Then I offer an analysis of the problems evident in many of the current Lutheran views of conscience. Finally, I conclude with my constructive proposal.

MARTIN LUTHER'S VIEW OF
CONSCIENCE: BOUND AND FREE

A contemporary Lutheran theology of conscience must employ Luther's understanding that the conscience is primarily an experience of judgment or evaluation between the individual and something or someone else.[18] It helps to begin by explaining what conscience is *not* for Luther. It is not an internal moral compass or inborn ethical awareness, nor is it a reflection of natural law. Furthermore, conscience is not a free choice made in the mind or brain of a rational, autonomous, subject. Nor is it an ability possessed by an individual. Like other themes in Luther's theology and anthropology, it helps to think of conscience not as an attribute or ability, but as a relationship.[19] For Luther, conscience is a dynamic relationship that always involves the individual and something (or someone) else to which the person is bound.[20]

Luther held that conscience involves judging one's actions and motivations in relationship to God, the law, God's Word, and the neighbor. "For conscience is not the power to do works, but to judge them. The proper work of conscience . . . is to accuse or excuse, to make guilty or guiltless, uncertain or certain. Its purpose is not to do, but to pass judgment on what has been done and what should be done, and this judgment makes us stand accused or saved in God's sight."[21] But this judging is not solely an act of intellect for Luther. In Luther's view, "conscience can at times perform in ways similar to both the intellect and the will. However, as a distinct power of the flesh, the conscience's proper work is to judge the activity of the whole person: the works of the will as well as the thoughts of the intellect."[22] Throughout his life, Luther understood conscience as that which senses or feels or experiences one's status before God and God's law (and Satan). "Though I lived as a monk without reproach, I felt that I was a sinner before God with an extremely disturbed conscience . . . . I hated the righteous God who punishes sinners . . . . Thus I raged with a fierce and troubled conscience."[23] For Luther, the conscience is like a feeling, but it is not only feeling. It involves thought, but it is not identical with intellect. It involves choice, but it does not correspond directly to the will. Furthermore, for Luther, conscience is always experienced in relationship to God's Word which contains the law that accuses, and it simultaneously contains the Word that frees. "When our conscience is troubled in the sense of the wrath of God, there is no other remedy than a good word, either a word which is spoken by a [sibling] who is present or a word which we recollect."[24] And, the accused conscience is also and only freed—ultimately—through Jesus Christ. Luther wrote, "How are we freed from all of this? Who will remove from our hearts . . . our evil conscience? No human being is able to do this . . . . We have the victory through Jesus Christ."[25]

Once the conscience is freed (and justified) in Christ by the promises in God's Word, it is simultaneously bound and free.[26] The conscience is bound (as demonstrated above) to God's Word, to the law, and to neighbor. But the conscience is free from self-justification, from fear of the devil, and from trying to meet the demands of the law. "Christian or evangelical freedom, then, is a freedom of conscience which liberates the conscience from works."[27] More importantly, the freely-bound conscience is bound to the neighbor. "Therefore the godly should remember that for the sake of Christ they are free in their conscience before God from the curse of the Law, from sin, and from death, but that according to the body they are bound; here each must serve the other through love . . . let everyone strive to do their duty in their calling and to help their neighbor in whatever way they can."[28] Finally, conscience also has a mystical (and perhaps erotic) dimension for Luther; it can be the place where Christ and the believer are joined to one another. "The conscience belongs to Christ and Christ to the conscience, and no one intrudes into the secret bedchamber of this spouse and his bride."[29]

Luther painted these broad strokes when framing what might be called his freely bound view of conscience. And typical to Luther's theology, there is a paradoxical dynamic. Conscience is free and is not free. It is bound and it is not bound. Here again, framing conscience as a relationship rather than as an attribute or moral awareness deepens one's understanding of Luther's view. This paradoxical character of conscience may also help explain why distinct Lutheran communities each claim to rightly interpret and employ Luther's view of the conscience to support their seemingly-opposing perspectives regarding the status of LGBTQIA+ persons in the ELCA. Nevertheless, I contend that these modern, Lutheran views of conscience are inadequate to contemporary theology and church life. They fail to employ contemporary insights (reason) that reveal how discourses constitute each person's experience of conscience, and they do not account for the way an individual's embodied experiences shape that person's experiences of conscience and moral judgments. Before offering a critique of these views of conscience, I present a brief summary of how the ELCA employed the concept of conscience and conscience-bound beliefs in "Human Sexuality: Gift and Trust."

BOUND CONSCIENCE AND CONSCIENCE-BOUND BELIEFS IN THE ELCA

Lutherans in the United States began discussing and debating a Lutheran view of conscience when the ELCA started drafting "Human Sexuality: Gift and Trust." This authoritative social statement contains frequent references to the conscience and conscience-bound beliefs. Numerous Luther scholars, theologians, and historians weighed in on what they considered to be the "correct" or "Lutheran" interpretation of conscience.[30] Some supported the way the ELCA employed conscience in HSGT, while others rejected it. Based on my own study of the social statement and the accompanying academic debates, it appears like the ELCA was trying to use conscience and conscience-bound beliefs as a framework or a boundary that would allow both progressive and conservative Lutherans to stay under the ELCA umbrella. The appeal to conscience was intended to include and appease many types of Lutherans (and to keep them in the ELCA). "This social statement draws upon this rich understanding of the role of conscience and calls upon this church, when in disagreement concerning matters around which salvation is not at stake, including human sexuality, to bear one another's burdens (Galatians 6:2), honor the conscience, and seek the well-being of the neighbor."[31] A few other excerpts from HSGT demonstrate how the social statement tried to create a space for a variety of views.

- "On the basis of conscience-bound belief, some are convinced that same-gender sexual behavior is sinful."[32]
- "On the basis of conscience-bound belief, some are convinced that homosexuality . . . reflect[s] a broken world."[33]
- "On the basis of conscience-bound belief, some are convinced that . . . neighbor and community are best served when same-gender relationships are honored . . . but they do not equate these relationships with marriage."[34]
- "On the basis of conscience-bound belief, some . . . believe that the neighbor and community are best served when same-gender relationships are held to the same rigorous standards . . . as heterosexual marriage."[35]
- "Although . . . this church lacks consensus . . . it encourages all people to live out their faith . . . with profound respect for the conscience-bound belief of the neighbor."[36]

If Martin Luther read HSGT, I think he *would* hear echoes of his own view of conscience in the social statement. But my goal here is not to debate the "Lutheranness" of conscience in the statement. Rather, I offer a reconstruction of a Lutheran view of conscience that resonates with Luther's understanding and augments it with contemporary findings which demonstrate that conscience is constrained by discourse and embodied. If Lutherans are going to effectively employ conscience as a foundation for their theological anthropology, ecclesiology, and advocacy work, they must update their ahistorical view of conscience with insights from reason. If Lutheran teachings and views of the human person are to remain useful in the future, they must arise from the gospel, be grounded in Lutheran theology, and be consonant with findings from the social and natural sciences. The ELCA *did* rely upon and utilize current scientific and sociological research in its social statements on genetics and criminal justice, but it *did not* look to recent scholarship regarding conscience, will, cognition, and how individuals make moral decisions when crafting HSGT.[37] Before offering my constructive proposal, I highlight what I see as the significant and ongoing weaknesses in the ELCA's current appeal to bound conscience. And some of these weaknesses also exist in Luther's understanding of conscience and endure in both progressive and conservative appeals to conscience.

PROBLEMS WITH LUTHER'S AND
LUTHERAN VIEWS OF CONSCIENCE

In Luther's writings about the plague, military service, secular authority, and monastic vows, he consistently argued that no one should be compelled to go against their conscience.[38] So when HSGT states that people of good faith can reach different conclusions based on conscience, the ELCA *does* echo Luther's claims. Nevertheless, I have identified ten significant and ongoing problems in the way that the ELCA as well as progressive and conservative Lutherans appeal to conscience and conscience-bound beliefs. (1) To begin, in the 2009 social statement (and following) the ELCA did very little to help Lutherans who take opposing viewpoints regarding the role of LGBTQIA+ persons in the church to engage in potentially transformative dialogue on issues related to biological sex, gender, human sexuality, marriage, and ordination. (2) Many contemporary Lutherans falsely equate conscience with some sort of inborn moral awareness of right and wrong or an internal sense of natural law. However, Luther did not view conscience this way.[39] (3) In the U.S. context, appeals to conscience—especially related to biological sex, gender, and sexual relations—are frequently equated with feeling. Although feelings of anxiety, judgment, and freedom are a part of the experience of conscience, Luther did not associate conscience primarily with feeling and emotion. (4) Conscience—as Luther taught—always involves judging one's self, one's views, and one's practices in light of the needs of the neighbor and the claims of Scripture.[40] Yet, many Lutheran discussions of conscience don't involve a call for critical self-appraisal of one's own identity, moral values, or underlying truth claims. Whenever one judges the beliefs, practices, and identities of others, one should always practice honest self-assessment in light of the law and the gospel. (5) Furthermore, the experience of conscience is not necessarily trustworthy. Too often people believe that their own beliefs and values (regarding the Bible or sex or gender) are beyond question precisely because they have strong personal feelings about an issue. However, Luther taught that conscience is not entirely trustworthy and that it does not always grasp the truth.[41]

(6) The ELCA's current HSGT statement doesn't help individuals and faith communities choose or judge whether it is more important to exercise one's conscience or to serve the needs of the neighbor. In "Whether One May Flee from a Deadly Plague," Luther stated that strong Christians may choose to stay and help others who are sick. While weak Christians may flee "as long as they do not neglect their duty toward their neighbors."[42] Christians are bound to care for the sick if no one else can care for them—even if one's own life is put in danger. Luther's advice here is self-respecting, practical, and ultimately

based on neighbor-love. In her commentary on "Whether to Flee," scholar Anna Marie Johnson says that, for Luther, "the only law a Christian must follow is the law of love . . . caring for the sick, maintaining public services, and tending to spiritual needs."[43] Luther consistently argued that performing acts of neighbor-love should be more important than following rules or exercising one's individual conscience and conscience-bound beliefs. (7) Another significant weakness in many Lutheran views of conscience is that they fail to recognize that individuals do not possess equal power, agency, and privilege when exercising their conscience-bound beliefs. Most of the time there are important differences in the amount of power, agency, and/or privilege that an individual or a group has in contrast with the power and agency possessed by another person or community. This means that in Lutheran debates about LGBTQIA+ ordination and marriage, most straight, cis, married, and child-producing persons have and exercise more power and agency than do many LGBTQIA+ persons.[44]

The next two concerns bring me to the heart of my criticism of existing Lutheran understandings of conscience. They fail to integrate scientific findings regarding embodiment and theoretical insights regarding the constraining function of discourse (reason) into their views of conscience. Recall that Luther said that his own theology must be convinced by clear reason. I am not suggesting here that Luther's view of conscience be laid aside because it is not scientifically (and theoretically) up-to-date. Rather I contend that contemporary Lutheran views of conscience must integrate modern scientific and theoretical findings into their concept of conscience.[45] (8) None of the Lutheran views of conscience that I encountered utilize the contemporary theoretical insight that every person (subject) comes to be who they are within a field of competing discourses. These discourses about race, sex, medicine, religion, or class, for example, profoundly constrain and influence the way an individual exercises their conscience, frames their self-identity, and makes moral judgments. Conscience can no longer be viewed as a possession or private experience of the supposed free, choosing, elite individual subject. Rather, as I show, insights from philosophy and critical theory persuasively reveal how discourses constrain the exercise of conscience. (9) In addition, most contemporary Lutheran views of conscience are not informed by current scientific findings which demonstrate that the exercise of conscience and the making of moral judgments are embodied activities of the whole person. These findings challenge any appeals to conscience that are based on internal truths, gut feelings, reason without emotion, or rely solely upon the Bible. As I demonstrate, even a person whose conscience has been freed by the power of the gospel does not exercise their conscience unbound from their embodied experiences.

(10) Finally, in an often-ignored move, HSGT says that competing claims of conscience should be honored since "salvation is not at stake" regarding the status of LGBTQIA+ persons in the church. "This social statement draws upon this . . . understanding of the role of conscience and calls upon this church, when in disagreement concerning matters around which salvation is not at stake, including human sexuality, to bear one another's burdens . . . honor the conscience, and seek the well-being of the neighbor."[46] The ELCA's claim that "salvation is not at stake" is false. When LGBTQIA+ persons are not welcome in an ELCA church, when they cannot pursue their vocations in ministry, when their relationships are not honored and celebrated, when they suffer violence and discrimination—their salvation is very much at stake. They know that they are created in God's image and they trust that God's loves them. But they need to hear these same good Words from their siblings in Christ and be welcomed into a faith community. In spite of the many shortcomings in Luther's and in today's Lutheran views of conscience and conscience-bound beliefs, I contend that conscience is still a useful insight and tool that Lutherans should retain and employ. The experience of conscience (self-judgment in relationship to God, the Word, the law, the neighbor, and the gospel) is central to the Christian faith. And exercising one's conscience lies at the heart of each Christian's vocation to serve the neighbor in the world. In the following pages I propose that in order to serve all neighbors, a contemporary Lutheran view of conscience should frame conscience as constrained by discourse, embodied, and (as Luther said) bound and free.

CONSCIENCE IS CONSTRAINED BY DISCOURSE

"Human Sexuality: Gift and Trust" tries to guide Lutherans as they make judgments about biological sex, gender, and sexual relations, and about LGBTQIA+ marriage and ordination. But the document is not particularly helpful in presenting a Lutheran view of conscience because it employs a 16th century understanding of conscience. This ahistorical understanding no doubt contributes to the lack of precision regarding "conscience" in HSGT and to the dearth of transformative conversations about sex, gender, sexuality, ordination and marriage in the ELCA. This situation is made more difficult by the reality that many U.S. Lutherans still view conscience as the possession or ability of a free, autonomous, judging, and rational subject. And thus, conscience is privatized and seen as the expression of an inner truth rather than as an act of self-judgment in relation to God, creation, law/gospel, and the neighbor. Today however, countless contemporary theorists and philosophers reject this view of self, agency, and conscience. Instead, they demonstrate that individuals come to be who they are within a confluence of competing discourses (race, sex, medicine, etc.) that actually constrain the way individuals (and groups) understand themselves, use language, exercise power, and make judgments about self and others. This means that Lutheran appeals to conscience regarding the status of LGBTQIA+ persons in the church are profoundly constrained by broader discourses about biological sex, gender, marriage, and sexuality. These discourses actually set the boundaries of the conversation, establish the grammar used, and provide the language employed to discuss biological sex, gender, race, marriage, and so on.

There are numerous definitions of discourse, but the following is succinct and clear. "Discourse is a set of rules for producing knowledge that determines what kind of intelligible statements can be circulated within a given economy of thought. For example, in the discourse on gender, you can only say meaningful things about two kinds of bodies that will make sense."[47] What scholar Riki Wilkins means is that in dominant heteronormative ways of thinking about biological sex and gender, most of the language available is premised on the false and binary assumption that all humans are either "male" or "female." Persons from the intersex community however resist binary discourses regarding biological sex. They are expanding language and cognition about biological sex to include three categories of female, male, and intersex.[48] In addition, emerging discourses about the diversity of biological sex are expanding into legal discourses (laws). For example, six U.S. states now allow individuals to select a third option—often X—as opposed to only (M)ale or (F)emale when applying for a driver's license.[49] This is an example of how binary medical and legal discourses that assume only two biological sexes are being resisted and changed into discourses that allow for a third option.

Discourses actually shape the language available to persons and therefore constrain and influence the way individuals understand the world and make judgments about it (exercise conscience). What this means for this analysis of a Lutheran view of conscience is that reason (here critical theory and philosophy) demonstrates that the exercise of conscience is constrained by the myriad discourses in which a person exists. For example, laws (legal discourses) that hold that there are only two biological sexes actually shape the way people think and speak about biological sex, gender, and sexuality. As Wilkins describes, "only two kinds of bodies make sense." Therefore, the exercise of conscience (making moral judgments) is never "pure" or "autonomous." Nor is the exercise of conscience an expression of an inner truth. Rather, conscience-bound beliefs about sex, gender, and marriage are constituted by contemporary discourse(s).

The assumptions and discourses used in HSGT actually set and establish the grammar, vocabulary, and rules for thinking about sex and gender in the social statement. And the vocabulary employed in the document actually constrains the way individual Lutherans think about and make judgments about sex, gender, and marriage. For example, HSGT states, "On the basis of conscience-bound belief, some are convinced that homosexuality and even lifelong, monogamous homosexual relationships reflect a broken world."[50] Elsewhere, the statement reads, "On the basis of conscience-bound belief, some are convinced . . . that the neighbor and the community are best served when same-gender relationships are honored."[51] Notice the vocabulary used in the text: homosexuality, monogamous, relationship, and same-gender. Each term constitutes a certain way of understanding biological sex and gender and human relationships. The unspoken assumptions are that there are only two sexual orientations, monogamy is divinely-prescribed, there are only two biological sexes, and there are only two corresponding genders. These binary and heteronormative ways of understanding sex and gender and relationships in HSGT are built upon legal, religious, and medical discourses. This means that the individual who reads HSGT, and who experiences a conscience-bound belief, and then makes a moral judgment is profoundly constrained by the language in and myriad discourses undergirding HSGT.

Framing conscience as constrained by discourse actually resonates with Luther's view. As I argued previously, Luther understood conscience in terms of relationship—free in Christ while bound to God, the Word, the law, and the neighbor. Similarly, this discourse analysis demonstrates that even though conscience may be justified by grace, liberated from the power of sin, and freed from the futility of satisfying the law; conscience is also and always constrained by the competing web of discourses in which the individual exists and makes moral judgments. So any appeals to an individual's interior experience of conscience or even appeals to Scripture alone are no longer plausible. For example, let's say that Jamie is a thoughtful Lutheran who says, "On . . . the basis of conscience-bound belief, I am convinced that homosexuality reflects a broken world." Jamie may say that their conscience-bound belief is based only on the Bible. But, if we recognize that Jamie exists within a field of competing medical, legal, economic, and religious discourses, then we must concede that Jamie's conscience-bound judgments regarding biological sex, gender, sexual relations, and ordination and marriage are actually constrained by numerous discourses. From medical discourse, Jamie has accepted the assumption that there are only two biological sexes. From legal discourse, Jamie has internalized the view that state-sanctioned marriage should only occur between a male and a female. From (pre-1973) psychological discourses, Jamie has accepted that same-sex desire is a mental disorder.[52] From Christian discourses, Jamie has assented to the claim that God's intention for humans is bonded, reproductive, heterosexual pairs. Jamie's conscience is free in Christ from satisfying the law, and bound to God's

Word, reason, and the neighbor. But Jamie's conscience is simultaneously constrained by secular and religious discourses that provide the vocabulary and constitute the very way Jamie reasons about biological sex and gender, and the ordination and marriage of LGBTQIA+ persons in the ELCA.

CONSCIENCE IS EMBODIED

When Luther defended his theology, he said that unless he was persuaded by Scripture or reason he would not go against his conscience. Yet, few Lutherans have explored what the sciences (reason) are discovering about how humans make moral judgments (exercise conscience). Today, many scholars in cognitive psychology, philosophy, and the neurosciences contend that an individual's moral judgments are never purely based on reason alone nor located solely in the brain or mind. Rather, ethical decisions are grounded in the individual's experience of embodiment. Findings from the field of embodied cognition deepen and make-more-reasonable Lutheran views of conscience by helping Lutherans better understand and articulate how experiences of body-mind shape the way individuals make judgments about biological sex, gender, marriage, or ordination.[53]

There are several different approaches to embodied cognition, but most share the fundamental tenet that "thinking is not something that is divorced from the body; instead thinking is an activity strongly influenced by the body and the brain interacting with the environment . . . . Cognition exists to guide action . . . . This concern for action contrasts with standard cognitive psychology that . . . considers action (and the body) as secondary to cognition."[54] Scientists and philosophers in this field reject the supposed split between mind and body and challenge the false assumption that moral judgments are unfettered by an individual's experience of embodiment. In contrast, they argue that embodied experiences form the material and metaphorical basis for cognition, moral judgements, and the exercise of conscience. Mark Johnson and George Lakoff (whose research guides my own use of embodied cognition) contend that embodied experiences are extended into metaphors and into cognition. For example, an infant's repeated experience of watching a person or object move towards and past them is expressed in the primary metaphor "time is motion."[55] The embodied experience of motion is then extended in the well-known metaphor "time flies." "Spatial concepts are embodied in various ways . . . . Concepts like *front* and *back* . . . arise from the body, depend on the body, and would not exist if we did not have the kinds of bodies we have."[56] In a similar way, the association of 'up' with happiness (or something good) is grounded in an infant's repeated experience of looking up at parents and having a positive encounter. This embodied pattern of looking up is then extended into the primary metaphor "happy is up." This alignment of "up" and something positive is echoed in the familiar expression of "being on top of the world." This phrase is more than a figure of speech; it reflects "underlying cognitive processes."[57] So when it comes to conscience and ethical reasoning, one's embodied experiences with self, environment, and others profoundly shape the way humans think and make ethical choices.

Recent studies in embodied cognition actually demonstrate that moral judgments (the exercise of conscience) are significantly influenced by an individual's embodied experiences, such as encountering a disgusting smell or unpleasant taste. In one experiment, participants were asked to look at photos of people from different groups (elderly, Asian American, gay men, etc.) and then instructed to make moral judgments about the people in the photos. When a disgusting smell was present in the room, participants evaluated the gay men in the photos more negatively than when no unpleasant odor was present. (The foul smell did not affect judgments about other groups represented in the images.)[58] Thus a moral judgment about a specific group of people was affected by a disgusting smell. This illustrates that the exercise of conscience is not merely a mental function of the intellect, mind, or brain. Rather it is an action-oriented activity of the whole person in a specific environment.

In another experiment, participants were asked to read morally "good" or morally "bad" stories and then instructed to drink a liquid and judge whether the beverage was sweet, neutral, or disgusting. Participants found the beverages to be more disgusting after encountering the morally "bad" vignette. Once again, the exercise of conscience—making a moral judgment—was affected by an embodied experience. This research "supports the central tenets of the conceptual-metaphor theory . . . by demonstrating how abstract concepts like morality could originate from sensory experiences and how intuitions and feelings play fundamental roles in moral processing."[59] In an additional study, subjects were asked to recall an "unethical" memory and an "ethical" memory. Participants who recalled an "unethical" act reported that they felt like their body weighed more than it actually did. After recalling an "ethical" memory, the participants' estimates of their own weight were more accurate. (Other self-estimates of height and ability were not affected.) "Extending the metaphor that guilt is a heavy weight on people's conscience . . . demonstrated that immoral acts led to reports of increased subjective body weight."[60]

The pattern of these results indicates that the relationship between embodiment and making judgments—exercising conscience—goes both ways. It is bidirectional. An embodied experience influences a moral judgment and vice versa.[61] But more importantly for my analysis and proposal, these experiments demonstrate that exercising conscience and making moral judgments are *always* embodied. It is no longer reasonable to say that an individual's judgments about biological sex, gender, marriage, and sexuality are exclusively guided by one's experiences, singularly grounded in one's own identity, or solely informed by the Bible. For example, let's imagine that a faithful Lutheran named Blair reads HSGT and then states, "On the basis of conscience-bound beliefs, I believe that LGBTQIA+ persons should be able to be married and ordained in ELCA congregations." Research in embodied cognition helps us understand that Blair's exercise of conscience is influenced to some degree by Blair's embodied experience prior to and during the time when Blair made their moral judgment about LGBTQIA+ marriage. Perhaps Blair's more progressive judgment was influenced by a positive moral story Blair read on the web. Or maybe Blair was drinking a glass of sweet tasting orange juice and sitting near a table that had a vase of fragrant flowers on it while reading HSGT. Findings from embodied cognition demonstrate that the positive moral story, the sweet taste, and the pleasing aroma influenced Blair's conscience-bound and fully embodied belief regarding same-sex marriage in the ELCA.

These insights from embodied cognition strengthen a Lutheran view of conscience because they illustrate that conscience can no longer be viewed as a private experience or as the expression of a purely rational, autonomous mind or brain. Second, the embodied nature of conscience and judgment resonates harmoniously with Luther's and Lutheran commitments that humans are whole persons (*totus homo*), that physical matter is a good, and that God is (incarnationally) present in humans and creation.[62] Finally, affirming the embodied character of conscience aligns nicely with Luther's understanding of conscience. In both proposals conscience and the making of moral judgments are primarily relational. Conscience is always related to and profoundly influenced by God, the law, one's embodied experiences, one's material conditions, one's community, and the neighbor.

A LUTHERAN VIEW OF CONSCIENCE: BOUND AND FREE AND CONSTRAINED BY DISCOURSE AND EMBODIED

In contrast to Lutheran views of conscience that do not utilize contemporary theoretical insights and scientific findings (reason) or those that erroneously assume an overly autonomous (white, western) view of the human person, I contend that conscience is bound and free, constrained by discourse and embodied. There are many advantages to this reason-grounded Lutheran model of conscience. To begin, several elements are consistent with Luther's view of conscience. It is solidly grounded in reason, since it is based on present-day findings from the sciences (embodied cognition) and from critical theory and philosophy (discourse). This updated model of conscience is also decidedly Lutheran because it rejects the claim that conscience is the exercise of free choice based on an individual's private feeling or emotions. Furthermore, conscience is never fully trustworthy and it is always exercised within a particular environment and specific community. Earlier I argued that Luther's view of conscience should be framed relationally since the exercise of conscience is in dialogue with the law, Scripture, God, and neighbor. The model of conscience proposed here is even more thoroughly relational, because conscience is always embodied and is in constitutive relation with body-mind and other humans. The claim that conscience is constrained by discourse also resonates with Luther's relational framing of conscience, because the very language a person speaks and the discourses available to them constrain and influence the way they experience conscience and make moral judgments.

There are other advantages to viewing conscience as constrained by discourse and embodied. This reformed, Lutheran model of conscience may prove more useful for interfaith conversations, since the commitment to conscience is no longer based exclusively on Christian theology, the Bible, or Martin Luther's teachings. It is also more attentive to the dynamics of power and privilege because it recognizes that persons possess power and agency in different ways and to different degrees. In addition, since the theory of conscience proposed here holds that body-mind is one and that conscience is always an enfleshed experience of the whole person, it affirms materiality more than other Lutheran views of conscience. And insights from embodied cognition deepen this materiality because the body-minds of others (family for example) profoundly shape individuals and their moral judgments. Furthermore, this reformed understanding of conscience is also more neighbor-centered because conscience always involves self-judgment in relationship to the neighbor's needs. The exercise of conscience can no longer be based upon a person's feelings, pure reason, or upon the Bible. Finally, claiming that conscience is bound and free, and that it is constrained by discourse and embodied is more resistant and liberating for LGBTQIA+ Christians than previous views of conscience. Because of its reliance on embodied cognition and discourse analysis, this model resists negative views of embodiment and the binary and heteronormative language and discourses that have too often constrained the way Lutherans (and many other Christian groups) understand biological sex, gender, body-mind, marriage, and sexuality.

CONCLUSION: "THE ONLY SAFE GUIDE IS LOVE"

As I develop this chapter, a 2018 survey of approximately 1,700 adults in the U.S. reveals that "More non-LGBT adults responded that they were 'very' or 'somewhat' uncomfortable around LGBTQ people in select scenarios."[63] This is a shift from three previous annual surveys which showed increasing acceptance.[64] And F.B.I. data reveals that the number of hate crimes against LGBT persons in the United States has increased in the last few years.[65] These grim statistics demonstrate the growing violence and oppression that LGBTQIA+ persons suffer every day. It is time for the ELCA—one of the eight largest groups of Christians in the United States with approximately 3.5 million members[66]—to move beyond defending its ahistorical view of conscience and the conscience-bound beliefs of its individual members and move toward neighbor-justice for all.[67] HSGT states, "This church also will attend to the need for equal protection, equal opportunities, and equal responsibilities under the law, and just treatment for those with varied sexual orientation and gender identity."[68] And it also argues that the church and its members oppose "all forms of verbal or physical harassment and assault based on sexual orientation. It supports legislation and policies to protect civil rights and to prohibit discrimination in housing, employment, and public services."[69]

What LGBTQIA+ persons need today are neighbors, faith communities, and a national church body to accompany them, honor them, support them as they advocate for their legal and economic equity, fight for their physical safety, insist on equitable access to health care, and protect and shelter LGBTQIA+ youth. A fundamental shift is needed from bound-conscience to neighbor-justice. And a new understanding of conscience is required to advance this shift. Protecting the lives, vocation, dignity, and health of LGBTQIA+ neighbors is far more important that defending one's allegiance to one's conscience and to individual conscience-bound beliefs regarding biological sex, gender, marriage, ordination, and human sexuality.

How might a faithful Lutheran be moved in their conscience to fight for justice for LGBTQIA+ neighbors? By—dare I say it—following Luther's teachings! He wrote about complex ethical issues—the plague, marriage, military service, and serving secular authorities—where there were no clear answers for Christians. Luther consistently encouraged his readers to rely on fairness (equity) and love of neighbor. When discussing whether or not Christians could rebel against unjust authorities, he wrote, "[T]he law ought to yield and fairness reign in its place."[70] And a few lines later, "This virtue, or wisdom, which can and should direct and moderate the severity of law in accordance with each case, and which judges the same deed to be good or evil according to the differences in intentions and the heart, is called *epieikeia* in Greek. In Latin, it is *aequitas* [equity]; I call it *Billichkeit* [fairness] in German."[71] When asked if Christians were obligated to care for their neighbors during the plague, Luther again appealed to responsibility for the neighbor; he did not instruct persons to merely follow their conscience. "To flee from death and to save one's own life is a natural tendency . . . and not forbidden unless it be against God and neighbor."[72] And in Luther's reflection on the value of monastic vows he wrote, "When it comes to the mitigation of laws and their right interpretation the only safe guide is love. Whatever is contrary to love can in no circumstances be imposed . . . . To put it another way. Whatever is not against love is a matter of free choice [conscience], permissible and sanctioned, especially in cases of necessity."[73] In his commentary on Galatians, Luther described the nobility and universal value of loving neighbor. "[N]o creature toward which you should practice love is nobler than your neighbor . . . nothing could be regarded as worthier of love in the whole universe than our neighbor."[74]

If the "only safe guide is love," then all Lutherans can and should follow the paths of love, equity, and neighbor-justice with respect to LGBTQIA+ persons within the ELCA and the broader society. Staying true to one's conscience is important. Living out one's conscience-bound beliefs is valuable. But asserting one's commitments of conscience while ignoring the needs of the neighbor is hard to reconcile with a Lutheran view of the gospel, with Luther's understanding of Christian vocation, and with his commitment that reason inform the life and choices of Christians. Theoretical and philosophical insights demonstrate that even the most deeply held moral judgments are constrained by discourses and language. And research from embodied cognition reveals that conscience-bound beliefs are grounded in one's experiences of body-mind, one's encounters with others, and one's environment. The reformed, Lutheran model of conscience I propose here is decidedly Lutheran. Conscience is the dynamic act of judging one's self in relationship to God and others. Conscience is free; free in Christ and free to serve the neighbor. Conscience is bound; bound to the law, to Scripture, and bound to the neighbor. And conscience is convinced (to use Luther's word) and based upon reason. It is constrained by discourse and it is embodied. It is my hope that this reformed view of conscience will encourage Lutherans to employ a theoretically and scientifically-grounded understanding of conscience that empowers them to live out their conscience-bound beliefs in a complex ethical world in service to *all* of their neighbors.

NOTES

1. "ELCA Assembly Opens Ministry to Partnered Gay and Lesbian Lutherans," Evangelical Lutheran Church in America, accessed July 1, 2019, https://www.elca. org/News-and-Events/6587.

2. "Human Sexuality: Gift and Trust," Evangelical Lutheran Church in America, accessed July 1, 2019, https://download.elca.org/ELCA%20Resource%20Repository/ SexualitySS.pdf.

3. The decision to allow ELCA clergy to perform marriages for LGBTQIA+ persons was established at the 2009 ELCA Churchwide Assembly, and the text is found in the "Resolutions Related to Ministry Policies as Adopted by the 2009 Churchwide Assembly," See "2009 ELCA Churchwide Assembly Addresses Variety of Topics," Evangelical Lutheran Church in America, accessed July 3, 2019, https://www.elca. org/News-and-Events/6218?_ga=1.107752834.1287315157.1433951594.

4. By "conservative" perspectives, I mean groups and individuals who view LGBTQIA+ persons as inherently disordered and sinful. By "progressive," I mean those who support the full inclusion of LGBTQIA+ persons in the Lutheran communion. Lutheran CORE is an example of a conservative group. The June 2019 director's letter specifically discusses "Human Sexuality: Gift and Trust." See "Lutheran Core Letter from the Director," CORE, accessed July 9, 2019, https://myemail.constantcontact.com/Lutheran-CORE-Letter-from-the-Director. html?soid=1120670649512&aid=-Y1ujuhenZ4. ReconcilingWorks is an example of a progressive group: "About," ReconcilingWorks, accessed July 9, 2019, https:// www.reconcilingworks.org/.

5. Rev. Dr. William Russell, "Martin Luther's Understanding of the Conscience, *'Coram Deo'* and the ELCA's Sexuality Study," *Journal of Lutheran Ethics* 5, no. 7 (July 2005): https://www.elca.org/JLE/Articles/654.

6. I have used current preferred terms for discussing sex and gender and identity, these will change over time. See the "GLAAD Media Reference Guide, 10th ed.," GLAAD, accessed July 1, 2019, https://www.glaad.org/reference.

7. "Human Sexuality: Gift and Trust" does not use the terms gay or lesbian. The language used is "homosexual" and "lifelong, monogamous, same-gender relationships." "Human Sexuality," Evangelical Lutheran Church in America, accessed October 11, 2020, https://download.elca.org/ELCA%20Resource%20Repository/ SexualitySS.pdf.

8. Ibid., 19.

9. As of 2013, 643 congregations had been officially removed from the ELCA roster of congregations. "Always Being Made New: 25 Years Together in Christ, 2013 Pre-Assembly Report, Report of the Secretary, Section II, 10 (2013), " Evangelical Lutheran Church in America, accessed June 29, 2019, http://download.elca.org/ELCA%20 Resource%20Repository/02c_Report_of_the_Secretary_20130806e.pdf.

10. Reconciling in Christ refers to the ReconcilingWorks program. "Your community explicitly states a welcome to people of "all sexual orientations, gender identities, and gender expressions" or "LGBTQIA+." "About the RIC Journey,"

ReconcilingWorks, accessed January 18, 2021, https://www.reconcilingworks.org/ric/aboutric/.

11. In a previous publication I wrote, "I employ queer in three ways. First, queer refers to an identity that persons claim for themselves when their sexual or gender identity and practices are deemed deviant by dominant heterocolonial discourses. Queer is also a method or way to 'transcend, transgress, alter, blur, or confuse the usual categories of gender.' Finally, I understand queer as a subaltern position (or location) from which an individual or group resists heteronormative religious and legal discourses." Mary Elise Lowe, "The Queer Body-Mind in Martin Luther's Theology: From Subaltern Sodomite to Embodied *Imago Dei*," in *The Alternative Luther. Lutheran Theology from the Subaltern*, ed. Else Marie Wiberg Pedersen (New York: Lexington Books/Fortress Academic, 2019), 119–120. The quotation within this quotation is taken from, Monica Joy Cross, *Authenticity and Imagination in the Face of Oppression* (Eugene, OR: Resource Publications, 2016), 67.

12. The ELCA's current definition of sexuality is useful. "Sexuality: A complex individual and social concept. Individually, sexuality includes the romantic and/or sexual feelings and desires that a person experiences. A person's sexuality is also influenced by the social and cultural forces in which they find themselves." "Faith, Sexism, and Justice: A Lutheran Call to Action, 80" Evangelical Lutheran Church in America, accessed July 1, 2019, https://download.elca.org/ELCA%20Resource%20Repository/Faith_Sexism_Justice_Social_Statement_Adopted.pdf?_ga=2.83342163.47161602.1592517489-1587583221.1592517489.

13. "New Report on Youth Homeless Affirms that LGBTQ Youth Disproportionately Experience Homelessness," Human Rights Campaign, accessed January 20, 2021, https://www.hrc.org/news/new-report-on-youth-homeless-affirms-that-lgbtq-youth-disproportionately-ex.

14. Elliott Kozuch, "HRC REPORT: Startling Data Reveals Half of LGBTQ Employees in the U.S. Remain Closeted at Work," Human Rights Campaign, accessed, January 15, 2021, https://www.hrc.org/news/hrc-report-startling-data-reveals-half-of-lgbtq-employees-in-us-remain-clos.

15. Petula Devorak, "The Murder of Black Transgender Women is Becoming a Crisis," *The Washington Post*, June 17, 2019, https://www.washingtonpost.com/local/the-murder-of-black-transgender-women-is-becoming-a-crisis/2019/06/17/28f8dba6-912b-11e9-b570-6416efdc0803_story.html?utm_term=.f89d0b6be669; Doha Madani, "Police Investigate 11th Murder of a Black Transgender Woman this Year," NBC News, June 27, 2019, https://www.nbcnews.com/feature/nbc-out/police-investigate-11th-murder-black-transgender-woman-year-n1023526.

16. Future research could offer a detailed analysis of newsletters, web pages, devotional materials, and advocacy literature generated by progressive and conservative Lutherans. After ten years of reading this literature, I have found that both groups employ an ahistorical, autonomous, choice-centered, and private view of conscience that is not based on findings from contemporary theory, philosophy, psychology, or the neurosciences.

17. Martin Luther, "Luther at the Diet of Worms (1521)," in *Luther's Works, Volume 32, Career of the Reformer II,* ed. George W. Forell, trans. Roger A. Hornsby (Philadelphia: Fortress Pres, 1958), 112.

18. Helpful sources on Luther's view of conscience include: George Forell, "Luther and Conscience," in *Encounters with Luther: Lectures, Discussions, and Sermons at the Martin Luther Colloquia 1970–1974,* ed. Eric W. Gritsch (Gettysburg: Institute for Luther Studies, 1980), 218–35; Bernhard Lohse, "Conscience and Authority in Luther," in *Luther and the Dawn of the Modern Era,* ed. Heiko A. Oberman (Leiden: E.J. Brill, 1974), 158–83; Martha Ellen Stortz, "*Solus Christus* or *Sola Viscera*? Scrutinizing Lutheran Appeals to Conscience," *Dialog: A Journal of Theology* 44, no. 2 (Summer 2005): 146–51.

19. "And this is the reason why our theology is certain: it snatches us away from ourselves and places us outside ourselves, so that we do not depend on our own strength, conscience, experience, person, or works but depend on that which is outside ourselves." Martin Luther, "Lectures on Galatians, 1535, Chapters 1–4," *Luther's Works, Volume 26, Lectures on Galatians, 1535, Chapters 1–4,* eds. Jaroslav Pelikan and Walter Hansen, trans. Jaroslav Pelikan (St. Louis: Concordia Publishing House, 1963), 387.

20. Matt Ley, "Luther's Understanding of the Bound Conscience," *Journal of Lutheran Ethics* 10, no. 11 (2010): https://www.elca.org/JLE/Articles/246.

21. Martin Luther, "Judgment of Martin Luther on Monastic Vows (1521)," in *Luther's Works, Volume 44, The Christian in* Society, eds. James Atkinson and Helmut T. Lehmann, trans. James Atkinson (Philadelphia: Fortress Press, 1966), 298.

22. Randall C. Zachman, *The Assurance of Faith: Conscience in the Theology of Martin Luther and John Calvin* (Minneapolis: Fortress Press, 1993), 24.

23. Martin Luther, "Preface to the Complete Edition of Luther's Latin Writings (1545)," in LW 32, 336–37; see also *Luther's Works, Volume 20, Lectures on the Minor Prophets III, Zechariah,* ed. Hilton C. Oswald, trans. by Richard J. Dinda (St. Louis: Concordia, 1973), 13; "Lectures on Titus (1527)," in *Luther's Works, Volume 29, Lectures on Titus, Philemon, and Hebrews,* eds. Jaroslav Pelikan and Walter A. Hansen, trans. Jaroslav Pelikan (St. Louis: Concordia Publishing House, 1968), 11. Elsewhere Luther wrote, "For one must know how one stands with God, if the conscience is to be joyful and be able to stand . . . . For this confidence and good conscience is the real, basically good faith, which the grace of God works in us." See "Sermons at Leipzig and Erfurt, 1519; 1521," in *Luther's Works, Volume 51, Sermons I,* ed. John W. Doberstein (Philadelphia: Fortress Press, 1959), 59.

24. Martin Luther, "Explication of Psalm 51," quoted in Uuraas Saarnivaara, "Written and Spoken Word," *Lutheran Quarterly* 2 no. 2 (1950): 172.

25. Martin Luther, "The Fourth Sermon on the Verse from the Prophet Hosea [13:14], 1 Corinthians 15:54–57 (1545)." In *Luther's Works, Volume 58,* ed. Christopher Boyd Brown, trans. Aaron M. Moldenhauer (St. Louis: Concordia Publishing House, 2010), 159.

26. It is beyond the scope of this essay to summarize Luther's view of Christian freedom. Luther argued that Christians are free in Christ from the power of sin and that they are free from the need to fulfill the law. Yet this freedom is to be used in

service to the neighbor (freedom *from* and freedom *for*). Luther did not understand freedom as the possession or ability of a rational, autonomous, choosing subject. This contemporary (Western and elite) model of freedom is inconsistent with Luther's understanding that every Christian should live out their evangelical freedom in service to the neighbor. For nice overviews of Luther's understanding of freedom, see Gerhard Forde, "Called to Freedom: Opening Address," in *Lutherjahrbuch: Organ der Internationalen Lutherforschung—Liberation and Freedom, Martin Luther's Contribution*, 62, (Göttingen: Vandenhoeck & Ruprecht, 1995): 13–27; Kristin Johnston Largen, "Freedom *from* and Freedom *for*: Luther's Concept of Freedom for the Twenty-First Century," *Dialog: A Journal of Theology* 52, no. 3, (September 2013): 232–43.

27. Luther, LW 44, 298; on 'royal freedom' see "The Bondage of the Will (1525)," in *The Annotated Luther, Volume 2 Word and Faith*, ed. Kirsi I. Stjerna, trans. Philip S. Watson, Benjamin Drewery, and Volker Leppin (Minneapolis: Fortress Press, 2015), 181.

28. Martin Luther, "Lectures on Galatians (1535), Chapters 5–6," in *Luther's Works, Volume 27, Lectures on Galatians, 1535, Chapters 5–6, Lectures on Galatians 1519, Chapters 1–6*, eds. Jaroslav Pelikan and Walter Hansen, trans. Jaroslav Pelikan (St. Louis: Concordia Publishing House, 1963), 49–50; Luther also wrote, "I will give myself as a kind of Christ to my neighbor . . . . I will do nothing in this life except what I see will be necessary, advantageous, and salutary for my neighbor." "Freedom of a Christian (1520)," in *The Annotated Luther, Volume 1*, ed. Timothy J. Wengert, trans. W.A. Lambert and Harold Grimm (Minneapolis: Fortress, 2015), 524; Elsewhere Luther wrote, "Godliness is nothing else but service to God. Service to God is indeed service to our neighbor." "Whether One May Flee from a Deadly Plague (1527)," in *The Annotated Luther, Volume 4, Pastoral* Writings, ed. Mary Jane Haemig, trans. Anna Marie Johnson (Minneapolis: Fortress Press, 2016), 400.

29. Luther, LW 44, 303–04.

30. Ley, "Luther's Understanding,"; Stumme, "Conscience-bound Beliefs."

31. "Human Sexuality," 41.

32. Ibid., 20.

33. Ibid.

34. Ibid.

35. Ibid.

36. Ibid., 21.

37. See "Genetics, Faith and Responsibility" Evangelical Lutheran Church in America, accessed December 18, 2020, http://download.elca.org/ELCA%20Resource%20Repository/GeneticsSS.pdf; "Hearing the Cries: The Church and Criminal Justice," Evangelical Lutheran Church in America, accessed November 12, 2020, http://download.elca.org/ELCA%20Resource%20Repository/Hearing_The_Cries_Faith_And_Criminal_Justice.pdf.

38. Martin Luther, "Whether One May Flee from a Deadly Plague (1527)," in TAL 4, 390–402; See also, Luther, LW 44, 251–400; Luther also wrote, "How one believes or disbelieves is a matter for everyone's own conscience . . . . For faith is a free act, to which no one can be forced." "On Secular Authority: To What Extent It Should

Be obeyed (1523)," in *The Annotated Luther, Volume 5, Christian Life in the* World, ed. Hans J. Hillerbrand, trans. J.J. Schindel, Walter I. Brandt, and James M. Estes (Minneapolis: Fortress Press, 2017), 111.

39. Martin Luther, "The Babylonian Captivity of the Church (1520)," in *Luther's Works, Volume 36, Word and Sacrament II,* ed. Abdel Ross Wentz, trans. A.T.W. Steinhäuser and revised by Frederick C. Ahrens and Abdel Ross Wentz (Philadelphia: Fortress Press, 1959), 84; and "Receiving Both Kinds in the Sacrament (1522)," LW 36, 248.

40. "Luther understood the word [*conscientia*] literally as a kind of 'knowing with' . . . . he could not imagine conscience working properly without conversation . . . . There is here no declaration of individual conscience, but rather an observation of its dependence on the mutual conversation and consolation of brothers and sisters." Stortz, *"Solus Christus,"* 150.

41. Zachman, *The Assurance of Faith,* 47; see also Luther, LW 26, 315; Elsewhere Luther wrote, "Such is the nature of conscience. Although it feels sin and the heart is terrified and agitated . . . it nevertheless does not confess its transgression." "Lectures on Genesis Chapter 42," in *Luther's Works, Volume 7, Lectures on Genesis, Chapters 38–44,* eds. Jaroslav Pelikan and Walter Hansen, trans. Paul D. Pahl (St. Louis: Concordia Publishing House, 1963), 273; Luther expressed a similar idea in "A Sermon on the Three Kinds of Good Life for the Instruction of Consciences (1521)," LW 44, 237.

42. TAL 4, 394.

43. Anna Marie Johnson in TAL 4, 394, note 14.

44. Cis or Cisgender: "Cisgender: A term used by some to describe people who are not transgender. 'Cis-' is a Latin prefix meaning 'on the same side as,' and is therefore an antonym of 'trans-.' A more widely understood way to describe people who are not transgender is simply to say nontransgender people. "GLAAD Media Reference Guide."

45. "We believe that God also provides insights to us through reason, imagination, the social and physical sciences." "Human Sexuality," 10.

46. Ibid., 41, n. 26; A related ELCA document reads, "Is this matter of conscience so central that it determines whether one is saved? No, it does not. While these questions about morality and ministry practice are significant . . . one's faith is not at stake." "Frequently Asked Questions about Bound Conscience in Documents from the Task Force for ELCA Studies on Sexuality," ReconcilingWorks, accessed January 20, 2021, http://www.reconcilingworks.org/images/stories/downloads/resources/026_FAQBoundConscience.pdf, 3; Although this document is currently available on the ReconcilingWorks website, it was originally on the ELCA website. It is no longer available on the ELCA's website. The original document was issued by the Studies Department, Program Unit for Church and Society of the ELCA.

47. Riki Wilkins, *Queer Theory, Gender Theory: An Instant Primer* (Los Angeles: Alyson Books, 2004), 59; See also "Discourses are out in the world and history as coordinations ('a dance') of people, places, times, actions, interactions, verbal and nonverbal expression, symbols, things, tools, and technologies that betoken certain identities and associated activities. Thus, they are material realities. But Discourses

also exist as the work we do to get people and things recognized in certain ways and not others, and they exist as maps that constitute our understandings. They are, then, social practices and mental entities, as well as material realities." James Paul Gee, *An Introduction to Discourse Analysis: Theory and Method* (New York: Routledge, 1999), 23.

48. According to the Intersex Society of North America, "If you ask experts at medical centers how often a child is born so noticeably atypical in terms of genitalia that a specialist in sex differentiation is called in, the number comes out to about 1 in 1500 to 1 in 2000 births." "How Common is Intersex?" Intersex Society of North America, accessed January 15, 2021, http://www.isna.org/faq/frequency.

49. Amy Harmon, "Which Box Do You Check? Some States are Offering a Nonbinary Option," *New York Times,* May 29, 2019, https://www.nytimes.com/2019/05/29/us/nonbinary-drivers-licenses.html.

50. "Human Sexuality," 20.

51. Ibid.

52. Jack Drescher, "Out of DSM: Depathologizing Homosexuality," *Behavioral Sciences* 5, no. 4 (December 2015): 565–75, https://doi.org/10.3390/bs5040565.

53. "I have often used Dewey's term, 'the body-mind,' which is intended to capture the fact that what we call 'mind' and 'body' are not two separate and ontologically distinct entities or processes, but instead are aspects . . . of an interactive . . . process." Mark Johnson, *The Meaning of the Body: Aesthetics of Human Understanding* (Chicago: University of Chicago, 2007), 274.

54. Arthur M. Glenberg, K. Witt, and Janet Metcalfe, "From the Revolution to Embodiment: 25 Years of Cognitive Psychology," *Perspectives on Psychological Science* 8, no. 5 (2013): 573, http://amplab.colostate.edu/reprints/Glenberg_etal_2013_PoPS.pdf; Christian Gärtner, "Cognition, Knowing and Learning in the Flesh: Six Views on Embodied Knowing in Organizational Studies," *Scandinavian Journal of Management* 29, no. 4 (December 2013): 338–52, https://doi.org/10.1016/j.scaman.2013.07.005; "Embodied Cognition," Stanford Encyclopedia of Philosophy, accessed January 13, 2021, https://plato.stanford.edu/entries/embodied-cognition/.

55. For a list of representative primary metaphors see George Lakoff and Mark Johnson, *Philosophy in the Flesh: The Embodied Mind and its Challenge to Western Thought* (New York: Basic Books, 1999), 50–54.

56. Ibid., 36.

57. Simone Schnall and Peter R. Cannon, "The Clean Conscience at Work: Emotions, Intuitions and Morality," *Journal of Management, Spirituality & Religion* 9 no. 4, (2012): 299, https://doi.org/10.1080/14766086.2012.742749.

58. Yoel Inbar, Paul Bloom, and David A. Pizarro, "Disgusting Smells Caused Decreased Liking of Gay Men," *Emotion* 12, no. 1 (2012): 23–27, http://dx.doi.org/10.1037/a0023984.

59. Kendall J. Eskine, Natalie A. Kacinik and Jesse J. Prinz, "A Bad Taste in the Mouth: Gustatory Disgust Influences Moral Judgment," *Psychological Science* 22, no. 3 (March 2011): 298, https://doi.org/10.1177/0956797611398497; see also Cristina-Elena Ivan, "On Disgust and Moral Judgments: A Review," *Journal of European Psychology Students* 6, no.1 (2015): 25–36, http://doi.org/10.5334/jeps.cq; Joshua

May rejects the research (above) that connects disgust with harsher moral judgments, in "Does Disgust Influence Moral Judgment?" *Australasian Journal of Philosophy* 92, no. 1 (2014): 125–41, https://doi.org/10.1080/00048402.2013.797476.

60. Martin V. Day, and D. Ramona Bobocel, "The Weight of a Guilty Conscience: Subjective Body Weight as an Embodiment of Guilt," *PLOS ONE* 8, no. 7 (July 2013): 1–7, https://doi.org/10.1371/journal.pone.0069546.

61. Another experiment showed that Christians judged a beverage as disgusting after reading a passage written by an adversarial atheist. Ryan S. Ritter and Jessie Lee Preston, "Gross Gods and Icky Atheism: Disgust Responses to Rejected Religious Beliefs," *Journal of Experimental Social Psychology* 47, no. 6 (November 2011): 1225–1230, https://doi.org/10.1016/j.jesp.2011.05.006.

62. Luther frequently used the phrase *totus homo* to express his commitment that persons are whole—a unity of body, soul, and spirit. See Mary Elise Lowe, "The Queer Body-Mind in Martin Luther's Theology."

63. "Accelerating Acceptance, 2018, Executive Summary: A Survey of American Acceptance and Attitudes Toward LGBTQ Americans." GLAAD, accessed January 28, 2021, https://www.glaad.org/publications/accelerating-acceptance-2018.

64. The 2019, Accelerating Acceptance report showed, "general attitudes toward LGBTQ people are stable." GLAAD Accelerating Acceptance Report, accessed January 28, 2021, https://www.glaad.org/sites/default/files/Accelerating%20 Acceptance%202019.pdf.

65. Grace Hauck, "Anti-LGBT Hate Crimes are Rising, the FBI Says. But it Gets Worse," *USA Today*, June 28, 2019, https://www.usatoday.com/story/news/2019/06/28/ anti-gay-hate-crimes-rise-fbi-says-and-they-likely-undercount/1582614001/.

66. "ELCA Facts," Evangelical Lutheran Church in America, accessed January 16, 2021, https://www.elca.org/News-and-Events/ELCA-Facts.

67. An early draft of the proposed ELCA 2019 social statement on sexism defines neighbor-justice. "This neighbor-justice approach to reading the Bible puts into action two ideas from Lutheran thought: 1) The Bible contains both law (demand) and gospel (promise) and 2) the central importance of seeking the neighbor's good." "Faith, Sexism, Justice: Conversations Toward a Social Statement," Evangelical Lutheran Church in America, accessed January 20, 2021, http://download.elca.org/ELCA%20 Resource%20Repository/FAITH_SEXISM_JUSTICE_Conversations_toward_a_ Social_Statement.pdf.

68. "Human Sexuality," 33.

69. Ibid., 19.

70. Martin Luther, "Whether Soldiers, Too, Can Be Saved (1526)," in *The Annotated Luther, Volume 5, Christian Life in the* World, ed. Hans J. Hillerbrand, trans. Charles M. Jacobs, Robert C. Schultz, and John D. Roth (Minneapolis: Fortress Press, 2017), 198.

71. Ibid., 199.

72. TAL 4, 394.

73. LW 44, 393; Luther also wrote, "[I]n all of one's works a person should in this context be shaped by and contemplate this thought alone: to serve and benefit others

in everything . . . having nothing else in view except the need and the advantage of the neighbor." "The Freedom of a Christian (1520)," TAL 1, 520.

74. LW 27, 58.

BIBLIOGRAPHY

Evangelical Lutheran Church in America. "Faith, Sexism, and Justice: A Call to Action." Accessed January 1, 2021. https://download.elca.org/ELCA%20 Resource%20Repository/Faith_Sexism_Justice_Social_Statement_Adopted.pdf.

———. "Faith, Sexism, Justice: Conversations Toward a Social Statement." Accessed June 29, 2019. http://download.elca.org/ELCA%20Resource%20Repository/ FAITH_SEXISM_JUSTICE_Conversations_toward_a_Social_Statement.pdf.

———. "Human Sexuality: Gift and Trust." Accessed July 1, 2019. https://download. elca.org/ELCA%20Resource%20Repository/SexualitySS.pdf.

Day, Martin V. and Ramona Bobocel. "Does Disgust Influence Moral Judgment?" *Australasian Journal of Philosophy* 92, no. 1 (2014): 125–141. https://www. tandfonline.com/doi/abs/10.1080/00048402.2013.797476.

Drescher, Jack. "Out of DSM: Depathologizing Homosexuality." *Behavioral Sciences* 5, no. 4 (December 2015): 565–75. https://doi.org/10.3390/bs5040565.

Eskine, Kendall J., Natalie A. Kacinik, and Jesse J. Prinz. "A Bad Taste in the Mouth: Gustatory Disgust Influences Moral Judgment." *Psychological Science* 22, no. 3 (March 2011): 295–99. https://doi.org/10.1177/0956797611398497.

Forde, Gerhard. "Called to Freedom: Opening Address." In *Lutherjahrbuch: Organ der Internationalen Lutherforschung*, 62, 13–27. Göttingen: Vandenhoeck & Ruprecht, 1995.

Forell, George W. "Luther and Conscience." *Encounters with Luther: Lectures, Discussions, and Sermons at the Martin Luther Colloquia 1970–1974*, edited by Eric W. Gritsch, 218–35. Gettysburg: Institute for Luther Studies, 1980.

Gärtner, Christian. "Cognition, Knowing and Learning in the Flesh: Six Views on Embodied Knowing in Organizational Studies." *Scandinavian Journal of Management* 29, no. 4 (December 2013): 338–52. https://doi.org/10.1016/j. scaman.2013.07.005.

Gee, James Paul. *An Introduction to Discourse Analysis: Theory and Method*. New York: Routledge, 1999.

GLAAD. "Accelerating Acceptance, 2018, Executive Summary: A Survey of American Acceptance and Attitudes Toward LGBTQ Americans." Accessed January 6, 2021. https://www.glaad.org/files/aa/Accelerating%20Acceptance%20 2018.pdf.

Glenberg, Arthur M., Jessica K. Witt, and Janet Metcalfe. "From the Revolution to Embodiment: 25 Years of Cognitive Psychology." *Perspectives on Psychological Science* 8, no.5 (2013): 573–85. https://doi.org/10.1177/1745691613498098.

Harmon, Amy. "Which Box Do You Check? Some States are Offering a Nonbinary Option." *New York Times,* May 29, 2019. https://www.nytimes.com/2019/05/29/us/ nonbinary-drivers-licenses.html.

Inbar, Yoel, Paul Bloom, and David A. Pizarro. "Disgusting Smells Caused Decreased Liking of Gay Men." *Emotion* 12, no. 1 (2012): 23–27. http://dx.doi.org/10.1037/a0023984.

Ivan, Christina-Elena. "On Disgust and Moral Judgments: A Review." *Journal of European Psychology Students* 6, no.1 (2015): 25–36. http://doi.org/10.5334/jeps.cq.

Johnson, Mark. *The Meaning of the Body: Aesthetics of Human Understanding.* Chicago: University of Chicago, 2007.

Lakoff, George and Mark Johnson. *Philosophy in the Flesh: The Embodied Mind and its Challenge to Western Thought.* New York: Basic Books, 1999.

Largen, Kristin Johnston. "Freedom from and Freedom for: Luther's Concept of Freedom for the Twenty-First Century." *Dialog: A Journal of Theology* 52, no. 3 (Fall 2013): 232–43.

Ley, Matt. "Luther's Understanding of the Bound Conscience." *Journal of Lutheran Ethics* 10, no. 11 (2010). https://www.elca.org/JLE/Articles/246.

Lohse, Bernhard. "Conscience and Authority in Luther." In *Luther and the Dawn of the Modern Era,* edited by H.A. Oberman, 158–83. Leiden: E.J. Brill, 1974.

Lowe, Mary Elise. "The Queer Body-Mind in Martin Luther's Theology: From Subaltern Sodomite to Embodied *Imago Dei.*" In *The Alternative Luther: Lutheran Theology from the Subaltern,* edited by Else Marie Wiberg Pedersen, 118–36. Lanham, MD: Lexington Books/Fortress Academic, 2019.

Luther, Martin. "The Babylonian Captivity of the Church (1520)." In *Luther's Works, Volume 36, Word and Sacrament II,* edited by Abdel Ross Wentz, translated by A.T.W. Steinhäuser and revised by Frederick C. Ahrens and Abdel Ross Wentz, 3–126. Philadelphia: Fortress Press, 1959.

———. "The Bondage of the Will (1525)." In *The Annotated Luther, Volume 2 Word and Faith,* edited by Kirsi I. Stjerna, translated by Philip S. Watson, Benjamin Drewery, and Volker Leppin, 153–258. Minneapolis: Fortress Press, 2015.

———. "The Fourth Sermon on the Verse from the Prophet Hosea [13:14], 1 Corinthians 15:54–57 (1545)." In *Luther's Works, Volume 58,* edited by Christopher Boyd Brown, translated by Aaron M. Moldenhauer, 148–60. St. Louis: Concordia Publishing House, 2010.

———. "The Freedom of a Christian (1520)." In *The Annotated Luther, Volume 1, The Roots of Reform,* edited by Timothy J. Wengert, translated by W.A. Lambert and Harold Grimm, 467–538. Minneapolis: Fortress, 2015.

———. "Judgment of Martin Luther on Monastic Vows (1521)." In *Luther's Works, Volume 44, The Christian in Society,* edited by James Atkinson and Helmut T. Lehmann, translated by James Atkinson, 243–400. Philadelphia: Fortress Press, 1966.

———. "Lectures on Galatians (1535), Chapters 5–6." In *Luther's Works, Volume 27, Lectures on Galatians, 1535, Chapters 5–6, Lectures on Galatians 1519, Chapters 1–6,* edited by Jaroslav Pelikan and Walter Hansen, translated by Jaroslav Pelikan, 3–149. St. Louis: Concordia Publishing House, 1963.

————. "Lectures on Genesis, Chapter 42." In *Luther's Works, Volume 7, Lectures on Genesis, Chapters 38–44,* edited by Jaroslav Pelikan and Walter Hansen, translated by Paul D. Pahl, 216–305. St. Louis: Concordia Publishing House, 1963.

————. "Lectures on Titus (1527)." In *Luther's Works, Volume 29, Lectures on Titus, Philemon, and Hebrews,* edited by Jaroslav Pelikan and Walter A. Hansen, translated by Jaroslav Pelikan, 1–90. St. Louis: Concordia Publishing House, 1968.

————. "Luther at the Diet of Worms (1521)." In *Luther's Works, Volume 32, Career of the Reformer II,* edited by George W. Forell, translated by Roger A. Hornsby, 101–31. Philadelphia: Fortress Press, 1958.

————. *Luther's Works, Volume 20, Lectures on the Minor Prophets III, Zechariah,* edited by Hilton C. Oswald, translated by Richard J. Dinda. St. Louis: Concordia, 1973.

————. *Luther's Works, Volume 26, Lectures on Galatians, 1535, Chapters 1–4,* edited by Jaroslav Pelikan and Walter Hansen, translated by Jaroslav Pelikan. St. Louis: Concordia Publishing House, 1963.

————. "On Secular Authority: To What Extent It Should Be Obeyed (1523)." In *The Annotated Luther, Volume 5, Christian Life in the* World, edited by Hans J. Hillerbrand, translated by J.J. Schindel, Walter I. Brandt, and James M. Estes, 79–129. Minneapolis: Fortress Press, 2017.

————. "Preface to the Complete Edition of Luther's Latin Writings (1545)." In *Luther's Works, Volume 32, Career of the Reformer II,* edited and translated by Lewis W. Spitz, 323–38. Philadelphia: Fortress Press, 1960.

————. "Receiving Both Kinds in the Sacrament (1522)." In *Luther's Works, Volume 36, Word and Sacrament II,* edited and translated by Abdel Ross Wentz, 237–67. Philadelphia: Fortress Press, 1959.

————. "A Sermon on the Three Kinds of Good Life for the Instruction of Consciences, 1521." In LW 44, 231–242.

————. "Sermons at Leipzig and Erfurt, 1519; 1521." In *Luther's Works, Volume 51, Sermons I,* edited by John W. Doberstein, 51–66. Philadelphia: Fortress Press, 1959.

————. "Whether One May Flee from a Deadly Plague (1527)." In *The Annotated Luther, Volume 4, Pastoral* Writings, edited by Mary Jane Haemig, translated by Anna Marie Johnson, 385–409. Minneapolis: Fortress Press, 2016.

————. "Whether Soldiers, Too, Can Be Saved (1526)." In *The Annotated Luther, Volume 5, Christian Life in the* World, edited by Hans J. Hillerbrand, translated by Charles M. Jacobs, Robert C. Schultz, and John D. Roth, 183–233. Minneapolis: Fortress Press, 2017.

May, Joshua. "Does Disgust Influence Moral Judgment?" *Australasian Journal of Philosophy* 92, no. 1 (2014): 125–41. https://doi.org/10.1080/00048402.2013.79 7476.

Ritter, Ryan S. and Jessie Lee Preston. "Gross Gods and Icky Atheism: Disgust Responses to Rejected Religious Beliefs." *Journal of Experimental Social Psychology* 47, no. 6, (November 2011): 1225–30. https://doi.org/10.1016/j. jesp.2011.05.006.

Russell, William. "Martin Luther's Understanding of the Conscience, '*Coram Deo*' (. . . and the ELCA's Sexuality Study)." *Journal of Lutheran Ethics* 5, no. 7 (July 2005). https://www.elca.org/JLE/Articles/654.

Schnall, Simone and Peter R. Cannon. "The Clean Conscience at Work: Emotions, Intuitions and Morality." *Journal of Management, Spirituality & Religion* 9 no. 4 (2012): 299. https://doi.org/10.1080/14766086.2012.742749.

Stortz, Martha Ellen. "*Solus Christus* or *Sola Viscera*? Scrutinizing Lutheran Appeals to Conscience." *Dialog: A Journal of Theology* 44, no. 2 (Summer 2005): 146–51.

Stumme, John R. "'Conscience-bound Beliefs' Rule and the 'Conscious-bound-belief' Rule." *Journal of Lutheran Ethics,* 10, no. 11 (November 2010). https://www.elca.org/JLE/Articles/245.

Wilkins, Riki. *Queer Theory, Gender Theory: An Instant Primer*. Los Angeles: Alyson Books, 2004.

Wilson, Robert A. and Lucia Foglia, "Embodied Cognition," The Stanford Encyclopedia of Philosophy (Spring 2017 Edition), Edward N. Zalta (ed.), https://plato.stanford.edu/archives/spr2017/entries/embodied-cognition/.

Zachman, Randall C. *The Assurance of Faith: Conscience in the Theology of Martin Luther and John Calvin*. Minneapolis: Fortress Press, 1993.

Chapter 3

The Obligations We Bear with One Another

A Reply to Lowe and Riswold on Questions of Conscience, Domination, and Love

Anthony Bateza

Read together, the chapters offered here by Mary Elise Lowe and Caryn D. Riswold raise valuable and thought-provoking questions about Lutheran theology and the moral challenges facing Christians more broadly. Each author is fundamentally concerned not only with how to best understand Luther's thought, but with what his theological legacy might offer us as we seek to understand ourselves and to serve our neighbors. What does it mean to be bound by one's conscience, and to what extent do we treat conscience as an emotional certainty divorced from reasons that provide cover for committing injustice? Have we become overly individualistic at the expense of communal systems and responsibilities for others? Do we know when power has been corrupted by the desire for domination? Lowe and Riswold raise these important questions with respect to the status and treatment of LGBTQIA+ people in the United States, specifically the response to sexuality and ordination that has developed within the Evangelical Lutheran Church in America (ELCA) and the issues surrounding the denial of goods and services for purported reasons of religious freedom.

In what follows, I will identify some of the strong contributions these chapters make, highlighting their unflinching scrutiny of the motivations and conceptual confusion at work in Lutheran and Christian moral reflection. I will also offer my own critical suggestions where I believe each argument could be improved through greater attention to what their own concepts entail, where ideas about domination, oppression, the social construction of values and the normative burdens of neighbor love need to be articulated more clearly. Ultimately, I affirm the goals of both Lowe and Riswold but offer a different path to reach these goals, one that I hope gets at some of the complexities and difficulties that appear in Lutheran theology and the lived realities facing us today.

WHEN MOTIVES MATTER

It is common, and usually counterproductive, to begin with questions about someone's motivations or intentions. This is not because intentions are mysterious or unimportant, but rather that beginning here often signals an effort to excuse or exculpate when a challenge is made. Charges of heterosexism, gender discrimination, or racism are too quickly evaded by claims of good intentions or simple ignorance. What I *meant* to say or do is offered up as the primary way that my sayings and doings should be interpreted, thereby dividing whatever harm they might have caused from me as the source of this harm. To their credit, Lowe and Riswold offer us a different way of understanding intentions. Both carefully interrogate the individual and collective motivations at work in the words, policies, and laws Christians have enacted. They accomplish this through careful attention to the phrases found in ELCA teaching documents and legal arguments offered inside the courthouse and the larger courtroom of public and political appeal. Behind the words used there are important, often unacknowledged, presuppositions that require careful explication. In both instances, we are allowed to see a worldview where Christianity is somehow threatened by the work for the social and legal equality of LGBTQIA+ peoples, whether this be business owners invoking their Christian values or a church body that employs ambivalence to avoid the risk of conflict and disunity.

I am drawn to Mary Elise Lowe's trenchant assessment of what is at stake in the ELCA's teaching and guiding documents regarding the ordination of individuals in noncelibate gay and lesbian relationships. Lowe points to a deep complexity in the church's response. On the one hand, the conversations and policy changes opened the door for recognizing and celebrating the ministerial gifts of LGBTQIA+ persons within the Lutheran church. If this is an instance of justice being served, which I believe it is, then the arc of the universe is bent ever so slightly in the right direction. On the other hand, Lowe shows us how the approach taken by the ELCA also signaled a painful and challenging reality that, put bluntly, the church was motivated by a deep and abiding desire to avoid offending or driving off those who deny the wholeness, dignity, and equality of LGBTQIA+ persons. The various appeals to conscience on offer created and honored a space for those who see homosexuality and other forms of sexual and gender identity as sinful and wrong. The harm to be avoided was the exclusion of those opposed to full inclusion, not the repeated violence and harms that have been committed against excluded LGBTQIA+ individuals, families, and those who love and support them.

Following Riswold's lead in making comparisons between white privilege and Christian privilege, we might engage in a simple thought experiment to sharpen the point here. Imagine the church taking a similar approach to the inclusion of Black members in the full life and leadership of the church as the approach taken for LGBTQIA+ persons. How might we respond if the church took up the position that some Christians, in good conscience, held to the biblically warranted and traditionally endorsed position that Black peoples are inferior to their neighbors who believe themselves to be white? While officially the church might move forward with plans for the full inclusion of Black people, how would Black people respond if in the same breath it was made clear that those who do not wish to call a Black pastor or who hold that Black people are cursed descendants of Ham, that they struggle with unnatural sexual desires, or that miscegenation posed a threat to traditional marriage?

Of course, the situation I describe is not some fanciful imagined possibility, it is recent and durable history, a part of the Christian inheritance. And, of course, shifting the frame from LGBTQIA+ issues to race and racism could be question begging. One might say that the matter under discussion is precisely how to discern the right political or religious stance on LGBTQIA+ issues, and that the moral and theological consensus on racism has been established while questions about sexuality and gender are part of a valid and ongoing debate. Given this, the pivot to racism will be seen as unhelpful at best and misleading at worst. But what Lowe and Riswold show is that the framing offered by Christians privileges those who question the status of LBGTQ+ persons or, at the very least, see the issues as a matter of indifference that is up for discussion. Furthermore, in the case of the ELCA's documents and debates, one can suspect the extent to which feared losses of members and money lurk as motives for the cautious and questionable stance taken. Attempting to appease conservative members comes at the expense of real LGBTQIA+ people. Whether or not salvation is at stake in an eschatological sense, Lowe argues persuasively that immanent damnation wrought by homophobia and heterosexism cannot be overlooked or dismissed by appeals to Christian conscience.[1]

INTERROGATING THEOLOGICAL CONCEPTS

In our efforts to think, communicate, and understand ourselves and one another, we often lack the time to sit with and critically examine our words and concepts. Indeed, such efforts would derail conversations and invite the charge of pedantry. Nevertheless, Lowe and Riswold show us why theological reflection is strengthened when time and attention are devoted to more carefully explicating the meaning within and behind the language we use. The two central concepts under investigation in these chapters are conscience and freedom, concepts that have a long life and deep connections to our theological and political traditions. As I read them, these authors make at least three important contributions to our understanding of these words.

Given the pull of individualism in western societies, where the solitary subject is given priority over the communal or structural facets of life, it is not surprising to see how this individualism affects the meaning of conscience and freedom. What is refreshing is the way these chapters flesh out unfettered individualism's distortion of these concepts. Looking at conscience, Lowe carefully excavates Martin Luther's usage of the term while adding insights gleaned from modern psychological research and moral reflection. Instead of viewing conscience as an inner source of assurance, she pushes us to see how Luther saw in conscience not confidence but critique, a source of self-judgment and not self-justification. Turning too quickly to conscience as a personal matter allows us to avoid weighty issues of power and privilege. Riswold makes a similar argument about freedom becoming a matter of individual power untethered from social forces and inequalities. We might describe both authors as criticizing a convoluted and unequal construal of freedom, where one enjoys negative freedom (freedom from) while turning positive freedom (freedom for) into a burden only others bear.[2] My liberty is experienced as a lack of interference from others that simultaneously authorizes my interference in the lives of others through the denial of services, standing, or other social goods such as marriage, adoption, or employment.

In addition to the meaning of conscience and freedom, we are invited to take note of how these concepts function in our discourse and debates. It is not just that the definitions of conscience and freedom are inadequate, but that they are being deployed in ways that are unjustified. Conscience is invoked by church bodies to avoid taking a stronger position on a question of moral weight, baptizing ambivalence. Freedom, understood as individual liberty, becomes the highest possible value and the hardest possible cudgel.[3] Freedom allows discriminatory treatment in the economic and political realms that would be ruled out of hand without the cloak of religion. Combined these efforts result in an unacknowledged hierarchy of values, where conscience and freedom for historically dominant groups trump appeals to other values on behalf of the historically marginalized. As an alternative, Lowe and Riswold display a variety of values and goods under consideration, showing that conscience, for example, concerns judgments about the good and does not spring from an unassailable source in natural law or divine declarations.

Through these efforts we are gifted with a powerful example of the ongoing importance of theological concepts and histories. While they do not make this point explicit, it is worth noting how these authors demonstrate the ways that contemporary social debates can be better understood and enriched by examining the traditions of the church and the living, breathing communities that carry these traditions in the present. While the common image of religion in debates about LGBTQIA+ issues is antagonistic, where people of faith are a continuing source of pain and an obstacle to justice, the image here is more dynamic and complicated. If theological concepts and ecclesial communities are sources of trouble and woe for the work of justice, they might and, as Lowe and Riswold show, should be sites of serious inquiry, ameliorative criticism and, perhaps, reparation and reconciliation.

WHOSE DOMINATION, WHICH OPPRESSION?

Addressing the dynamic, constructed meaning of our beliefs, values, and affective responses is an important move when engaging in most forms of ideological critique. It is particularly effective when a concept seems to evade appraisal because it is taken as a given, either because it enjoys an aura of durability in a community in an unreflective sense or it is defended as hardwired into the cosmos as an immutable law, natural or divine. This is certainly the case with many of the sentiments and arguments concerning LGBTQIA+ recognition and rights. Critics of evolving interpretations on these issues suggest that there is no room for change, and certainly no room for progress, as ideas about human sexuality and gender identity are purportedly written into our genetic code and articulated in the sacred scriptures. Lowe and Riswold challenge this move, pushing for a historically and culturally sensitive hermeneutical strategy that examines the development of our ideas about conscience and freedom while also inviting the reader to reconsider the relationship between meanings given in religious communities, scriptural texts, and sociopolitical contexts.

When discussing concepts like freedom and conscience these authors provide us with the some much-needed clarity and precision, making their overall arguments about the mistakes surrounding current Christian practices all the more convincing. That said, there are moments when key terms are used without the same attention to depth or meaning. One important case involves the understanding of domination and oppression, concepts both Lowe and Riswold appeal to throughout their work. This shortcoming does not affect the quality of their arguments, and to state the obvious, no chapter or article could ever cover every permutation of meaning for every concept deployed. In this instance this lack suggests an area where further development of the concepts in question would provide more charitable reading of those groups and positions the authors criticize and might allow for the arguments to have a greater impact on audiences disinclined to agree with their stated goals of furthering cause of justice for LGBTQIA+ persons.

Domination and oppression are always negative words, by which I mean they are immediately recognized as bad and disavowed. Nobody suggests domination as an appropriate course of action. Instead, I believe, people debate how domination is understood and whether or not the action or arrangement under dispute is an instance of domination. In many cases we move along quite smoothly while presupposing a shared understanding of such words. If I point to the treatment of black and brown bodies during the era of chattel slavery in the United States, or the actions of Adolf Hitler and the German National Socialist apparatus in twentieth century, I can describe these as examples of domination and oppression and expect pushback only from extreme positions outside the overwhelming mainstream where slave masters and Nazis are paradigmatic instances of dominators and oppressors. The situation becomes more complicated, and more contested, the further I move away from these examples and look to apply these terms to other cases. Can a straight line be drawn from slavery, through the Jim Crow south, up to and including contemporary instances of police brutality and other forms of violence disproportionally inflicted upon black and brown bodies today?

My short answer is yes, I can draw such a line and make these connections. I answer this way because of how I understand domination and oppression, and how I understand these historical and present-day realities. Following the work of Philip Pettit, I understand domination as the possibility of arbitrary interference in the choices of another.[4] Staying with the paradigmatic case of slavery, the master is able to constrain the life of the slave without seeking the slaves' opinion or fearing repercussions for his actions toward the slave. We might be tempted to say that domination is not at work if the master is not prone to interfere in the slaves' life, giving the slave wide leeway in making their own choices, or even showing relatively kindness and benevolence toward the slave in ways that appear to seek their good. This might make the situation better for this slave when compared with the conditions endured under the violent and brutal master down the road, but this relative improvement does not make the situation any less dominating. The slave remains cut off from their agency, beholden to the choices and will of the master, insecure and exposed.[5]

Oppression is a concept with similar weight and connotations as domination, yet remains distinct from it. As Iris Marion Young argues, domination is best construed as the arbitrary or asymmetric exertion of power of one group over another, as we find in cases of political tyranny. Young explains that the meaning of oppression has undergone an expansion across the twentieth century, moving from the realm of tyranny to the broader, everyday institutions and practices people encounter in purportedly democratic, liberal societies. Oppression is understood as a structural feature of a society whose "causes are embedded in the unquestioned norms, habits, and symbols, in the assumptions underlying institutional rules and the collective consequences of following those rules."[6] Young furthers her analysis by defining the idea of "social groups" and outlining five different categories of oppression with different social impacts and interactions: exploitation, marginalization, powerlessness, cultural imperialism, and violence.[7] Each category has its own dynamic, with exploitation tracking material loss of labor and the goods of one's work as people are used by systems, while marginalization describes the situation of those the system "cannot or will not use," those who are "expelled from useful participation in social life and thus potentially subject to severe material deprivation and even extermination."[8] Under these categories, racism appears not as a distinct category of oppression but as the confluence of many, in ways that touch on the intersections of social group identity, class, politics, and ideology.

This brief foray into different definitions of domination and oppression is offered not to belabor fine, academic variations of meaning, but rather to show what kind of labor is required to help clarify meaning and to connect arguments to audiences. Would those on the other side of issue agree with the definitions of domination and oppression presented here? Would the conservative Christian baker or Lutheran opponent to the ordination of non-heterosexual pastors describe the situation facing LGBTQIA+ persons in our society as one of domination and oppression? To be clear, we might reject out of hand the quality or value of their beliefs on these questions, just as I am inclined to dismiss white supremacist defenders of slavery and holocaust deniers. Not every objection, especially one offered in bad faith, warrants a response. But if we choose to respond in this case, the picture becomes murkier. Presumably these bakers and congregants see themselves as subjected to some form of oppression, being pushed along political and social forces that they resist towards conclusions that they reject. They might hold that the kind of goods being denied to LGBTQIA+ persons in these instances, a dessert in one instance, an ordination in another, do not rise to level of tyrannical domination or some category of oppression.

If my goal is to convince opponents of LGBTQIA+ rights, then addressing these fundamental differences in how terms are understood gets at a fundamental difference in how the world is understood. I will need to slowly and methodically move the other side to expand their view of domination and oppression to include the treatment of LGBTQIA+ people in bakeries, congregations, and beyond. I might also want to demonstrate that I grasp the complexities behind their own feelings of oppression and marginalization, neither endorsing nor dismissing their experiences. If my goal is to encourage proponents of LGBTQIA+ rights, then addressing these fundamental differences in how domination and oppression are understood is also a worthwhile endeavor. Providing conceptual clarity and valuable insights into the beliefs and feelings of my opponents serves to sharpen our arguments and wards off the possible threat of merely "preaching to the choir." Instead of pointing to, and presuming, that domination and oppression are operative, I can better articulate the dynamics and intersections of power. Furthermore, recognizing our own psychological proclivity to be more attuned to changes in our subjective experiences rather than tracking objective changes is important as well. We judge happiness and wealth in relationship to our past experiences and those around us, and similarly an experience of increased anti-Christian hostility marks a significant change for those unaccustomed to challenging stress, even as the objective power and privilege enjoyed by Christians remains overwhelming.[9]

WHERE DOES LOVE GUIDE US?

Both Lowe and Riswold believe that contemporary Christians have lost their way, either through narrow and misguided views on conscience and freedom that have led them away from central Lutheran and Christian insights, down the path of power to a place of domination and oppression. As Riswold puts it, what is being sought is "glory, triumph, and certainty, in contrast to service, humility, and incarnational living of even one of the acts of mercy detailed in Matthew 25."[10] The way back from this place is difficult to discern, but the proper goal should be lives of service and love ordered to the needs of the neighbor. In Luther and the Christian tradition these authors see a repeated call toward humility, putting aside narrow self-interest because one has put on Christ and taken on the burdens and needs of others. Building on Luther's comments in his argument against the medieval views on monastic vows and the proper response to the dangers of a pandemic, Lowe extends the idea that "love is the only guide" to make a compelling case for the prioritization of care for LGBTQIA+ peoples over the painfully common Christian practices of condemnation, exclusion, or at *best*, the kind of ambivalence and indifference enjoyed by the privileged and detached.

The turn to love of neighbor, embodied in concrete service on the neighbor's behalf and for their own flourishing, is an important and moving appeal that has a firm foundation in Luther's writing and lived example. It also, I fear, exposes one of Luther's greatest potential shortcomings. As I read him, Luther generally assumes that Christians have a solid grasp of what it is that their neighbor needs. The examples given by the Reformer tend to center on immediate physical or biological necessities. We know, he thinks, when our neighbor is lacking food, shelter, and clothing. We might need a stern reminder to also take note of their need for medical treatment and emotional care when a plague is ravaging the town or a melancholic bout of depression has settled into their soul.[11] If we have a consensus about what justice requires, what my neighbor is due and how I am able to provide what is needed, then the appeal to love will hopefully enkindle my spirit and move my limbs into action. But Luther is less helpful when the cases are less clear or when he himself questions what the neighbor needs.

One of the most obvious examples of this comes in Luther's response to the German peasants during the events of 1524–1525, known as the German Peasants' War or the Revolution of the Common Person, the nomenclature depending on your own political persuasion and views on the events.[12] The situation was one in which peasant farmers, miners, disaffected knights, and urban tradesmen banded together to make economic and political demands of their local rulers, the motley collection of secular dukes and margraves working in concert with powerful abbots and bishops. Recent legal arrangements had supplanted customary legal practices with ancient Roman law, with the results favoring the powerful and stripping the common person of access to land, food, inherited wealth, and the possibility of release from bonds of debt and serfdom. The groups of people that gathered in protest were eclectic, their aims shifting from one region to another, and their use of armed, violent resistance was celebrated by some but feared by many.

When they appealed to "God's justice," looking to the freedom had in Christ and the message for the poor found in the Bible, some invited Luther and other reform minded religious leaders to offer guidance and, hopefully, support for their cause. Luther famously demurred at first, and then infamously denounced the peasants' cause, casting his lot with the princes whose wonton violence both put down the rebellion and went beyond to make a lasting example of those who might take up the peasants' cause in the decades to follow. While I believe that Luther's initial response is more complicated than many recognize as he denounces the princes for their wickedness and lays at their feet the blame for the peasants' uprising, his views on the situation reveal many weaknesses in his theological and political thought.[13] To recall Young's categories for oppression, the peasants railed against economic exploitation. Luther is confusingly ambivalent, both agreeing with their plight while also suggesting that they are looking to have two cows when one should be sufficient. The peasants complain about being made more power-less, being denied customary legal recourse for their grievances, and Luther seems to suggest that powerlessness is their lot given the political and eco-nomic hierarchies established by God. When violence is inflicted on bodies, Luther laments the violence done to rulers and clergy more than the horrors perpetrated against the common people.

I rehearse these details not to suggest that Luther should be tossed aside, that his moral insights should be discarded because of his ethical failings. Rather, this example brings into the light what is often obscured by appeals to the power of loving one's neighbor. If I am inclined to agree that love looks like one particular economic arrangement and not another, then the appeal to love can strengthen my resolve. If I am not so inclined, or to put it more strongly, fiercely opposed to the cause in question, appeals to love will fall flat. Alternatively, it is just as likely that those on the other side of an issue will take themselves to be acting in love toward their neighbor, even when their actions appear to be anything but loving from my perspective. Undoubtedly some take themselves to be acting out of love *coram hominibus et deo*, serv-ing their neighbor and God through a reading of the Bible and a political positioning of the Church. They might believe that viewing homosexuality as a sin, for example, is an act of neighbor love, both toward the homosexual and toward the larger society. I do not find this view irrational even though, because of my own beliefs and commitments, I find it egregiously wrong and deeply fallacious. I would compare this with those arguments that were so often wrapped in Christian thought, where the alleged deficiencies in Black people and the preposterous benefits claimed from enslavement and control were proffered in defense of slavery. Nevertheless, this sharp divergence in how we describe the situation and our obligations is not tied to a different abstract goal (love of neighbor) but to very different views about what love looks like, what it demands, and who counts as my neighbor.

This suggests to me that appealing to love of neighbor is potentially con-fusing and ineffective without attention to, and argument about, the require-ments of love. It is not enough to say that the other side has failed to live out love of neighbor without *also* addressing how love might shape their approach and how their view of love is in need of refinement, correction, or wholesale renovation.[14] Without this hard work contrasting one side as loving and the other as failing to love the neighbor too easily evades the place where beliefs diverge and where intervention is needed.

There is also the need to articulate one's own position, the alternative being offered to those who seem to lack the correct understanding of love and its demands, and I think that Lowe and Riswold do some of this work. Highlighting the disproportionate harms inflicted upon LGBTQIA+ persons as they are pressed out of church and familial spaces ought to give pause to any seeking to cast these outcomes as examples of faithful service to Christian ideals or gospel love of neighbors. Pressing further on why being targeted and excluded from mundane activities, like securing a wedding cake, shows both the vulnerability of LGBTQIA+ persons and the concrete privileges cis, heterosexual people take for granted. These efforts, if framed rightly, can also identify the harm without reducing LGBTQIA+ people to case studies in suffering, setting out a telos of love marked by lives filled with quotidian joys and flourishing.

While I contend that invoking Christian notions of service and neighbors will not do the kind of moral work that Lowe and Riswold suggest without greater attention to the messy examples and multifaceted meaning of these concepts and ideals, there is one further benefit to their turn to love. Making a liberated conscience and autonomous freedom the driving forces has a tendency to push toward exculpation instead of expiation, disavowing guilt at the expense of repentance, repair, or reconciliation. Foregrounding love, instead of conscience and freedom, places relationships front and center. At times, we use the language of love metaphorically or analogically to say we love ideals or institutions, expressing our attraction and commitment to justice or the systems that support it, but the proper home for talk of love is embodied in relationships shared with others. Attending to love invites us to consider how we are attached to others in individual and communal ways, relationships that are personal and impersonal. Asking what love requires, as a person of faith rooted in a tradition that speaks of loves divine and human as central to our being *coram hominibus et deo,* in heart, soul, and mind, provides a valuable intellectual and affective invitation to reconsider our connections.

This Christian concern with love and relationships also has much to learn from non-Christian sources. The moral philosopher Elinor Mason, whose work investigates responsibility and related concepts, provides us with some helpful tools for challenges at hand. Mason constructs a typology of praise and blame that distinguishes ordinary, detached, and extended varieties. Blameworthiness in the ordinary sense applies when an individual who is a member of our moral community, and thus accountable to the same shared norms and standards, commits some wrong that they would recognize as such. Detached blameworthiness describes our holding those outside of our community to our standards, standards they would not recognize and that we are not in a position to directly communicate with them. This variety of blame is employed primarily for our own needs, to make our expectations clear to ourselves as we solidify or modify our ethical commitments. Thinking about Mason's use of these ordinary and detached instances of blame potentially provides us with language to more carefully evaluate the audience for Lowe and Riswold's criticisms, to ask who is a part of which community and for what purposes are we offering accusations or accolades. But for present purposes I am more interested in Mason's views on extended blameworthiness.

The need for extended blameworthiness arises, Mason argues, when "an agent has acted wrongly, and understands the wrongness, but has acted wrongly entirely inadvertently."[15] Some paradigmatic cases here concern socially weighty matters, such as the effects of implicit bias that generate sexist and racist acts, and more limited situations such as accidents, omissions, or oversights. In these situations, Mason suggests that the individual who committed some wrong can take on responsibility even if alternative explanations or mitigating circumstances might rightly be invoked to diminish culpability. This responsibility and blame are not embraced for the sake of the wrongdoer, out of an exaggerated sense of self-worth or a misguided desire for self-abnegation. "We voluntarily extend our responsibility zone in order to secure the respect and trust of others, and as a way of showing commitment and investment in our relationships."[16]

Mason constructs the helpful example of someone borrowing, and then losing, a piece of jewelry on loan from a friend. The borrower, who she calls "Perdita," goes back to her friend and apologizes for having lost a necklace. After the apology, a conversation continues with the friend asking for more explanation for what happened. At this point, Perdita could explain emphasizing the accidental, nonmaliciousness of the loss. She is not prone to loosing things, she did not toss it into an empty field in a fit of anger, let's say, or carelessly take it on and off in a crowded subway or concert hall. This was a momentary "glitch" where she "spaced out," the kind of mishap too familiar to us all. The explanation offered in this instance might well be true and accurate, but a problem lingers insofar as the explanation builds an argument for why Perdita should be excused for her loss. Mason points out that this conversation is not just about explaining causes but also concerns how Perdita "thinks the loss of the necklace should be taken . . . In not taking responsibility in this case, Perdita would be showing that she is more concerned with her friend."[17]

The conversation between Perdita and her friend could proceed differently by moving in the direction of extended responsibility. This would make clear to the friend that Perdita cares about her friend's loss, and concomitantly that Perdita values or understands how concern and investment in the other are central features of friendship itself. Here "Perdita shows her respect and love for her friend by accepting that the action is her own, and feeling remorse. Perdita need not feel full blown guilt . . . . Likewise, Perdita's friend need not engage in deep and lasting resentment. The point is that the friend needs to see that Perdita is engaging with her, responding to her being hurt, and to the fact that Perdita hurt her."[18]

A lost necklace is one thing, the standing and dignity of LGBTQIA+ persons is quite another, but weightiness of the latter does not mean that dissimilar issues are at work in the work that love requires. Bringing Mason into conversation with Lowe and Riswold allows us to put a different edge on the demand to respond in and for love. A church body, like the ELCA, presenting conscience and freedom as exculpating reassurances to its individual members and for its own actions as a corporate body, lays bare a lack of concern driven by love and held in relationship. It communicates how a Christian friend thinks the loss of standing and dignity of LGBTQIA+ persons should be taken. Instead of saying that members of the church have simply failed to deliver the good to these friends, a failure marked by remorse that yearns for repair, the church approaches the question as justifiably contested, as one where the duties here remain up for debate.[19] Notice that this recognition of duties might come with a tragic acknowledgment of the limits of the church's jurisdiction. While congregational polity and theological principles about the priesthood of all believers mean that no individual church could or should be required to recognize and call an LGBTQIA+ pastor, this would be expressed as a sinful and lamentable limit, one where the neighbor is not served and Christ's love has been choked by thorns and thistles.

None of what has been offered here resolves the challenges posed above by considering and responding to those who would disagree with this description of their attitudes and actions about LGBTQIA+ persons, the audience that would characterize their choices to not ordain and to not prepare wedding cakes as neither dominating nor oppressive. Added to this, we could say that they would also be able to take on the language of love, whereby their actions remain committed to the good of these friends whom they believe to be in error. This reality needs to be acknowledged, in part, because it shows us that other actions and responses are also on the table. Just as is the case between friends who cannot resolve weighty disputes, so it is between Christians who have reached an impasse. We might let go of the issue by considering it *adiaphora* or inconsequential, willing to admit diverging positions without much sense of loss. This is certainly the stance many take on LGBTQIA+ issues, opting for a laissez faire attitude. This comes with some benefits but also entails great costs, especially for those for whom these are fundamental and defining issues. Here one might opt for tolerance in its most robust sense of the term, patiently enduring this objectionable difference to maintain a relationship.[20] We hold on to the seriousness, remaining committed to the rightness of our position while simultaneously remaining friends, members of a shared religious and political community.

Finally, we might decide that the costs of indifference or tolerance are too high, that the right response here is commitment to one set of ideals or relationships that risks or accepts the loss of others. While the spiritual estate does not wield the sword, it would be mistaken to think that power and coercion are not at the church's disposal.[21] Judgments are made about what is to be believed and done, and when these are enforced members protest, churches divide and denominations split. Those on either side will take themselves to be in the right, and those in the middle can become confused and consternated by such developments. The confusion will likely increase as the different sides appeal to similar ideals of love in defense of opposing viewpoints. Love provides less safety than we might desire, and less guidance that we might imagine, in moments of conflict and loss. But knowing this does not diminish its value, and the opportunities to test this love and our commitments to those claimed as our beloveds, should be embraced in the ways Lowe and Riswold commend. It is not clear that this will resolve our disputes, but it certainly makes clear what and who we are fighting for.

NOTES

1. David Gushee gives an impassioned and cogent example of what this kind of argument can look like in his "Reconciling Evangelical Christianity with our Sexual Minorities: Reframing the Biblical Discussion," *Journal of the Society of Christian Ethics* 53, no. 2 (Fall/Winter 2015): 141–58.

2. This is an oblique reference to Isaiah Berlin's well-known distinction between positive and negative freedom or liberty. See "Two Concepts of Liberty," in *Four Essays on Liberty,* 2nd ed. (Oxford: Oxford University Press, 1990).

3. At the time of this writing troubling debates about requirements to wear masks in public spaces during the COVID-19 pandemic have made the issue of individual liberty especially polarizing and, I would argue, dangerous.

4. See Philip Pettit, *Republicanism: A Theory of Freedom and Government* (Oxford: Clarendon Press, 1997), especially pages 21–27. The view of choices here is intentionally broad so as to capture the various ways that individuals might be constrained—from material and bodily concerns (food, shelter, relationships, education, wealth, sex, bodily security and life) to the more abstract or institutional (ideals and values such as dignity, honor, and self-worth, etc.) For a helpful addition, see Thomas Wartenberg's distinction between "domination from below," where those in a superior social position exercise control of the bodies and possessions of those in a subordinate position, versus "domination from above" where ideologies and ways of thinking and feeling are shaped. *The Forms of Power* (Philadelphia: Temple University Press, 1990), here chapter six.

5. For a penetrating look at the complicities and vicious capriciousness of so-called kind masters, see Frederick Douglass, *Narrative of the life of Frederick Douglas, an American Slave* (Boston: Anti-Slavery Office, 1849), 19f.

6. Iris Marion Young, *Justice and the Politics of Difference* (Princeton, NJ: Princeton University Press, 2011), 41.

7. Young, *Justice and the Politics of Difference,* 48–63.

8. Young, *Justice and the Politics of Difference,* 53.

9. Given Riswold's use of Robin DiAngelo's work on white fragility, it would be interesting to note some similar affective, and frequently gendered, similarities in response to the work of antiracism and in challenging Christian privilege. Drawing from her observations as a workshop facilitator, DiAngelo notes how white men frequently become angry and belligerent when confronted with their own racism. In contrast, she describes a more intimately pained response in white women, whereby they take offense at accusations and cry. Both responses have intellectual and emotional components, and both take attention away from any harm done to people of color and redirect it towards whites and the alleged harms done to them. DiAngelo describes this dynamic as "white fragility, which is "a state in which even a minimum amount of racial stress becomes intolerable, triggering a range of defensive moves. These moves include the outward display of emotions such as anger, fear, and guilt, and behaviors such as argumentation, silence, and leaving the stress-inducing situation. These behaviors, in turn, function to reinstate white racial equilibrium." Applying this same stress and equilibrium dynamic strikes me as a fruitful way to further the interrogation of Christian responses to a feared loss of privilege and the defense moves that might arise when Christians are accused of enjoying their privilege and not acknowledging the harm done to others. *White Fragility: Why It's So Hard for White People to Talk about Racism* (Boston: Beacon Press, 2018), 103.

10. Riswold, 19.

11. Martin Luther's "A Simple Way to Pray, for Master Peter the Barber," available in *Luther's Spirituality*, ed. Philip D. W. Krey and Peter D. S. Krey (New York: Paulist Press, 2007): 217–34.

12. The literature and opinions on the German Peasants' War are both voluminous. For helpful anglophone introductions see *The German Peasants' War: A History in Documents,* ed. Tom Scott and Bob Scribner (Amherst, New York: Prometheus Books, 1991), Robert Scribner, *The German Peasant War of 1525: New Viewpoints* (London: Unwin Hyman, 1979), Peter Blickle, and *The Revolution of 1525: The German Peasants' War from a New Perspective* (Baltimore: The Johns Hopkins University Press, 1991).

13. For more on longer explanation of my views, see Anthony M. Bateza, "Reconciling Rapacious Wolves and Misguided Sheep: Law and Responsibility in Martin Luther's Response to the German Peasants' War," *Political Theology 19,* no. 4 (2018): 264–81.

14. Taking on the other side's position, and responding to their potential objections to my own, does of course grant their position more standing that I might want to grant. As I noted above, not every objection warrants a response, but I choose to not engage a position under certain conditions. Some of these are minor conditions of time and space. Is this the right moment for that issue, or must I leave it to the side for present purposes? Some of these conditions are more substantive than practical. Is the other side taking a position or offering questions in bad faith, as a distraction or rhetorical trap? Will entertaining a debate give undue credence to a position in ways that might signal that a settled question is still being hotly contested? Am I concerned about what taking up this question, offered in good faith and in the midst

of an ongoing moral deliberation, will do to those who have been harmed, such that the cost of repeated trauma outweighs the benefits of creating space for public contestation? I would consider debates about the reality of human caused climate change and, in some instances, the enduring life of sexism and antiblack racism to be topics that are often contested in bad faith or in ways that quickly and flippantly dismiss the ongoing damage being done to real people.

15. Elinor Mason, *Ways to Be Blameworthy: Rightness, Wrongness, and Responsibility* (Oxford: Oxford University Press, 2019), 2.

16. Mason, *Ways to Be Blameworthy*, 185.

17. Mason, *Ways to Be Blameworthy*, 194.

18. Mason, *Ways to Be Blameworthy*, 195.

19. It should be noted that I have presented a less robust distinction between individual, personal relationships and collective, impersonal ones than Mason endorses in her articulation of these issues. This invites some confusion as I do not address whether or not it is proper to consider the relationship between a church body, the ELCA, and LGBTQIA+ people, a social group marked by a shared identity, however dynamic and contested that identity might be. I believe that this lack of precision is warranted insofar as Christian ecclesial bodies have complicated personal and impersonal dimensions that are not easily demarcated by words like individual, church, synod, or the like. Furthermore, the church's texts and traditions also blur these distinctions in complicated ways. Jesus' words speak of individuals bound together to God and to one another, as branches to a vine and sheep in a flock, to say nothing of the heavy use of friendship and love language. To take on these issues would require a deeper examination of the interpretive and ecclesiological issues on the table, which is beyond the limitations and scope of this chapter.

20. My views on tolerance are indebted to John Bowlin's *Tolerance Among the Virtues* (Princeton, NJ: Princeton University Press, 2016).

21. I take issue, in part, with Riswold's observation that "The heart of the Christian religion is not about human power and domination . . . " (p. 12). I suspect my objection here is a difference of interpretation and a matter of degree and not kind. I would affirm her warnings about the use of political coercion by Christians insofar as religious reasons for enforcing policy decisions create troubling theological and legal issues in the United States. That said, the state's use of power is something that I endorse, as happens when governmental actors enforce requirements of nondiscrimination in voting, employment, education, and other areas. Power is distinct from domination, as explained above, and I take it that forms of coercion are also permitted under varying conditions, understanding coercion in a broader sense than brute physical force.

BIBLIOGRAPHY

Bateza, Anthony M. "Reconciling Rapacious Wolves and Misguided Sheep: Law and Responsibility in Martin Luther's Response to the German Peasants' War." *Political Theology* 19, no. 4 (2018): 264–81.

Berlin, Isaiah. *Four Essays on Liberty,* 2nd ed. Oxford: Oxford University Press, 1990.

Blickle, Peter. *The Revolution of 1525: The German Peasants' War from a New Perspective.* Baltimore, MD: The Johns Hopkins University Press, 1991.

Bowlin, John. *Tolerance Among the Virtues.* Princeton, NJ: Princeton University Press, 2016.

DiAngelo, Robin. *White Fragility: Why it's so Hard for white People to Talk about Racism.* Boston: Beacon Press, 2018.

Douglass, Frederick. *Narrative of the life of Frederick Douglas, an American Slave.* Boston: Anti-Slavery Office, 1849.

Gushee, David. "Reconciling Evangelical Christianity with our Sexual Minorities: Reframing the Biblical Discussion." *Journal of the Society of Christian Ethics* 53, no. 2 (Fall/Winter 2015): 141–58.

Luther, Martin. "A Simple Way to Pray, for Master Peter the Barber." In *Luther's Spirituality*, edited by Philip D. W. Krey and Peter D. S. Krey, 217–34. New York: Paulist Press, 2007.

Mason, Elinor. *Ways to be Blameworthy: Rightness, Wrongness, and Responsibility.* Oxford: Oxford University Press, 2019.

Pettit, Philip. *Republicanism: A Theory of Freedom and Government.* Oxford: Clarendon Press, 1997.

Scribner, Robert. *The German Peasant War of 1525: New Viewpoints.* London: Unwin Hyman, 1979.

Scribner, Robert and Tom Scott, eds. *The German Peasants' War: A History in Documents.* Amherst, New York: Prometheus Books, 1991.

Wartenberg, Thomas. *The Forms of Power.* Philadelphia: Temple University Press, 1990.

Young, Iris Marion. *Justice and the Politics of Difference.* Princeton, NJ: Princeton University Press, 2011.

Chapter 4

Retrieving Luther's Critique of Idolatry for Our Fragmented World

Whiteness, Greed, and the Environment

Benjamin Taylor

"If there is one single deep conviction which I have acquired in El Salvador, it is that such idols are real; they are not the inventions of so-called primitive peoples but are indeed active in modern societies. We dare not doubt this, in view of such idols' innumerable victims: the poor, the unemployed, the refugees, the detainees, the tortured, the disappeared, the massacred."[1]

As Moses receives the Decalogue on Mount Sinai, the Israelites decide to build a golden calf, which they promptly begin to worship after they have completed it. When the God of Israelites warns Moses about the actions of Moses' fellow wanderers, Moses proceeds to go down the mountain and throw down the tablets in disgust. This narrative, a seminal moment in the Israelites' self-understanding, is a story about faithfulness, jealousy, production and ultimately, forgiveness and grace. Three millennia later, Martin Luther often took this narrative up as the archetypal narrative for the phenomenon of idolatry. Through Luther's writings, Luther returns again and again to the problem of idolatry and what idolatry means in his own society. We find him using the language of idolatry to talk about the abuses of the Roman Church, the abuses of the "merchants," and the concentration of power in German society. Yet, although Luther often talked about the problem of idolatry, there is relatively little discussion of idols or idolatry in the scholarship of Luther's life and works.

My opening quotation from the liberation theologian Jon Sobrino might help us understand why there is a dearth of Lutheran discussion about the phenomenon of idolatry: namely, idols are often understood to be products of "so-called primitive peoples," and therefore, idols may have not seemed to be worthy as a subject in traditional Lutheran theological discourse. However, in recent years, there has been a new generation of Luther scholars who have sought to read Luther contrapuntally, whether that means by highlighting places in which Luther speaks to our present cultural and political moment anew or by lifting up themes that have been submerged within Lutheran scholarship.

This present essay seeks to lift up Luther's critique of the idol in order to see how Luther might speak to us in our current social and political moment. This work requires both a theological excavation of Luther's theology as well as a theoretical reading of what Luther's critique of idolatry might mean for us today. To these ends, this essay unfolds in four parts. In the first part, I will introduce Martin Luther's critique of the idol by looking at his definition of the idol in his Large Catechism. In the second part, I will further define Luther's critique of the idol by reading it as both a "commodity" and as a "master signifier." In this second part of the essay, I will also explain how the idol presents itself in contemporary U.S. society. The understanding of the idol as both a "commodity" and a "master signifier" intersect with each other in the contemporary problem of "environmental racism," which is the focus of the third part of this essay. In this third part of the essay, I argue that both "whiteness" and "greed" serve as idols in today's society, which come together in the contemporary problem known as "environmental racism." Finally, then, the last part of the essay argues that Luther's *theologia crucis* subverts the construction of idols in today's society. Using Luther's *theologia crucis* as an epistemological criterion for the construction of knowledge, Luther's *theologia crucis* becomes ground for an ideological critique of the idols of greed and whiteness in today's society. In so doing, Luther's *theologia crucis* calls our human constructions into question and points us toward the love and awe of God's good creation.

LUTHER AND THE IDOL

We turn first to an introduction of Luther's critique of the idol. In the *Large Catechism*, as part of his commentary on the first commandment, Martin Luther rhetorically asks "what does it mean to 'have a god.'" In answering this question, Luther writes: "A 'god' is the term for that to which we are to look for all good and in which we are to find refuge in all need. *Therefore, to have a god is nothing else than to trust and believe in that one with your whole heart.* As I have often said, it is the trust and faith of the heart alone that make both God and an idol."[2] Luther believed that all people inherently relied on "something" beyond themselves (*extra nos*), in which they put their faith. Luther continues, "Anything on which your heart relies and depends, I say, that is really your God."[3] Luther's analysis is subtle here: Luther understands that we are given to create "false gods" in whom we place our faith and trust. Luther believed that these idols or "false gods" have an outsized role in our lives. Idols organize or shape our experience of the world. In a sense, the problem of idolatry becomes the problem of ideology in that we are being shaped by social norms and political narratives beyond our control.[4] For Luther, then, not only did idols create a kind of "false consciousness" that he found deeply problematic, but idols also directed us away from placing our faith in God. Luther's caution against idolatry reminds us that we ought to place our faith in the God who has revealed God's self in the person of Christ, even as that revelation remains concealed "under the opposite" (*sub contrario specie*). When we realize that we are putting too much stock on what we might define as success or happiness, then we are not relying on the God in whom we trust. We are instead honoring an idol.

In general, Luther believed that there are two forms of idolatry. In the first form of idolatry, individuals turn God into a thing. In turning God into a thing, they worship an idol, not God. An example will make this more concrete. In his commentary of the First Commandment, Luther writes:

> There are some who think they have God and everything they need when they have money and property; they trust in them and boast in them so stubbornly and securely that they care for no one else. They too have a god—mammon by name, that is, money and property—on which they set their whole heart. This is the most common idol on earth.[5]

For Luther, these people put their faith in "money and property," which means that "money and property" becomes their God. The second form of idolatry is that individuals attempt to turn themselves into God. Luther often used "good works" or "indulgences" as an example for this form of idolatry. Luther writes, "The idols, or work of their hands, are now those works which they perform according to their own righteousness, not knowing the righteousness of God. And thus, they produce their own works in opposition to God and to faith in Christ. This is their idolatry to the present day."[6] Luther believes that when humans buy indulgences or do "good works" to merit their own salvation, they attempt to turn themselves into God. Luther says that indulgences are a means of "usurping" the power of God. God is the One who justifies; by justifying ourselves, we are attempting to take God's place.

The individual falls into idolatry in these two ways, either by the individual's turning God into a thing or by the individual's placing themselves in the role of God. Even as these forms of idolatry seem to be concerned with the relationship between God and the individual, I argue that these forms of idolatry have deep political and cultural significance because these claims have to do with what we deem to be of ultimate value. In order to tease out the political and cultural significance of these claims, we now turn to the work of theorizing what idolatry means for us today. In doing so, we turn to two themes: the idol as commodity and the idol as master signifier.

MANIFESTATIONS OF IDOLATRY: THE COMMODITY AND THE MASTER SIGNIFIER

We have looked at how Luther conceptualized the issue of idolatry in his own day. Luther understood that humans implicitly rely on something *extra nos*, which organizes the way that humans experience their lives. In his own day, Luther believed that this "something else" should be God but he also understood that many people rely on idols, which leads them to turn away from God. What does this mean for us today? In this section, we will turn our attention to two theoretical concepts: the commodity and the master signifier. These two concepts are important for our purposes because they help us to theorize or to contextualize what we might mean by "the idol" in today's society. By identifying how the idol functions like a commodity or a master signifier, we can better grasp how the idol manifests itself in our society.

The Idol as Commodity

In this section, we consider Luther's first form of idolatry, which is the attempt to turn God into a thing. Luther often claimed individuals produce "the idol of mammon," which obscures their relationship with God. This critique remains valid for today; only in today's language, we call this concern the critique of the commodity. In the analysis of political economies, a commodity is an object that has been produced by the forces of the marketplace. The commodity is a depersonalized and dehumanized object that replaces the dynamic relationships that were commonplace in more agrarian societies. In these more agrarian societies, individuals would trade and barter their goods *qua* individuals in the public square. In the age of commodities, the dynamic public square becomes a static marketplace where individuals trade things for money. In thinking about the idol as a commodity, we can come to the following conclusions.

First, the idol as reified becomes the object of devotion. This is what happens when the Israelites construct the golden calf in Exodus 33. The Israelites' devotion is transferred from God onto a thing, the golden calf. As the devotion is transferred to the calf, the idol obscures the presence of the divine. In his groundbreaking essay, "The Work of Art in the Age of Mechanical Reproduction," the German theorist Walter Benjamin explains how something similar happens to an artwork when it is reproduced through the use of technology. Benjamin argues that as the artwork is mechanically reproduced, the artwork loses its "aura," by which he means its authenticity or its essence. Benjamin writes, "To pry an object from its shell, to destroy its aura, is the mark of a perception whose 'sense of the universal equality of things' has increased to such a degree that it extracts it even from a unique object by means of reproduction."[7] This is why, for instance, the artworld does not value forgeries as much as it does the original artwork——the original artwork has an aura which the forgery does not. What is important for our purposes is that the reproduction of artwork pretends to reproduce the value of the artwork and fails. The reproduction reifies or objectifies (literally, turning it into an object) the aura of the artwork. For his part, Luther also recognized the same dynamic at play in the production of indulgences, which he understood to be "the chief idol." Luther believed that the buying and selling of indulgences was idolatrous because indulgences objectify the grace and love of God. Instead of the grace and love of God being present in and through the experience of the individual's dynamic encounter with God (*coram Deo*), the experience is objectified into a commodity that can be bought and sold. Put differently, Luther believed that indulgences objectified a relationship that was to be both dynamic and processual.

Second, as a commodity, the idol becomes subject to greed, wealth, and class dynamics in power-laden societies. In market societies, the product becomes subject to the fluctuations and whims of the market. In his *Ninety-Five Theses*, Luther railed against the buying and selling of indulgences and the ways in which this buying and selling put a market value on God's love.[8] Luther's critique of greed and wealth is most pronounced in his economic writings. In the previous section, we saw how Luther identified mammon as "the most common idol" on earth. In *On Trade and Usury*, Luther turns his critique toward the practices of the then-emergent forms of market economies among the German public. We can get to the heart of Luther's critique of "the merchants" by looking at what he derisively termed "the rule of the merchants." Luther explains "the rule of the merchants" in this way: "Among themselves the merchants have a common rule which is their chief maxim and the basis of all their sharp practices, where they say, 'I may sell my goods as dear as I can.' They think that this is their right."[9] This "rule of the merchants" (i.e., that businesses sell their products for as much value as they can) is basic to the functioning of market economies. However, Luther believes that these practices lead to greed and idolatry. Luther furthers this argument in his explanation of the Seventh Commandment ("You Shall Not Steal").

> For to steal is nothing else than to acquire someone else's property by unjust means. The few words include taking advantage of our neighbors in any sort of dealings that result in loss to them. Stealing is a widespread, common vice, but people pay so little attention to it . . . . Stealing is not just robbing someone's safe or pocketbook but also taking advantage of someone in the market, in all stores, butcher shops, wine and beer cellars, workshops and, in short, wherever business is transacted and money is exchanged for goods or services.[10]

For Luther, the practice of taking advantage of another's property is stealing because these practices treat the other as the means to an end rather than the end in itself. The merchants objectified the Other. Said otherwise, Luther understood the merchants to be idolatrous because they were beholden to the idol of mammon, which manifests itself as greed. Because we are made in the image of God, Luther argued that this objectification of the other is an objectification of God.

By looking at the idol as commodity, we have seen one component of the significance of Luther's critique of idolatry. In seeing the idol as a commodity, we have emphasized how Luther argued that dynamic processes are reduced or objectified into a thing. Later on, we will see how Luther's understanding of idolatry is at work in humanity's relationship with nature, as humans reduce the rich tapestry of the environment into a thing for their own profit. I now turn to another way of thinking about Luther's critique of idolatry: the idol as a master signifier.

The Idol as Master Signifier

In this section, I consider the second form of idolatry; specifically, the individual's attempt to turn themselves into God. In doing so, we pick up on Luther's economic critique in *On Trade and Usury*. After Luther introduces "the rule of the merchants," Luther offers his advice for how the merchants should act towards their neighbor. Luther writes, "The rule ought to be . . . 'I may sell my wares as dear as I ought, or as is right or fair.' For your selling ought not to be an act that is entirely within your own power and discretion, without law or limit, as though you were a god and beholden to no one."[11] This passage is important for a number of reasons. Not only does Luther argue for a more charitable understanding of the economy (an economy in which the merchants prioritize justice and fairness over profit), but Luther also notes that the merchants should not act "as if they were a god."[12]

In other words, Luther argues that the economic practices of the merchants constitute a form of idolatry in which they "act as if they were a god." Luther's language about "the neighbor" in his critique of economic practices is especially noteworthy. As we have said, Luther believes that these practices objectify the neighbor. But they also do something more. Luther maintains that these economic practices hurt the neighbor because they put the merchant's well-being over and above the well-being of the neighbor. Luther writes, "This selling of yours is a work that you perform toward your neighbor, it must be so governed by law and conscience, that you do it without harm and injury to your *neighbor*, and that you be much more concerned to do him no injury than to make large profits."[13] The individual who puts their own well-being over the well-being of their neighbor falls into idolatry because they act as "if they were a god."

Another way of conceptualizing this form of idolatry is to think about it in terms of Jacques Lacan's term "master signifier."[14] For Lacan, humans try to make sense out of their messy existence by inventing language, which is simply a set of signifiers that organizes the world by referring to the world through signs. Put differently, Lacan believed that humans understand the world through the process of naming it through language. However, because each system of language is simply a self-referential series of signifiers, language in itself does not have a given meaning. But, of course, Lacan believed that humans create meaning by orienting language around what he termed the master signifier. The master signifier, in a sense, organizes human experience by language. Thus, the psychoanalytic theorist Kalpana Seshadri-Crooks argues that the master signifier "establishes a structure of relations, a signifying chain that through a process of inclusions and exclusions constitutes a pattern for organizing human difference."[15] In Luther's theology, the notion of the human as *curvatus in se* approximates this patterning in the sense that human makes sense of the self by organizing all of reality around the self. The self, as idol, has this way of founding, orienting or organizing human experience. This is what Luther means by the phrase "to have a god" or by rhetorically asking "what does it mean to have a god?" Luther believes that the idol determines the individual's existence in a manner akin to the master signifier. When the self becomes an idol, the idol often preempts the individual acting in love towards one's neighbor. We have already seen how this form of idolatry plays itself out in Luther's critique of "rule of the merchants." Luther believed that money served as the merchant's master signifier, which accounted for their "stealing" from their neighbors.

Luther would often make this similar argument when he was talking about the Roman Church and their preoccupation with indulgences or the Pope.

For example, Luther writes that the Roman Church "set up the idols of indulgences and Masses. This is by far the richest source of gain."[16] In this example, the indulgence is a master signifier that overdetermines the meaning of the relationship between the individual and God. With the introduction of indulgences, the relationship between the individual and God is oriented by the idol, rather than being oriented by the grace of God as manifested on the cross.

Today, we might think of whiteness as an idol. To say that whiteness is an idol is to say that whiteness is a self-referential norm that funds a racial and economic hierarchy that prioritizes white people over people of color. In recent years, critical race scholars have begun to talk about "white privilege" and "white fragility" as ways in which whiteness functions in today's society.[17] Whiteness, in this sense, is not a neutral term; rather, whiteness is a structural regime that upholds the cultural and political status quo.[18] Peggy McIntosh famously notes in her seminal essay "White Privilege: Unpacking the Invisible Knapsack" that white people often have to "unpack" their own relationship to whiteness in order to see clearly the ways in which their own whiteness or their internalized racism impacts others. In my own work, I argue that whiteness is an idol that has been normalized in the cultural, political and theological discourse of the United States. This work builds off the work of thinkers like James Baldwin and Franz Fanon who argue that whiteness functions as a kind of gaze that solidifies an in-group by creating the Other.[19] We will turn to this theme in a moment as we discuss the phenomenon known as "environmental racism."

ENVIRONMENTAL RACISM

Critical race scholars argue that whiteness oppresses people of color in a myriad of ways by securing its own benefits for white people. One of these ways is the cultural or sociological phenomenon known as "environmental racism."[20] In recent years, environmental scholars and cultural theorists have introduced the term "environmental racism" to talk about the ways in which societies' use and abuse of environmental resources disproportionately affects people of color. Environmental racism manifests itself in different ways in different communities.

A well-known example of environmental racism is the series of events that occurred in Flint, Michigan. In late 2015 and 2016, citizens of Flint began to realize that their tap water suddenly turned into a brownish color, which left their skin to be itchy. After years of investigative reporting and lawsuits, it was discovered that the water in Flint became contaminated after Republican Governor Rick Snyder appointed a city manager with the task of looking for ways to save the city money. The crisis began when the city manager decided that the city could pump water from the Flint River rather than continuing the practice of providing fresh water from Detroit in order to save money. Once the crisis began, many Flint residents felt as if Snyder did not care about the crisis. We can see how the "Flint water crisis" serves as an example of environmental racism: the civic leaders in Flint prioritized money over the well-being of the residents of Flint, which had a disproportionate impact on people of color.

There are many other examples of what we might think of as environmental racism. In the winter of 2019, Nina Lakhani, an environmental justice reporter for *The Guardian*, documented contemporary examples of environmental racism in a series of reports that the paper named "Our Unequal Earth." Lakhani's series included the following examples:[21]

- The murder of a land-rights activist in Costa Rica
- The existence of "hot spots," a geological phenomenon that warms areas of land, that are linked to formerly red-lined neighborhoods in Oregon, which led to the deaths of people of color.
- The use of harmful chemicals used in hair products that are targeted to and used by African American women
- The depletion of well water in a middle-class Pennsylvania town as a result of "fracking"
- The construction of President Trump's border wall on burials of indigenous Native Americans

As seen by the breadth of these examples, it can be difficult to settle on a single definition for the term "environmental racism." However, in the effort "to call a thing what it is," we might identify environmental racism as *a set of ideological practices that prioritizes money and power over the lives of individuals, many of whom are people of color*. Environmental racism is a pernicious problem in the developed world because of the profound intersections of geography, class, and race. As Bourma-Prediger puts it, racial inequality and environmental degradation "are of a piece. Humans treated unjustly by virtue of race often suffer inordinately the negative effects of our exploitation of the earth. Poor and oppressed unite—an oppressed earth and humans oppressed because of their skin color. Put more positively, ecological harmony and racial justice are interdependent goals."[22]

What does environmental racism have to do with idolatry? I believe that Luther's understanding of idolatry lies at the heart of environmental racism. Environmental racism, as I have suggested, occurs when people in power prioritize money and power over the well-being of people, which leads to a situation that disproportionately affects the lives of people of color. In

Luther's understanding of idolatry, individuals understand place themselves at the center of a set of social relations, which we referred to earlier as a master signifier. Environmental racism, I want to suggest, is the result of the idol of whiteness. When whiteness becomes an idol within a political economy of space, especially in the economy of social space, the idol of whiteness leads widespread environmental racism.

We can see environmental racism manifest itself either in the pernicious history of "Redlining,"[23] just as we can in the Flint Water Crisis. In both cases, policymakers prioritized the idol of whiteness (or money and power) to disastrous effects for the most marginalized in society. When cities or businesses decide where to dispose of their waste with only a view to their bottom line or the (lack of) political opposition that such a decision engenders, these cities or businesses idolize money and power over the people in their communities. By reading the dynamics of environmental racism through the lens Luther's critique of idolatry, we can provide a proper theological reading of this social and political problem. This theological reading is important for the harnessing of political power.

Yet, there is another way that Luther's understanding of idolatry lies at the heart of environmental racism. Above, we explained that Luther believed that individuals commit idolatry when they turn God into a thing; for example, when the Israelites attempt to worship the Golden Calf or when Luther's contemporaries worshiped "mammon." In this form of idolatry, humans objectify something that is inherently dynamic. This form of idolatry happens when humans look at the natural world as an object or a thing that they can exploit for their own money and power. This idolatry clearly manifests itself in the rise of the fossil fuel industry in the twentieth century as well as the production of natural gas today. The earth is understood as an object for which humans can exploit. This exploitation of nature becomes an instance of environmental racism as it fundamentally reshapes people of color's relationship with the natural world. The black feminist scholar bell hooks makes this argument in her 2009 book *Belonging: A Culture of Place.* In *Belonging,* bell hooks argues that black southerners always maintained a spiritual and a political connection to the natural world before the Great Migration of the twentieth century, a time in which thousands of African Americans moved from the rural South to the industrial cities of the North. In her reflections about her grandfather's (Daddy Jerry's) intimate connection to nature, hooks writes, "Daddy Jerry taught me to cherish land. From him I learned to see nature, our natural environment, as a force caring for the exploited and oppressed black folk living in the culture of white supremacy. Nature was there to teach the limitations of humankind, white and black. Nature was there to show us god, to give us the mystery and the promise."[24] In a separate reflection, she writes:

This profound belief in divine order allowed Daddy Jerry to experience whole-ness and integrity despite the forces of white supremacist exploitation and oppression surrounding him. His love of the soil, the solace that he found in nature enabled him to have an open mind and an uplifted heart. Despite the suf-ferings he experienced living in the world of Jim Crow, subjected to the cruel whims of a white supremacist patriarchal regime, he found a culture of belong-ing in the natural world, with the earth as his witness.[25]

hooks argues that nature provided African Americans a "foundation of our counter-hegemonic black subculture."[26] hooks's analysis on her own grand-father's relationship to nature clues us in on the importance of nature for African Americans. In the midst of white supremacist world, nature serves as a kind of equalizer, the ground of spiritual and political sustenance that is needed in everyday life. For many African Americans, this connection to the earth had been severed not only by the Great Migration but also by the epistemic and social conditions of the hegemonic dominant culture. To work in a factory in the North in the hopes of achieving "the American Dream" was to take on the dominant culture's relationship vis-a-vis nature. Along with their white counterparts, African Americans began to approach nature as a "thing" to be processed. Instead of being infused with a sense of the mysterious divine, nature becomes a commodity to be bought and sold. The aura of nature, which had previously served as a resource for an oppositional cultural politics, undergoes a profound erasure. Through this reification, nature is transformed into the idol of the marketplace as a form of environ-mental racism.

CONCLUSION: LUTHER'S *THEOLOGIA CRUCIS* AND THE GROANING OF THE EARTH

In the previous sections of this paper, I introduced different forms of how Luther conceptualized idolatry in his day. In doing so, I have sought to explain contemporary manifestations of these forms of idolatry. In this way, I have shown that contemporary idols are connected with the idols that Luther identified in his day. In Luther's time, he dealt with idols with his theologi-cal conviction that God reveals God's self most fully in Christ's death on the cross—a theological conviction Lutheran scholars refer to as *theologia crucis* (theology of the cross).

Luther outlines his *theologia crucis* in the eighteenth to twenty-second theses on Luther's *Heidelberg Disputation* (1519). In this disputation, Luther argues that humans should look for God in and through the cross of Jesus Christ rather than in the speculation of divine things, which he terms *theologia gloriae* (or, the theology of glory). Because God is to be known in the suffering of the cross, it follows that (1) God reveals God's self "indirectly and incompletely"[27] and that (2) God reveals God's self to be One in solidarity with all those who suffer. Luther's *theologia crucis* proclaims a God who calls into question the "human ensconced values" that we attribute to God.[28] In other words, Luther's *theologia crucis* problematizes all idols that we create because the cross reminds us that God never shows up in the places for which we prepare ourselves. Instead, Luther argues that God reveals God's self "under the opposite" (*sub contrario specie*).[29] Mary Solberg puts a fine point on this argument when she writes that humans "believe and act as if they have the power to invent, name, describe control and dispense God."[30] When they do so, they are simply creating an idol. Seen in this light, idols are produced by theologians of glory. The practice of the theologian of the cross is to "name a thing what it actually is." This practice often means calling out idols as human constructions. As Walter Altmann writes, "God is against the idols. God is a radical critique of all the idols who want to ideologically cover up a system that causes human suffering and death or that preserves the deadly established injustices."[31]

What, then, does Luther's *theologia crucis* mean for the problem of environmental racism that structures and conditions the lives of people of color? What does the theologian of the cross do about whiteness? I believe that Luther's *theologia crucis* and the Lutheran tradition calls us into a new way of being that might help us begin to answer these questions. Although I cannot offer policy suggestions, I offer here three proposals that might help us think more clearly about what it means to be "a community of the cross."[32]

First, Luther's *theologia crucis* calls us to adopt a hermeneutic of suspicion about the way that power operates in society. We have argued that idols are products of the rich and the powerful in today's world. As many Luther scholars have pointed out, Luther's *theologia crucis* offers a critique of power. The problem of environmental racism, like many of the problems in the world, arises from the concentration of political power. As a community of the cross, we must be more aggressive in standing up and questioning those in power.

Second, Luther's *theologia crucis* calls us to recognize God's presence in the suffering of God's creation. In his book *The Scandalous God*, the late Lutheran theologian Vítor Westhelle argued that Luther's *theologia crucis* forces us to look at the suffering of the earth, as well as the suffering of those around us.[33] There are many in the world, including those in power, who create fantastic illusions about the state of the environment and the natural world, including illusions about their own complicity in the ecological destruction that humans have wrought. By provoking us "to call a thing what it is," the community of the cross must expose these illusions and work together to build a more sustainable society.

Third, Luther's *theologia crucis* calls us to act out God's solidarity with the poor and the oppressed in love. By reminding us that God reveals God's self in the pain and suffering of the cross, Luther's *theologia crucis* shakes up any ideological construct or "human construction" that does not speak to the suffering of the world. This essay opened with Jon Sobrino's important reminder that idols are real to those who live in the margins of society. Idols condition, limit and oppress those who are identified as Other by the powerful. The community of the cross must act on Sobrino's reminder in order to stand with those who suffer in the world.

NOTES

1. Jon Sobrino, "Awakening from the Sleep of Inhumanity" *Christian Century*, April 3, 1991, 368–69.

2. Martin Luther, "Large Catechism," in *The Book of Concord: The Confessions of the Evangelical Lutheran Church*, eds. Robert Kolb and Timothy J. Wengert (Minneapolis: Fortress, 2000), 386. My emphasis.

3. At first glance, Luther's insistence that an individual believes in God or an idol might appear to be a false (or at least, an outdated) binary, but I believe that Luther is offering us a more nuanced analysis. Luther notes that there are often "idols" that attract our desire rather than our desire reaching to God. For Luther, these idols could be the idol of mammon, the idol of self-perfection or, as in the case of the Roman Church, the idol of power. In the words of Jean-Luc Marion, the idol "fixes our gaze," meaning that, in idolatry, we honor ourselves rather than God. Jean-Luc Marion, *God Without Being: Hors-Texte*, 2nd Edition (Chicago: University of Chicago Press, 2012), 12.

4. By "ideology," I am thinking about the ways in which cultural and political narratives affect the ways in which we live in the world. Mary Elise Lowe makes this point in her essay "Sin from a Queer, Lutheran Perspective," in which she suggests that we think of sin as a "discourse." Lowe writes that "Each of us exists in a field of competing discourses (just and unjust) that create and regulate the language, identities and practices available to us." Mary Elise Lowe, "Sin from a Queer, Lutheran Perspective." In *Transformative Lutheran Theologies: Feminist, Womanist and Mujerista Perspectives*, ed. Mary Streufert (Minneapolis: Fortress Press, 2010), 75. By trusting in a false god, we turn ourselves over to a (potentially unjust) discourse that affects the way we live in the world.

5. Luther, "Large Catechism," 387.

6. Martin Luther, "Lectures on Amos (1525)" in *Luther's Works, Volume 18, Lectures on the Minor Prophets I*, ed. Hilton Oswald, trans. Richard J. Dinda (St. Louis, Concordia Publishing House, 1975), 129.

7. Walter Benjamin, "The Work of Art in the Age of Mechanical Reproduction," in *Illuminations: Essays and Reflections* (New York: Schocken Books, 1968), 223.

8. Martin Luther, "Trade and Usury (1524)," in *Luther's Works, Volume 45, The Christian in Society II*, ed. Walther I. Brandt, trans. by Charles M. Jacobs, rev. Walther I. Brandt (Philadelphia: Fortress Press, 1962), 247.

9. Ibid.

10. Luther, "Large Catechism," 416.

11. LW 45, 248.

12. Ibid.

13. LW 45, 248–49.

14. For more on "master signifier," see Jacques Lacan, *The Seminar of Jacques Lacan: The Other Side of Psychoanalysis (Book XVII)*, trans. Russell Grigg (New York: WW Norton: 2007), especially 11–38. For a theological treatment of the "master signifier," see "Ideology Critique" in Adam Kostko, *Žižek and Theology* (London: T&T Clark, 2008), 19–42.

15. Kalpana Seshadri-Crooks, *Desiring Whiteness: A Lacanian Analysis of Race* (London: Routledge, 2000), 3.

16.Martin Luther, *Luther's Works, Volume 8, Lectures on Genesis, Chapters 45–50,* edited by Jaroslav Pelikan, translated by Paul D. Pohl (St. Louis: Concordia Publishing House, 1966),
320.

17. For more on "White privilege" and "White fragility," see the following works: George Yancy, *Black Bodies, White Gazes: The Continuing Significance of Race in America,* 2nd Edition (Lanham, MD: Rowman & Littlefield, 2017); Eduardo Bonilla-Silva, *Racism Without Racists: Color-Blind Racism and the Persistence of Racial Inequality in America*, 5th Edition (Lanham, MD: Rowman & Littlefield, 2018); Robin DiAngelo, *White Fragility: Why It's so Hard for White People to Talk About Racism* (Boston: Beacon Press, 2018).

18. Because whiteness is a structural power that benefits white people at the expense of people of color, many questions about the "morality" or "goodness" of white people obscures the nature of the discussion of whiteness. In other words, for a white person to ask "Am I a good person?" or "Am I racist?" misses the point of the nature of whiteness. Rather, the question should be, "Given that I live in a culture that values and honors whiteness, what have I done to check my own perception of the world and those around me as a white person?"

19. See George Yancy, *Black Bodies, White Gazes.*

20. For more on "environmental justice" or "environmental racism," I would suggest the following works: Laura Pulido, "Rethinking Environmental Racism: White Privilege and Urban Development in Southern California" *Annals of the Association of American Geographers* 90, no. 1 (March 2000): 12–40; *Confronting Environmental Racism: Voices from the Grassroots,* ed. Robert Bullard (Boston: South End Press, 1993). For a theological reading of "environmental racism," I would draw attention to Steven Bourma-Prediger, "Environmental Racism" in *Handbook for US Theologies of Liberation,* ed. Miguel De La Torre (St. Louis: Chalice Press, 2004), 281–87. For a treatment of environmental racism from a Lutheran perspective,

see Cynthia Moe-Lobeda, *Resisting Structural Evil: Love as Ecological-Economic Vocation* (Minneapolis: Fortress Press, 2013), especially 35–40.

21. Nina Lakhani "Our Unequal Earth." *The Guardian*, accessed February 28, 2020, https://www.theguardian.com/environment/series/our-unequal-earth.

22. Steven Bourma-Prediger, "Environmental Racism" in *Handbook for US Theologies of Liberation*, ed. Miguel De La Torre (St. Louis: Chalice Press, 2004), 284.

23. "Redlining" refers to the discriminatory practice in which banks and real estate firms discourage immigrants or people of color from living in a certain neighborhood or part of a city through discriminatory banking and civic practice. The practice occurred throughout the United States in the middle of the 20th century. For more on the history of "Redlining," see Ta-Nehisi Coates's, "The Case for Reparations," *The Atlantic*, accessed May 11, 2020, https://www.theatlantic.com/magazine/archive/2014/06/the-case-for-reparations/361631/.

24. bell hooks, *Belonging: A Culture of Place* (New York: Routledge, 2009), 42.

25. hooks, *Belonging*, 216.

26. hooks, *Belonging*, 8.

27. See McGrath's section on "the leading themes of Luther's 'theology of the cross' in *Luther's Theology of the Cross: Martin Luther's Theological Breakthrough* (Oxford: Wiley-Blackwell, 2011), 211–14.

28. See Karen Bloomquist, "Let God be God: The Theological Necessity of Depatriarchalizing God" in *Our Naming of God: Problems and Prospects of God-Talk Today*, ed. Carl Braaten (Minneapolis: Fortress, 1989), 58.

29. Walter Altmann writes, "God's love manifests itself not in an affirmation of the world but, on the contrary, in the weakness of Christ. It is *absconditas sub contrario.* Therefore God weeps, wails and groans. God in God's weakness, in poverty, in humility, in sacrifice, in the cross—not because God takes pleasure in all this, but because God wants to overcome the alienation and injustice of this world." Walter Altmann, *Luther and Liberation: A Latin American Perspective* (Minneapolis: Fortress, 2015), 34–35.

30. Mary Solberg, *Compelling Knowledge: A Feminist Proposal for an Epistemology of the Cross* (Albany, NY: SUNY Press: 1997), 74.

31. Altmann: *Luther and Liberation*, 43–44.

32. Douglas John Hall coined the term "Ecclesia Crucis" ("the church of the cross") in his *God and Human Suffering: An Exercise in the Theology of the Cross* (Minneapolis: Augsburg, 1986).

33. See chapter six, "Cross and Poetry: The Mask of God and Human Accountability Toward Creation" in Vítor Westhelle, *The Scandalous God* (Minneapolis: Fortress, 2006).

BIBLIOGRAPHY

Altmann, Walter. *Luther and Liberation: A Latin American Perspective.* Minneapolis: Fortress, 2015.

Benjamin, Walter. "The Work of Art in the Age of Mechanical Reproduction," *Illuminations*, 217–51. New York: Schocken Books, 1968.

Bloomquist, Karen. "Let God be God": The Theological Necessity of Depatriarchalizing God" in *Our Naming of God: Problems and Prospects of God-Talk Today*, edited by Carl Braaten. Minneapolis: Fortress, 1989.

Bonilla-Silva, Eduardo. *Racism Without Racists: Color-Blind Racism and the Persistence of Racial Inequality in America*, 5th Edition. Lanham, MD: Rowman & Littlefield, 2018.

Bourma-Prediger, Steven. "Environmental Racism" in *Handbook for US Theologies of Liberation,* edited by Miguel De La Torre. St. Louis: Chalice Press, 2004.

Bullard, Robert, ed. *Confronting Environmental Racism: Voices from the Grassroots.* Boston: South End Press, 1993.

Coates, Ta-Nehisi., "The Case for Reparations" *The Atlantic,* July 2014.

DiAngelo, Robin. *White Fragility: Why It's So Hard for White People to Talk about Racism.* Boston: Beacon Press, 2018.

Douglas, John Hall. *God and Human Suffering: An Exercise in the Theology of the Cross.* Minneapolis: Augsburg, 1986.

hooks, bell. *Belonging: A Culture of Place.* New York: Routledge, 2009.

Kostko, Adam. *Žižek and Theology*. London: T&T Clark, 2008.

Lacan, Jacques. *The Seminar of Jacques Lacan: The Other Side of Psychoanalysis (Book XVII)*, translated by Russell Grigg. New York: WW Norton: 2007.

Lakhani, Niki. "Our Unequal Earth." *The Guardian.* Accessed February 28, 2020. https://www.theguardian.com/environment/series/our-unequal-earth

Lowe, Mary Elise. "Sin from a Queer, Lutheran Perspective." In *Transformative Lutheran Theologies: Feminist, Womanist and Mujerista Perspectives*, edited by Mary Streufert, 71–86. Minneapolis: Fortress, 2010.

Luther, Martin. "The Large Catechism." In *The Book of Concord: Confessions of the Evangelical Lutheran Church*, edited by Robert Kolb and Timothy Wengert, 377–480. Minneapolis: Fortress, 2000.

———. "Lectures on Amos (1525)." In *Luther's Works, Volume 18, Lectures on the Minor Prophets I*, edited by Hilton Oswald, translated by Richard J. Dinda, 125–89. St. Louis, Concordia Publishing House, 1975.

———. *Luther's Works, Volume 8, Lectures on Genesis, Chapters 45–50*, edited by Jaroslav Pelikan, translated by Paul D. Pohl. St. Louis: Concordia Publishing House, 1966.

———. "Trade and Usury (1524)." In *Luther's Works, Volume 45, The Christian in Society II*, edited by Walther I. Brandt, translated by Charles M. Jacobs and revised by Walther I. Brandt, 231–308. Philadelphia: Fortress Press, 1962.

Marion, Jean-Luc. *God Without Being: Hors-Texte*, 2nd Edition. Chicago: University of Chicago Press, 2012.

McGrath, Allister. *Theology of the Cross: Martin Luther's Theological Breakthrough.* Oxford: Wiley-Blackwell, 2011.

Moe-Lobeda, Cynthia. *Resisting Structural Evil: Love as Ecological-Economic Vocation.* Minneapolis: Fortress, 2013.

Pelikan, Jaroslav and Helmut T. Lehman, eds. *Luther's Works*. Philadelphia: Fortress Press, 1955–1986.

Pulido, Laura. "Rethinking Environmental Racism: White Privilege and Urban Development in Southern California" *Annals of the Association of American Geographers* 90:1 (March 2000), 12–40.

Seshadri-Crooks, Kalpana. *Desiring Whiteness: A Lacanian Analysis of Race*. London: Routledge, 2000.

Sobrino, Jon. "Awakening from the Sleep of Inhumanity" *Christian Century*, April 3, 1991.

Solberg, Mary. *Compelling Knowledge: A Feminist Proposal for an Epistemology of the Cross* Albany, NY: SUNY Press: 1997.

Westhelle, Vítor. *The Scandalous God*. Minneapolis: Fortress, 2006.

Yancy, George. *Black Bodies, White Gazes: The Continuing Significance of Race in America*, 2nd Edition. Lanham, MD: Rowman & Littlefield, 2017.

Chapter 5

A Non-Universal Lutheran Theology

Contextual Theological Process in Namibia

Marit A. Trelstad

Two years after Namibia gained freedom from apartheid in 1990, I worked with a Lutheran church in a black township within the city of Mariental. It was 1992 and I was twenty-four. I had been raised in the shadow of a North American caricature of Lutherans as passive, apolitical Christians who sing and have church basement potlucks. But in Namibia, many black Lutheran churches were a base for guerilla fighting against South Africa. Others resisted South Africa nonviolently. Lutheran bishops and pastors were the main instigators and leaders of the independence movement, similar to leadership of Nelson Mandela in South Africa. They were arrested and tortured or killed during the independence struggle. In 1988, a black Lutheran Church headquarters in the capital, Windhoek, was bombed. A majority of Namibians, both black and white, were Lutheran Christians then and still are today.[1] Familiar with black and liberation theologies, I went to volunteer at a church and learn about the role of Lutheran theology and churches in opposing political, social and economic oppression. A year later in 1993, I furthered my theological study in southern Africa through a graduate school course in Zimbabwe. We studied the Lutheran church there and "land theology" that focused on the radical disparity of justice and the necessity of political activism.

In 2003, I returned to Namibia to specifically research the role of Lutheran theology in the political struggles of 1970–1990. I accessed local church

documents and academic sources and began interviewing independence leaders. In 2012, a student-faculty research project through my university allowed
this research to continue.[2] Kristin Lee, to whom this research is indebted, was
my student who travelled to Namibia to continue recording and transcribing
personal interviews. All of this is to say that the Lutheran church in Namibia
has long had a place in my heart. For decades, I have formally and informally
studied Lutheran theology's role in that particular time period in Namibia. I
set out to pinpoint Lutheran theological ideas that encouraged leaders in the
fight for independence.

My hypothesis had assumed that Lutheran theology was positively influential in the movement against apartheid because the wide majority of leaders
were Lutheran. By and large, this was proved wrong. However, Lutheran
practice and methodology, combined with non-Lutheran theologies of liberation, did support Lutheran resistance to apartheid. Specifically, Lutheran
and reformation methodologies that highlight scriptural authority and "biblical theology" ultimately backed the social and political liberation of black
Lutherans from apartheid. On the other hand, theological concepts familiar
to North American and European Lutherans were often used to support
apartheid or discourage political resistance. Even the foundation of Lutheran
theology, "justification by grace through faith," was used by white Lutherans
to support the status quo.

From this research process and the lived faith example of Lutheran
Namibians, I learned three primary lessons: (1) No idea in Lutheran theology
can be universally applied as good for all contexts. Not even the concepts that
one holds most dear. All theology is interpreted by its context. Additionally,
theology's ability to be good news is dependent on our awareness of this contextual specificity. Indeed, to borrow a term from German Lutheran biblical
scholar Herman Gunkel, we need to know the social, political, historical *Sitz
im Leben* (the setting in life) before ascribing theological terms. Our claims
are always contextually specific and non-universal. (2) Some concepts in
Lutheran theology have been particularly prone to supporting political and
social systems of oppression and warrant caution and increased precision
in application. While they are not always used abusively, they come with
"red flags" that should invoke heightened listening. (3) North American
and European Lutheran theologies have developed theological "shorthand"
phrases or categories that serve as a way of summing up larger concepts. While
the interpretation of these categories or phrases vary considerably, there are
common concepts such as: "law and gospel," "theology of the cross," "orders
of creation," "two kingdoms" and "priesthood of all believers" among others.
"Justification by grace through faith" is the most central. But filtering theology through these phrases carries its own blindspots. Lutheran theology in
other parts of the world may be carried through practices and other categories

of thought. Indeed, what I initially interpreted as a lack of Lutheran theological influence on the independence struggle revealed that I was searching for North American and European Lutheran categories of thought and thereby missing Namibian Lutheran leaders' own deep, Protestant prioritization of scripture's authority in the face of social and ecclesial oppression.

Often Lutheran theological categories are referenced as though they are self-explanatory and universally applicable. But Martin Luther himself offered caveats to such universal theological applications. For example, he claimed that the law needed to be contextualized, lest it be abused. The law, he claimed, was given to the proud while the gospel was for the broken-hearted.[3] While this approach to the law is not consistent throughout his theology, it reveals that Luther considered the role of context in interpreting theology.

In feminist theology, contextual interpretation has long been assumed. For example, feminist theologians Valerie Saiving Goldstein, Susan Nelson, and Judith Plaskow who each claimed that the sin of pride was not the luxury of women and disempowered men.[4] Susan Nelson wrote an article in 1982 that critiqued Reinhold Niebuhr's understanding of the sin of pride.[5] Nelson wrote that those with power in patriarchal systems may suffer from pride but not all people begin from an equal sense of entitlement or self-centeredness. She argued that women socialized to be other-centered or submissive may never have been allowed to be proud in the first place. Thus, a repeated exhortation to have less pride may redouble the oppression they already experience. Nelson offered that women may be more apt to suffer from a sin of hiding or self-diminishment than pride.

Considering these points, the thesis of this chapter follows: *A contextual and relational awareness in Lutheran theology may assist it to be increasingly socially responsible and speak gospel. Instead of applying neat categories and catchphrases, responsible Lutheran theology is a non-universal process of interrogating Lutheran theological categories from within particular contexts and in accordance to the voices of those most vulnerable.* In particular, this chapter examines the context of Namibia and how North American and European Lutheran theological categories often served to further the privilege of white Lutherans. Nevertheless, Lutheran methodologies that highlighted scriptural authority and a homegrown "biblical theology" ultimately backed the social and political liberation of black Lutherans from Apartheid.

A few words on privilege and perspective at the outset: I want to acknowledge the limitations of examining Namibian theology as an outsider. I am not seeking to propose a Namibian theology but to report on theological perspectives of Namibian Lutherans and to reflect on Lutheran theology's role in supporting or limiting liberation.[6] Grant-supported research allowed me to cultivate a wide set of sources from Namibia and the United States through libraries and churches. Thus, this chapter brings together recorded interviews with Lutheran apartheid leaders, as well as published and unpublished works by Namibian theologians. While some books have been published about the history of the Lutheran church in Namibia during the independence struggle, engagement specifically with Lutheran theology's role have been limited.

I look forward to learning more from my Namibian colleagues and a new generation of Namibian theologians about this era and beyond. During my research, Namibian theologians also described the most pressing concerns since the independence movement. Namibian theology has addressed issues of apartheid, land, growing poverty and urbanization, and AIDS in the last decades. This chapter does not address these important contemporary issues but focuses on the role of Lutheran theology in the independence struggle prior to March 21, 1990, the date Namibia's independence from South Africa was officially recognized.

BRIEF HISTORY OF NAMIBIA AND THE LIBERATION STRUGGLE

While Namibia has a relatively small national population of 2.3 million, it is richly diverse in cultures and languages. There are several ethnic groups including the Ovambo, Himba, Caprivians, Kavango, Damara, Herero, Nama, San, Basters, and Tswana. Starting in the late nineteenth century, European colonizers took the vast majority of land for white settlements and murdered tribal peoples in those areas over the course of decades of uprisings and revolutions against this domination. Between 1888 and 1907, for example, German soldiers attacked Herero and Nama people, decimating their populations. In World War I, South Africa joined British Allied Forces to occupy German "South West Africa," as it had come to be called. This occupation continued through World War II. Administrators of the land were appointed by South Africa and only white settlers were allowed to vote for national legislators and regional authorities. Against the advice of the United Nations, South Africa incorporated "South West Africa" by 1949 into its own holdings through a series of actions.

As an institution within Namibia, apartheid was implemented in 1962, when all non-white Namibians were divided into homelands and lost many human rights.[7] For example, towns were segregated into three areas: white, black, and colored. "White" referred to those with European ancestry, "black" referred to people from all the African tribes listed above, and "colored" included everyone who had racially-mixed heritage as well as people of Indian or Asian descent. Quality of education, housing, and legal rights differed enormously between townships: whites received all privileges, and African tribal members received the least. Those people designated to be "between" these groups or "colored" were assigned a median status but had significant disadvantages to those deemed "white." The areas of town were literally separated by open spaces and roads.[8]

Apartheid as an institution within Namibia was officially proposed under the Odendaal Commission of Inquiry in 1962. This report proposed to ethnically split Namibians into eleven different groups, each receiving their own homeland, with the white population remaining separate. South Africa laws were implemented, which removed political power from nonwhite citizens, required that all nonwhites register with their homeland, and monitored the movement and activities of nonwhite residents.[9] The earliest response by Namibians to this occupation and racial discrimination came from the South West Africa People's Organization (SWAPO). Founded by the Ovambo majority in northern Namibia in 1960, SWAPO's original aim was to peacefully resist apartheid, but after peaceful resistance failed to make an impact on the South African government, they believed they were forced to turn to armed resistance.[10] In June 1971, the International Court of Justice declared, "that the continued presence of South Africa being illegal, South Africa is under an obligation to withdraw its administration from Namibia immediately and thus put an end to its occupation of the Territory."[11]

The year 1971 marked the beginning of the involvement of the Namibian churches in the liberation struggle. Immediately after the International Court of Justice ruling on the illegality of the South African occupation of Namibia, the Lutheran churches responded with an Open Letter to South African prime minister Vorster and an accompanying pastoral letter to Namibian churches. In the letter to Vorster, the two black Lutheran churches in Namibia, the Evangelical Lutheran Church in the Republic of Namibia (ELCRN) and the Evangelical Lutheran Church in Namibia (ELCIN), asserted that the churches would no longer stand for the abuses of apartheid.[12] The pastoral letter to the churches explained the theological reasons behind why the churches were finally breaking their silence on the apartheid issue. South African theologian Christo Lombard wrote: "After the *Open Letter* to Vorster, the mainline churches, representing more than 80% of the Namibian population, consolidated their cooperation towards the liberation of the oppressed masses in Namibia and jointly launched a very impressive ecumenical programme."[13]

In 1973, Vorster met with the heads of the Lutheran churches in an attempt to regain the support of the churches. Initially, Vorster had offered cooperation as a "good Christian as long as the church sticks to her duty, which is preaching the Gospel. But if the church, to the contrary, understands her chief task to be getting involved in politics, then the cooperation is likely to suffer as a result."[14] However, Bishop Auala and Moderator Gowaseb, two leaders who had signed the Open Letter, held their ground and refused to back down.[15]

The churches created support groups for Namibians to come together, pool their resources, and work to end apartheid, and organized assemblies for different resistance groups.[16] The South African government responded harshly to these actions taken by the churches. Foreign church leaders working for liberation were deported, and local leaders were denied visas or passports to visit other countries to educate them about the Namibian situation. In addition, the Council of Churches in Namibia offices and the ELCIN printing press were bombed on several occasions.[17]

While negotiations for free elections and an independent Namibia began in 1988, Namibia was officially recognized as independent on March 21, 1990. Despite this, the seaport of Walvis Bay was held by South Africa until 1994 and South African diamond company DeBeers continued to manage and profit from large mines in southern Namibia.[18]

THEOLOGICAL MOTIVATIONS IN THE INDEPENDENCE MOVEMENT

My research focused on four areas of inquiry pertaining to Lutheran theology that I asked in a limited set of interviews with designated Lutheran leaders:

1. In what ways was the Lutheran Church involved in Namibian liberation and the anti-apartheid movement? 2. In what ways was your own resistance to apartheid and South Africa informed by your Lutheran identity and Lutheran theology in particular? What ideas in Lutheran theology are particularly useful to your understanding of social justice and social action? 3. In what ways was the church's resistance informed by Lutheran theology in particular? 4. Are there other theologians whose work featured prominently in providing a basis for the resistance movement? If so, who? In other words, which theologians were most quoted by Lutheran leaders in the struggle for Namibian Independence? What ideas of theirs were particularly influential?

Thus, in examining this Lutheran rebellion against injustice, I was seeking to identify which theological ideas provided the motivation for action on behalf of the oppressed.

The results of my research sadly revealed that Lutheran theological ideas were often used as a tool of white oppressors more than aiding the resistance movement. Looking back on the church and the independence struggle, some church leaders and theologians (such as Rev. Dr. Paul John Isaak) framed their later theological reflections in Lutheran terms, but very few claimed it as an impetus for action at the time. In particular, Lutheran understandings of justification, the two kingdoms, and orders of creation were used as weapons against the majority black population in Namibia. The life example of Lutheran theologian Dietrich Bonhoeffer and his interpretation of the two realms, however, were important theological moorings for a limited group of leaders. Beyond Lutheran sources, however, liberation and black theologies were claimed as positive influences for liberation.

Across interviews and texts, Lutheran leaders repeatedly pointed out ways that Lutheran theology was not helpful for their independence struggle. One complaint was that Luther's writing, situated within its specific European context, did not necessarily address the African struggle. In addition, more than one scholar and church leader mentioned that Luther had supported a feudal system and did not defend the peasants. This led some Namibians to feel that Luther could not support their objections to South African rule.[19]

Beyond this, specific theological ideas used commonly by North American and European Lutheran theologians were denounced as deleterious to independence movements. For example, the Lutheran concept of the "orders of creation" was used by white Lutherans to ascribe an inherent Christian command to obey one's government and the social and political structures in which one lives. In Namibia, the government and ruling class were white, cementing a hierarchy among the races. The biblical reference underlying this idea is based on a selective, uncontextualized reading of Romans 13:1–2: "Let every person be subject to the governing authorities; for there is no authority except from God, and those authorities that exist have been instituted by God. Therefore whoever resists authority resists what God has appointed, and those who resist will incur judgment." This biblical verse was strategically invoked against the Namibian independence movement. Bishop Zephania Kameeta wrote:

> We were accused of trying to falsify the Gospel . . . . This was very difficult, because the South African government claims to be a Christian government. So from their side they misused the Gospel, falsifying it, and telling the people that on the basis of the Gospel nobody has any right to say anything against the government. They contended that to speak against the government is to be a communist and a Marxist, for the government is ordained and given by God. They said that to oppose the government is to oppose God.[20]

Nineteenth century German "neo-Lutheran theologians" are credited for lifting up this idea of orders in society.[21] While admitting that all forms of social structure were faulty, this concept of divinely-granted orders among humans grew in usage in particular branches of Lutheran theology and was evoked perniciously and disastrously during the holocaust and World War II to fuel ideas of a naturally superior "Aryan" people. This is worth mentioning as the rise of this particular concept in some Lutheran theologies paralleled the

German attacks and justification of violence—even calling for extinction—of particular groups of indigenous people in Namibia, such as the Herero. By the middle of the twentieth century, this concept was used in Germany as a Lutheran justification of conquest and murder, while in Namibia it was used to support white domination, leading to passivity in the face of institutional-ized Apartheid.

While Luther did not use this exact phrase in his own writing, he used words like "orders" and "stations" and "estates" to refer to societal-relational structures in which people always exist. Yet, because of human sin, none of these orders are above God nor are they flawless or unchanging from the beginning of time. Indeed, Luther offered that one may need to challenge social and political orders in order to serve God and neighbor faithfully.[22] Similarly, Kameeta and other Namibian Lutheran theologians, such as Paul John Isaak, repeatedly emphasized that one's obligation to God's creation actually invokes one to counter apartheid: "If God is the Creator of heaven and Earth . . . and if Jesus Christ is the Founder and Head of the Church, why should the Church be silent and do nothing in the face of racism, exploita-tion, and violence, when these are committed in God's world? Alternatively, why should God withdraw from the history of this world, hand it over to the Devils, and restrict [Godself] to the Temples and Church buildings?"[23] Adding to this, Per Frostin, another researcher on the Lutheran church's action in Namibia, wrote: "admittedly, Luther claims that the main rule is that Christians should obey the government and not rebel. He maintains, however, that God often sends what he calls heroic [people] (*viri heroici*) who have God's mandate to break such a rule for the sake of justice. These 'heroic [people]' can in Luther's view be Christians or non-Christians."[24]

Lutheran theologians today invariably recognize the horrendous history of the concept of orders of creation over the last century. Though a few North American theologians defend "orders of creation" as redeemable and neces-sary,[25] many have seen that a theological defense of this concept cannot coun-ter the ease with which it is utilized for abuse of power and even genocide. In the context of Namibia, a Lutheran support of orders of creation was elided with Luther's discussion of the Two Kingdoms to provide a double theologi-cal sanction of Apartheid. The first sanctioned support and the second justi-fied passivity in regard to racial oppression in Namibia.

Namibians heartily critiqued Luther's *distinction between the two king-doms* and the colonial powers that used it. They repeatedly identified it as an obstacle to the independence movement. The theological concept of two kingdoms is based in Luther's writing about the "realms" of power, dis-tinguishing God's realm from the realm of the world until the eschaton. In Luther's sixteenth century context, where political and spiritual powers were indistinguishable, he saw this as a necessary separation. In the last century, however, it has been used to justify church inaction against oppressive regimes in Germany and Namibia. German and Finnish missionaries, from primarily white Lutheran congregations, used the Two Kingdoms doctrine to justify their support of the colonial and apartheid regimes. This functioned in two ways. First, it provided divine sanction for white efforts to rule all other races in Namibia. Second, through affirming that church matters are separate from political matters, this same doctrine set a standard of political non-involvement in the churches that was hard to break for generations.[26]

The impact of the two kingdoms doctrine in Namibia also had unexpected nuance. Earlier in Namibian history, a Nama King named Henrik Witbooi, a Lutheran convert, had used Luther's theology of the two realms to justify the Nama revolt against German occupation. He died as a Namibian hero and martyr in battle against German colonizers in 1905. Witbooi had said, "The Lord God has placed various kingdoms in this world, thus I know and believe that it is neither a sin nor a crime that I should wish to remain an independent chief of my own country and people."[27] Witbooi also cleverly supported the tenet that God institutes government over the people but clarified that this did not mean that God supported the rule of white government. Despite Witbooi's liberative use of this doctrine, the vast majority of black Lutheran leaders in the more recent independence struggle experienced this particular doctrine as toxic.[28] White church leaders claimed that Lutherans believe that Luther's concepts implies a dualism "between spirit and matter, between church and world, between the sacred and the secular or between God and humanity," and thus a "theological critique of injustice in social, political and economic structures is deemed as illegitimate. If the question of liberation and Christian life are related to two different spheres, it is impossible to formulate a theology of liberation"[29]

As with the orders of creation, black Lutheran theologians theologically-countered the Two Kingdoms in many different ways. Paul John Isaak developed the understanding of the *imago dei* (image of God) in all humanity in a manner similar to the Open Letter. From Genesis 1:26, one sees that God creates all humans in God's image, and Isaak argued therefore that the church had to be politically involved to protect all people in their dignity. Bishop Shejavali and Dr. Rev. Isaak[30] both explicitly and specifically included the charge of the church to protect the God-given integrity and rights of women. Isaak wrote that the church must practice what it preaches and therefore defend the inviolable human rights of all people. Kameeta added that God certainly instigated political action on behalf of the enslaved Israelites, insisting that the Pharoahs of the world hear the word of God to "Let my people go!"[31]

Justification by grace was the third commonly mentioned idea within Lutheran theology that served as a detriment to liberation in Namibia. From my perspective, this was most distressing as it reveals that even the most central Lutheran ideas can be oppressive, depending on their contextual application. Like Dietrich Bonhoeffer, Lutheran theologians and church members in Namibia struggled with explaining how justification necessarily wrought good actions on behalf of the neighbor. While the white Lutheran churches did not use the North American Lutheran pejorative phrase "works righteousness," they claimed that the Open Letter of 1971 was "purely politi-cal" and immediately dissociated themselves from the main black churches who supported the letter. Like Prime Minister Vorster's response, white privileged Namibians held that the church's business was spiritual, convey-ing the gospel and this did not have political ramifications. The preaching of justification encouraged a disconnection of church and state, gospel and politics.[32] Bonhoeffer had similarly encountered this reasoning when his theology demanded resistance to the German regime during World War II. In the words of Namibian scholars and leaders, the church's single-focus on jus-tification excused those responsible for apartheid while passively supporting continued oppression. Latin American liberation theologians, such as Juan Luis Segundo, had identified this separation of works of merit and faith as the Achilles Heel of Lutheran theology, rendering ethics unnecessary.[33] Reinhold Niebuhr also famously critiqued the ethical impact of the Lutheran concept of justification by faith.[34]

While justification was not a useful tool for resistance during the liberation movement, theologians and leaders later reflected on Luther's understanding of Christian calling to the world, based on various elements of Luther's work. Isaak called for a balance between the spiritual and political and offered that Luther calls Christians to a life of "faith seeking justice" in response to grace and states that "in Namibia, an evangelical religious tradition did not preclude political involvement; on the contrary, it was most often accompanied by an emphatic insistence on social justice. From the perspective of the Open Letter, political neutrality was tantamount to theological heresy: engagement in the affairs of this world was viewed as a Christian obligation."[35] Rev. Dr. Abasai Shejavali offered a similar comment, building on Luther's writing in *On the Freedom of the Christian* (1520). The "inner" person is transformed by grace and this leads necessarily to service to the neighbor and a life of discipline regarding one's "outer" person. One is made free to serve the neighbor.[36]

In terms of the research and literature, it was interesting that some com-mon theological concepts in North American and Europe did not appear in the literature or interviews. The "theology of the cross" that describes God's presence in suffering was not mentioned or present. Bishop Kameeta refer-enced the "cross of reconciliation" in his sermons but this is a different idea altogether.[37] The "priesthood of all believers," "law and gospel" and "civic versus theological understandings of the law" were also not mentioned. Also interesting, Luther himself was almost never quoted. One Lutheran pastor, Rev. Petrus VanZyl, theorized that this may be due to lack of access to texts at the seminary. During my work with his congregation in 1992 and interview in 2003, he explained that he did not recall reading Luther's own writings in seminary in Namibia, unlike his studies in the United States. While this is highly anecdotal, it was striking that Luther's writings were not often quoted or referenced.

OTHER THEOLOGICAL INFLUENCES: BONHOEFFER AND LIBERATION THEOLOGY

Although many Namibian Lutherans did not cite Luther's writings directly in their reflections during and after apartheid, several Namibians referenced Dietrich Bonhoeffer's language of a politically active "Confessing Church," directly drawing comparisons between the apartheid state and the Nazi state. The church in both settings was called to a place of resistance and direct ethical engagement. Bonhoeffer's life and writings encouraged church leaders to become involved in the struggle. Bonhoeffer had written, "There is no place to which the Christian can withdraw from the world."[38] Bishop Kameeta took this command to heart when he refused to flee his country, and was one of many leaders arrested and tortured.[39] By choosing to be directly involved in the resistance movements, the church saw itself as enacting Bonhoeffer's statement that Christians are called: "'not just to bandage the victims under the wheel, but to put a spoke in the wheel itself,' through direct political action."[40] This quotation was used regularly in Bishop Kameeta's writings and sermons.[41] The Namibian Lutheran churches also followed Bonhoeffer's understanding of the obligations of the state to its people, that he based on Luther's treatises *On Temporal Authority* (1523) and *To the Christian German Nobility* (1520). When the South African state failed to live up to the protective obligations of its responsibilities, the black Lutheran churches felt called to support victims of apartheid. South African Theologians also referenced Bonhoeffer in their struggle against apartheid.[42]

While my interview questions centered on the impact of Lutheran theology in the resistance movement, respondents often offered that the main sources of theological resistance to apartheid were from the work of black and Latin American liberation theologians. These were by far the most common theological inspirations offered at the start of most conversations. Martin Luther King Jr.'s passion for social justice, sermons, life example, and willingness to risk his life was an inspiration for many church leaders. Ngeno Nakamhela mentioned King in a 2011 interview,[43] and Kameeta quoted King as an illustration for the passion one embodies when standing up for justice:

If a man happens to be 36 years old, as I happen to be, and some great truth
stands before the door of his life, some great opportunity to stand up for that
which is right and which is just, and he refuses to stand up because he wants to
live a little longer and he is afraid his home will get bombed, or he is afraid that
he will lose his job, or he is afraid that he will get shot . . . he may go on and
live until he is 80, and the cessation of breathing in his life is merely the belated
announcement of an earlier death of the spirit. Man dies when he refuses to
stand up for that which is right. A man dies when he refuses to take a stand for
that which is true. So we are going to stand up right here . . . letting the world
know: WE ARE DETERMINED TO BE FREE.[44]

Beyond King, church leaders, bishops, and theologians *repeatedly* referenced
the importance of North American Black Theology, particularly the work
of James Cone. In fact, when asked about their theological foundations for
resistance, Namibian leaders almost invariably responded, "Have you heard
of James Cone?" Cone's U.S.-based Black Theology offered a direct application of theology and liberation to the global Lutheran church in the context of
racial oppression. It is one of many testimonies to Cone's theological legacy.

Latin American liberation theology also played a role in solidifying
the theological base for resistance. Abisai Shejavali referenced Gustavo
Gutierrez and his assertion that "to know God is to do justice."[45] Selma
Shejavali, influential in the liberation and women's movements, stated that
liberation theology "unchained the minds of the people" so that they saw that
God did not want them to suffer.[46] Some theologians or church leaders hesi-
tated to align themselves with liberation theology due to its connection with
communism or socialism. Directly north of Namibia, Angola was deep in its
own civil war, with Cold War interests such as the Soviet Union, Cuba and
the United States being deeply involved. Namibian church leaders affirmed
the ideas of liberation theology but many were cautious to affiliate with communist powers that eschewed religion.

Similar to liberation theologians, the question of nonviolent or violent
struggle against South Africa was especially challenging for Namibian
Lutherans. Some maintained a position of nonviolent but aggressive resistance while others took up arms and aligned themselves with SWAPO, the
main political resistance movement mentioned earlier.[47] Kameeta recalled the
perspective of Dr. Johannes Lukas de Vries, the first indigenous president of
the ELCRN from 1972 to 1979 and one of the persons credited with introducing black liberation theology to Namibian theology and the church. De Vries
was a committed pacifist and rejected violence as a means toward independence while also respecting those Christians who chose otherwise. Kameeta
added his own reflection that Christians in South Africa and Namibia did not

create the violent situation in their countries. Nonetheless, they may be forced into situations where violent response is inevitable, though always evil:

> If I am now deciding to take up arms, then the Word of God should not be misused by saying that it never permits such a step. We are aware that violence is evil. But there can be a time in the life of a nation when the only option for action that is left open is to turn to violence. We know that God will judge us one day. And it is with this knowledge and with a prayer for forgiveness that we have been taking up arms and will continue to do so.[48]

Church leaders took various positions during the independence movement and, later, spoke respectfully of their colleague's decisions even when they disagreed.

BIBLICAL THEOLOGY

As an alternative to liberation theology, some scholars and church leaders preferred the term "biblical theology." This was a persistent phrase and theme throughout interview responses and in published books, open letters and sermons. Namibian Lutherans described the independence movement as most influenced by the Bible and a biblical theology rooted in the image of God as liberator.[49] Biblical exegesis centered on the inherent equality of all humans, endowed by God in the process of creation. Other common biblical themes, shared with liberation theologies from the United States and Latin America, focused on God as a liberator of the oppressed, as seen in Exodus.

Several theologians and church leaders stated that their Christian faith and the Bible, more than specific Lutheran affiliation, provided the strongest motivation for Christian political resistance. Beginning in Genesis, Lutheran pastors and bishops emphasized that all people are made in God's image and therefore they needed to resist the apartheid state which institutionalized a hierarchy between the races.[50] Reminiscent of other liberation theologies, they stressed that God sided with the oppressed, as evident in Exodus.[51] Bishop Auala, another signer of the 1971 Open Letter, wrote a pastoral letter urging people to remember that Pharaoh was overthrown in favor of God's people. He wrote "Have no fear; stand firm and see the deliverance that the Lord will bring you this day."[52]

In addition to these examples, black leaders of the church offered a reinterpretation of Romans 13 which was used by whites to justify South Africa as a divinely appointed authority which must be obeyed. As stated earlier, Romans 13 was nefariously coupled with a Lutheran "Orders of Creation" concept in order to affirm a divine racial hierarchy. Namibian biblical theologians countered, "According to Romans 13, *all* authority is ordained by God. Nowhere does it say that only the 'white' authorities are intended. Neither does Romans 13 mean that the wrong of the authorities should be covered up."[53]

At synod meetings with many church leaders attending, they discussed the political consequences of the Gospel. Bishop Zephania Kameeta clearly centered his actions on his belief of God being a liberator of the oppressed. "For me, God, in his essence, is a God who liberates. It is not a matter of whether what I am saying is liberation or black theology, but what I believe God is. And, from the beginning to the end, he is the one who liberates."[54] Abisai Shejavali also talked about Christians being called to oppose injustice because "[God] is the liberator . . . . He is not for oppressions, exploitations, and human rights violations."[55] Likewise, Shejavali affirmed the biblical teaching of Jesus in the Gospels where he states that the one who serves the neighbor serves him (Matthew 25: 35–40). He discussed how Christians should become like Christ, standing up for those who are suffering.[56] Though not explicitly cited by Shejavali, Luther also wrote in *The Freedom of the Christian* on how Christians are to be Christ to the neighbor, serving them in all their needs.[57]

CONCLUSION

Protestant practice and theological methodology of countering political, ecclesial, and social oppression with scripture was deeply embodied in the Namibian resistance movement. The word of God, supporting the humanity and equality of black Namibians, was the most foundational and initial basis for resistance. At first glance, it appeared that the Namibian independence movement was primarily hobbled by its Lutheran heritage. Lutheran theology had been used deleteriously and Luther's own theological writings were rarely referenced. But a primary Lutheran practice of serious biblical exegesis combined with an insistence on scriptural authority was mightily influential in instigating church involvement in the liberation movement. This was evident in the "Open Letter" and subsequent texts and interviews. Protestant affirmation of scripture reading, biblical exegesis, and scriptural authority countered the logic of apartheid.

Based on the case study of Lutheran theology's role in Namibian struggles against racial injustice, this chapter offers some recommendations for Lutheran theology beyond the context of Namibia. First, there are some doctrines in Lutheranism that have developed an oppressive track record: namely, the orders of creation and the two kingdoms. While these may not always be problematic, they should be red flags to evoke a habit of listening more closely to their contextual application. A "hermeneutic of suspicion," made famous by Paul Ricœur, suggests a manner of reading and hearing for unflattering or dangerous aspects of seemingly innocuous and obvious "truths."

Second, I am increasingly wary of navigating Lutheran theology by catchphrases since it can lead to profound misunderstanding. Categories and catchphrases in North American and European Lutheran theology assume shared agreement on their meaning and, sometimes, application. But what we see again and again, as in Namibia, is that phrases can easily be made to serve the means of their speaker. Even when we choose to communicate through Lutheran theological "shorthand," it would be best to always clarify how we interpret it. Research in the Namibian context also drew to mind that Luther himself wanted his followers to call themselves Christians, rather than Lutheran. He did not seek to make himself the focal point of the Lutheran tradition but rather he continually sought to point to the Bible and Christ. Black Lutheran Namibians looked primarily to Christ and the Bible as the source for their strength and resistance. Lutheran Namibian theology reflects a reliance on biblical exegesis that can seem more faithful to Luther's theological method than typical North American or European proof-texting of Luther's works. Namibian biblical theology offers a compelling example of a contemporary Lutheran liberative method.

Lutheran theologians must always be attuned to the intersection of theology and context and be willing to critically analyze the various ways our theology supports oppression or condones hierarchies that do not serve but diminish and harm the neighbor. Lutheran theology must involve a perpetual critical process of theological norms, informed by those most impacted by its application. An examination of the Namibian context reveals that Lutheran theology may only be ethically accountable and theologically sound if it is grounded in a particular context and interpreted by that context. In particular, the work of James Cone and Dietrich Bonhoeffer were used to undermine a white, doctrinal Lutheranism that applied Luther's concepts to perpetuate oppression. No particular concept or commitment in Lutheran theology is ethically neutral or universal.

NOTES

1. "Namibian Population 2019," 2019 World Population Review, last modified August 28, 2019, accessed October 20, 2019, http://worldpopulationreview.com/countries/namibia-population/. One can contrast this to the United States where approximately 2 percent of the population is Lutheran.

2. My sincere thanks to Kristen Lee, student researcher, who interviewed leaders, obtained and researched documents and books as a part of a Kelmer-Roe Student-Faculty Research Grant at Pacific Lutheran University. Together, we read all sources available in North America and Namibia up to 2012 on the topic of the Namibian black Lutheran churches' theology and their leaders during the apartheid struggle.

3. Martin Luther urges restraint in preaching the Law to the afflicted in multiple disputations, for example, see Luther, "Second Disputation Against the Antinomians," in Holger Sonntag (ed.), *Only the Decalogue is Eternal: Martin Luther's Complete Antinomian Theses and Disputations* (Minneapolis, Minn.: Lutheran Press, 2008), 88–89. Likewise, in his classic text *The Proper Distinction Between Law and Gospel*, nineteenth-century Lutheran theologian, C. F. W. Walther echoes Luther's insistence on the contextualization of preaching. He warns against preaching the law to those who are already downtrodden and states that "to the broken-hearted not a syllable containing a threat or a rebuke is to be addressed, but only promises conveying consolation and grace, forgiveness of sin and righteousness, life and salvation." C. F. W. Walther, *The Proper Distinction Between Law and Gospel* (St. Louis, Mo.: Concordia, 1928), 101 (lecture 12, thesis 8). (Reference is to the English translation of the 1897 lectures.)

4. See the following three classic texts: Valerie Saiving Goldstein, "The Human Situation: A Feminine View," *Journal of Religion* 40, non2 (1960): 100–12; reprint in Carol P. Christ and Judith Plaskow (ed.), *Womanspirit Rising* (San Fransisco: Harper SanFransisco, 1992), 25–42; Susan L. Nelson, *Healing the Broken Heart: Sin, Alienation, and the Gift of Grace* (Atlanta, Ga.: Chalice, 1997); Judith Plaskow, *Sex, Sin, and Grace: Women's Experience and the Theologies of Reinhold Niebuhr and Paul Tillich* (Lanham, MD: University Press of America, 1980).

5. Susan Nelson Dunfee, "The Sin of Hiding: A Feminist Critique of Reinhold Niebuhr's Account of the Sin of Pride" in *Soundings: An Interdisciplinary Journal* 65, no. 3 (Fall 1982): 316–27.

6. Most of my research and experience with black Lutheran congregations was focused in Southern Namibia, in the city of Mariental, and the capital of Windhoek. The vast majority of Lutherans, however, are located north of the capital.

7. Bonganjalo Goba, "The Influence of Certain Political Movements in South Africa on the Church's Role in the Struggle for Liberation," in *The Politics of Religion and Social Change: Religion and the Practical Order, Vol. 2*, eds. Anson Shupe and Jeffrey K. Hadden (New York: Paragon House, 1986), 145.

8. Colin Leys and Susan Brown, eds., *Histories of Namibia: Living Through the Liberation Struggle* (London: The Merlin Press, 2005), 2.

9. Goba, "The Influence," 145.

10. Leys and Brown, "Histories," 2.

11. Paul John Isaak, *Religion and Society: A Namibian Perspective* (Windhoek, Namibia: Out of Africa Publishers, 1997), 41.

12. At the signing of this letter, the churches were known as the Evangelical Lutheran Church of Ovambo-Kavango (ELOK) and the Evangelical Lutheran Church in South West Africa (ELCSWA). The ELOK grew out of the early Finnish missionaries to northern Namibia, and eventually became the Evangelical Lutheran Church

in Namibia (ELCIN). The ELCSWA grew out of the German mission, and today is known as the Evangelical Lutheran Church in the Republic of Namibia (ELCRN). To lessen confusion, only the modern names and acronyms will be used in this chapter.

13. Christo Lombard, "The Role of Religion in the Reconstruction of Namibian Society: The Churches, the New Kairos and Visions of Despair and Hope," in *Journal of Religion and Theology in Namibia*, no. 1 (1999): 43.

14. Per Frostin, "The Theological Debate on Liberation," in *Religion and Politics in Southern Africa*, eds. Carl Fredrik Hallencreutz and Mai Palmberg (Uppsala, Sweden: The Scandinavian Institute of African Studies, 1991), 125–26.

15. Abisai Shejavali interview by Kristen Lee, Pacific Lutheran University Kelmer-Roe Research, April 27, 2011, transcript and recording, Pacific Lutheran University Chair of Lutheran Studies collection.

16. Selma Shejavali, interview by Kristen Lee, Pacific Lutheran University Kelmer-Roe Research, April 20, 2011, transcript and recording, Pacific Lutheran University Chair of Lutheran Studies collection.

17. Philip Steenkamp, "The Churches," in *Namibia's Liberation Struggle: The Two-Edged Sword*, eds. Colin Leys and John S. Saul (Athens: Ohio University Press, 1995), 96.

18. One of the best, condensed resources on Namibian history and the Lutheran churches is an undergraduate honors thesis: Katherine Caufield Arnold, "The Transformation of the Lutheran Church in Namibia" (Undergraduate Honors Theses, College of William and Mary, 2009), access February 21, 2021, https://scholarworks. wm.edu/cgi/viewcontent.cgi?article=1260&context=honorstheses.

19. A. Shejavali, interview, April 27, 2011.

20. Zephania Kameeta, "The Kairos of Liberation in Namibia and the Involvement of the Church," in *Towards Liberation*, ed. Jorg Baumgarten (Windhoek, Namibia: Gamsberg Macmillan Publishers Ltd., 2006), 77.

21. Bernhard Lohse, *Martin Luther's Theology: Its Historical and Systematic Development* (Minneapolis: Fortress, 1999), 245.

22. Carl E. Braaten, "God in Public Life: Rehabilitating the 'Orders of Creation,'" in *First Things: A Monthly Journal of Religion and Public Life* 8 (Dec 1990) paragraph 13, accessed October 18, 2019, https://www.firstthings.com/article/1990/12/god-in-public-life-rehabilitating-the-orders-of-creation.

23. Zephania Kameeta, "A Letter to Brothers and Sisters," in *Towards Liberation*, ed. Jorg Baumgarten (Windhoek, Namibia: Gamsberg Macmillan Publishers Ltd., 2006), 18.

24. Frostin, "Theological Debate," 137. Gendered-language correction mine.

25. Carl E. Braaten, for example, asserts that the preaching of the gospel can too quickly slide into liberation theologies that only equate the gospel with social liberation. Thus, he argues against an historical relativizing of an eternal gospel in Carl E. Braaten, "God in Public Life," paragraph 39. Many black Namibian Lutheran theologians, however, claim that love of neighbor and affirmation of justice and the God-created integrity of creation necessitate social justice on behalf of the neighbor. While one affirms the gospel's importance for faith, one is simultaneously and irrevocably drawn into the world, countering unjust systems.

26. Johannes Lukas de Vries, "Theological Consequences of the Historic 'Open Letter,'" in *That South West Africa May Become a Self-Sufficient and Independent State* (Windhoek, Namibia: United Lutheran Theological Seminary, 1996), 13.

27. Frostin, "Theological Debate," 133.

28. A. Shejavali, interview, April 27, 2011.

29. Frostin, "Theological Debate," 123.

30. Isaak, "Religion and Society," 52. And Abisai Shejavali, interview, April 27, 2011.

31. Zephania Kameeta, "South Africa's Illegal Presence in Namibia and the Confessing Church," in *Namibia in Perspective*, eds. Gerhard Totemeyer, Vezera Kandetu, and Wolfgang Werner (Windhoek, Namibia: Council of Churches in Namibia, 1987), 209.

32. Isaak, "Religion and Society," 46.

33. Juan Luis Segundo, *Liberation of Theology*, trans. John Drury (Maryknoll, NY: Orbis, 1976), 143–44.

34. Reinhold Niebuhr, "Germany," in *Worldview* 16 (June 1973) 14–15, as quoted by Segundo, *Liberation of Theology*, 143.

35. Isaak, "Religion and Society," 47.

36. Abisai Shejavali, interview with Marit Trelstad, June 3, 2003, notes held in Pacific Lutheran University Chair of Lutheran Studies collection.

37. Zephania Kameeta, "In Christ: Hope for the Church" in *Towards Liberation*, ed. Jorg Baumgarten (Windhoek, Namibia: Gamsberg Macmillan Publishers Ltd., 2006), 41.

38. Kameeta, "South Africa's Illegal Presence," 212.

39. A. Shejavali, interview, April 27, 2011.

40. Lombard, "The Role of Religion," 46.

41. Zephania Kameeta, "South Africa's Illegal Presence," 205–13.

42. John W. DeGruchy, *Bonhoeffer and South Africa: Theology in Dialogue* (Grand Rapids, MI: Eerdmans Publ. Co., 1984), 212.

43. Ngeno Nakamhela, interview with Kristen Lee, Pacific Lutheran University Kelmer-Roe Research, April 19, 2011, transcript and recording, Pacific Lutheran University Chair of Lutheran Studies collection.

44. Martin Luther King Jr. as quoted by Kameeta in *Towards Liberation*, 32.

45. A. Shejavali, interview, April 27, 2011.

46. S. Shejavali, interview, April 20, 2011.

47. For further reading on this subject see Leys and Saul, *Namibia's Liberation Struggle.*

48. Zephania Kameeta quoted in *Siegfried Groth, Namibia - the Wall of Silence: the Dark Days of the Liberation Struggle*, trans. Hugh Beyer (Wuppertal, Germany: Peter Hammer Verlag, 1995), 30–31. This book by Lutheran pastor Groth has been highly contentious due to its criticism of SWAPO over political detainees, even though Groth was a supporter of the independence movement. He personally chronicles the Lutheran church's involvement in the movement and its struggles over nonviolent and violent resistance.

49. One reason for this distinction may be the church leaders' interest in distancing themselves from potential Marxist or communist associations in SWAPO and liberation theology.

50. Shekutaamba Nambala, *History of the Church in Namibia*, ed. Oliver K. Olson (Grand Rapids, MI: Eerdman's Publishing Company, Lutheran Quarterly Books, 1994), 131.

51. A. Shejavali, interview, April 27, 2011.

52. Carl J. Helberg, *A Voice of the Voiceless: The involvement of the Lutheran World Federation in Southern Africa 1947–1977* (Lund, Sweden: Skeab/Verbum, 1979), 192. The quotation referenced by Helberg is Exodus 14:13–14.

53. J.L. de Vries, "Theological Consequences," 13.

54. Kameeta, *Towards Liberation*, 3.

55. A. Shejavali, interview, April 27, 2011.

56. A. Shejavali, interview, April 27, 2011.

57. Martin Luther, "The Freedom of the Christian" in Timothy F. Lull, *Martin Luther's Basic Theological Writings*, *Third Edition* (Minneapolis, MN: Fortress, 2012), 419.

BIBLIOGRAPHY

Braaten, Carl E. "God in Public Life: Rehabilitating the 'Orders of Creation.'" In *First Things: A Monthly Journal of Religion and Public Life* 8 (Dec 1990). Accessed October 18, 2019. https://www.firstthings.com/article/1990/12/god-in-public-life-rehabilitating-the-orders-of-creation.

DeGruchy, John W. *Bonhoeffer and South Africa: Theology in Dialogue*. Grand Rapids, MI: Eerdmans Publ. Co., 1984.

De Vries, Johannes Lukas. "Theological Consequences of the Historic 'Open Letter.'" In *That South West Africa May Become a Self-Sufficient and Independent State: Conference on the Occasion of the 25th Anniversary of the Open Letter of the Lutheran Churches in Namibia to John Vorster, Prime Minister of South Africa*, edited by Hans Lessing, 11–14. Windhoek, Namibia: United Lutheran Theological Seminary-Paulinum Ecumenical Institute for Namibia, 1996.

Frostin, Per. "The Theological Debate on Liberation." In *Religion and Politics in Southern Africa*, edited by Carl Fredrik Hallencreutz and Mai Palmberg, 123–139. Uppsala, Sweden: The Scandinavian Institute of African Studies, 1991.

Goba, Bonganjalo. "The Influence of Certain Political Movements in South Africa on the Church's Role in the Struggle for Liberation." In *The Politics of Religion and Social Change: Religion and the Practical Order, Vol. 2*, edited by Anson Shupe and Jeffrey K. Hadden, 141–159. New York: Paragon House, 1988.

Groth, Siegfried. *Namibia - the Wall of Silence: the Dark Days of the Liberation Struggle*. Translated by Hugh Beyer. Wuppertal, Germany: Peter Hammer Verlag, 1995.

Helberg, Carl J. *A Voice of the Voiceless: The involvement of the Lutheran World Federation in Southern Africa 1947–1977*. Lund, Sweden: Skeab/Verbum, 1979.

Isaak, Paul John. *Religion and Society: A Namibian Perspective*. Windhoek, Namibia: Out of Africa Publishers, 1997.

Kameeta, Zephania. "In Christ: Hope for the Church." In *Towards Liberation*, edited by Jorg Baumgarten, 39–50. *Windhoek*, Namibia: Gamsberg Macmillan Publishers Ltd., 2006

———. "The Kairos of Liberation in Namibia and the Involvement of the Church." In *Towards Liberation*, edited by Jorg Baumgarten, 65–79. Windhoek, Namibia: Gamsberg Macmillan Publishers Ltd., 2006.

———. "A Letter to Brothers and Sisters." In *Towards Liberation*, edited by Jorg Baumgarten, 14–37. Windhoek, Namibia: Gamsberg Macmillan Publishers Ltd., 2006.

———. "South Africa's Illegal Presence in Namibia and the Confessing Church." In *Namibia in Perspective*, edited by Gerhard Totemeyer, Vezera Kandetu, and Wolfgang Werner, 205–213. Windhoek, Namibia: Council of Churches in Namibia, 1987.

Leys, Colin, and Susan Brown, eds. *Histories of Namibia: Living Through the Liberation Struggle*. London: The Merlin Press, 2005.

Lohse, Bernhard. *Martin Luther's Theology: Its Historical and Systematic Development*. Minneapolis: Fortress, 1999.

Lombard, Christo. "The Role of Religion in the Reconstruction of Namibian Society: The Churches, the New Kairos and Visions of Despair and Hope," in *Journal of Religion and Theology in Namibia*, no. 1 (1999): 38–87.

Luther, Martin. "The Freedom of the Christian." In Timothy F. Lull, *Martin Luther's Basic Theological Writings, 3rd Edition.* Minneapolis, MN: Fortress, 2012.

———. "Second Disputation Against the Antinomians." In *Only the Decalogue is Eternal: Martin Luther's Complete Antinomian Theses and Disputations*, edited by Holger Sonntag, 83–124. Minneapolis, Minn.: Lutheran Press, 2008.

Nambala, Shekutaamba. *History of the Church in Namibia*, edited by Oliver K. Olson. Grand Rapids, MI: Eerdman's Publishing Company, Lutheran Quarterly Books, 1994.

"Namibian Population 2019," 2019 World Population Review, last modified August 28, 2019, accessed October 20, 2019, http://worldpopulationreview.com/countries/namibia-population/.

Nelson Dunfee, Susan. "The Sin of Hiding: A Feminist Critique of Reinhold Niebuhr's Account of the Sin of Pride." *Soundings: An Interdisciplinary Journal* 65, no. 3 (Fall 1982): 316–27.

Nelson, Susan L. *Healing the Broken Heart: Sin, Alienation, and the Gift of Grace.* Atlanta, GA: Chalice, 1997.

Plaskow, Judith. *Sex, Sin, and Grace: Women's Experience and the Theologies of Reinhold Niebuhr and Paul Tillich. Lanham, MD*: University Press of America, 1980.

Segundo, Juan Luis. *Liberation of Theology*, translated by John Drury. Maryknoll, NY: Orbis, 1976.

Saiving Goldstein, Valerie. "The Human Situation: A Feminine View," *Journal of Religion* 40, no. 2 (1960): 100–12.

Steenkamp, Philip. "The Churches." In *Namibia's Liberation Struggle: The Two-Edged Sword*, edited by Colin Leys and John S. Saul. Athens: Ohio University Press, 1995.

Chapter 6

A Variegated Lutheran Theology in the Context of Twenty-First Century Idols

Mary Philip a.k.a. Joy

> Either way, change will come.
> It could be bloody, or,
> it could be beautiful.
> It depends on us.[1]

The sun's rays were quite warm, and the leaves of the butterfly bushes were feeling it too, but the Monarch flitted in and out of the flower bunches as though she didn't have a care in the world. She seemed quite content teasing the nectar out of the tubular flowers while occasionally fanning her wings to keep cool! The Monarch was soon joined by a Great Spangled Fritillary, closely followed by the Canadian Tiger Swallowtail. Enjoying lunch in the company of these beautiful butterflies made me feel, even if only momentarily, as though all was well with the world. Were the pandemic and the death of George Floyd figments of my imagination? Alas, that was wishful thinking! George Floyd did cry out, "I cannot breathe." And, as of August 27, 2020, the death toll due to COVID-19 was 822,000. COVID-19 and racial discrimination continue to claim lives and are very much stark realities! Do I even want to think about Luther or Luther's theology amidst this pandemonium? But, then, how could I not!

Were there comparable calamities during the time of Luther? What were the idols of Luther's times?[2] Though whiteness per se may not have been an idol in Luther's time, I wonder if "Christianity" could be added to the list. Luther's hatred for the Jews and Muslims is well known fact. Or, maybe, it was only Luther who had the problem. But then, in the twelfth century,

Bernard of Clairvaux is believed to have encouraged the killing of Muslims. Shakespeare, who lived and wrote his plays in the sixteenth century, was quite negative and even derogatory in his depiction of Jews and people of African descent. Portrayal of his characters as "dog Jew," "blackfiend," or "an old black rap," would be familiar to readers of Shakespeare.

Luther's time also saw the devastation from the Black Death (Bubonic plague, continuing from the fourteenth century) and smallpox (introduced by the Europeans, claiming the lives of 95 percent of the original peoples of the Americas). While the entrance of Europeans into the Americas wiped out groups of people, it also created modern capitalism, the root of many an evil! "The mineral wealth exploited from 'the New World' in the form of gold and silver led to massive inflation in the Spanish Empire and the resulting 'price revolution' changed how money was valued, a crucial moment in the development of modern capitalism."[3] So, it is safe to assume that there were plenty of idols and demons to go around in Luther's time as well.

Throughout history, pandemics have caused humanity to ponder questions about life and so have societal evils like slavery, the caste system, the horrors of Auschwitz, and so on, but to what avail? So, what has changed now?

This pandemic, unlike the others, exposes and exacerbates inequalities and inequities within society. Unfortunately, rather than take responsibility, communities and nations are vying with each other to find a scapegoat. "The virus does not discriminate, but its impacts are felt more harshly among those who suffer the consequences of discriminatory laws and practices."[4] In other words, we can now add pandemic racism, for which an indulgence should be in the making. Now, where does this leave us as individuals, communities, nations, and the earth as a whole? Where are we heading to? Isn't it time to pause?

As I pen these words, the pandemic is in its eighth month since the outbreak was first identified in Wuhan, China (December 2019). While it has mounted a pile of dead bodies in its path, the pandemic has at the same time afforded a pause, a time of Sabbath, to the natural world. In the Indian state of Punjab, people posted pictures of the Himalayan mountain ranges, a sight to behold for the first time in three decades, thanks to a drop in air pollution because of the country's coronavirus lockdown. Wildlife, be it the doe with her fawns or the white-tailed eagle, have made a spectacular recovery in many parts of the world. These were signs of nature healing itself when people were not around to wound her. While air is undoubtedly less polluted because of a drop in the emissions of greenhouse gases, the impact of self-isolation on people is not as light as it was thought to be.

We are, indeed, in a time and space where crisis is the only constant. But as Wangari Maathai, the founder of the Greenbelt movement, said, "There are opportunities even in the most difficult moments."[5] So, what opportunity are we presented with amid COVID-19, when things change by the minute? James Baldwin also reminds us that "not everything that is faced can be changed; but nothing can be changed until it is faced."[6] So, maybe the more pertinent question is, "how do we face this crisis, this ever-changing time?" What are the rules and tools we are working with?

It goes without saying that without change there would be no butterflies. I would not be in the company of these exquisite creatures if it were not for the long and painful metamorphosis of the various stages through which they pass. Amid the long waiting period, the long Holy Saturday of the pandemic, what can we hope for? Maybe it is time to look into the idols of our times and the indulgences we are buying.[7] And, maybe it is time to look into what aspects of Lutheran theology or Lutheran concepts have relevance in the contexts we are in,[8] specifically in the pandemic-ridden world of the twenty-first century.

To conceal the idol of whiteness, whether in America or Canada, we resort to protest marches and sign up for webinars and antiracism workshops.

To camouflage the idol of colonialism, whether in Namibia—still dealing with the vestiges of colonial Lutheranism—or India, we resort to *neo*-colonialism.

Idolatry, whether "by the individual's turning God into a thing or by the individual's placing themselves in the role of God,"[9] essentially is about one's relationship with God and neighbor. "These idols . . . have an outsized role in our lives. Idols organize or shape our experience of the world. In a sense, the problem of idolatry becomes the problem of ideology in that we are being shaped by social norms and political narratives beyond our control."[10] Idols objectify a thing or a phenomenon so that it becomes a commodity with a market value. "To say that whiteness is an idol is to say that whiteness is a self-referential norm that funds a racial and economic hierarchy that prioritizes white people over people of color."[11] In other words, the idol of whiteness is bequeathed so very high a value that anything that is not white is rendered of less, or even no value or worth. It puts the wellbeing of one who is white over and above the wellbeing of those who are black, indigenous, or persons of color, leading to racial discrimination. Against the idol of whiteness, the lives of Chantal Moore and Breonna Taylor do not matter; they become disposable.

The idol of colonialism also has a similar modus operandi. This was especially true in the case of the role of Lutheran theology in the political struggles of the Namibians from 1970 to 1990.[12] "Theological concepts familiar to North American and European Lutherans were often used to support apartheid or to discourage political resistance. Even the foundation of Lutheran theology, "justification by grace through faith,' was used by white Lutherans to support the status quo."[13] In the twenty-first century, have things changed that much? Not really! There has been some contextualization of Lutheran theology to make it relevant to other times and places. However, the belief that Lutheran concepts can serve as the key to unlocking theological conundrums is still very much prevalent in Lutheran strongholds and circles. Indeed, "theology's ability to be good news is dependent on our awareness of this contextual specificity."[14] But, then, that awareness would mean losing control over the hegemonic Lutheran discourses, creating cracks in the dominant German, Scandinavian, and North American framework of doing theology, and making space for the hitherto subjugated or hidden Lutheran theologies that arise from the contexts in which it has taken root.

Amidst these idols that freeze our gaze, limit our gait, and stop our breath, what can we hope for? Amidst this pandemic, where we are dangerously close to normalizing hatred, inequity, violence, and discrimination, what is there to be hopeful about?

Richard Rohr, in a recent devotional piece, voiced this question, posed by many amidst the scary issue of climate change. "How can you know all these facts [about climate change] and still have hope?" Rohr then goes on to say that for him,

> Faith and hope are rooted in the conviction that, regardless of how bad things may be, a new story is waiting to take hold—something we have not yet seen or felt or experienced . . . . God is calling us . . . to work with God and others to champion that new story. For the vast majority in our society, that new story remains unseen. Wrestling our future from the grip of fossil fuel seems impossible—our addiction is too strong, affordable options are too few, and the powers that defend the status quo are mighty, indeed . . . . We cannot be freed by chipping away at this millstone. We must begin to live into a new story by changing the human prospect [of destruction] and restoring creation's viability.[15]

These words could not be more applicable in the time of this pandemic. It is time to live into a new story, to be engaged in a new theology, one that is aimed at listening to and acting on the "plea of the supplicant" or "lifting the underside of history."

So, how can we live into this new story? How and where does Luther's theology fit into the weaving of this story? Luther's theology, be it the two-kingdom doctrine, the theology of the cross, or the law/gospel dialectic, the foci of a mammoth amount of literature—this is not a matter of one-size-fits-all. As mentioned earlier, Luther's theological concepts are often viewed as a key, but for what? "If we receive it only to construct locks to fit the key, it will not open anything other than the lock itself . . . The key is a real gift if, and only if, it opens the lock that holds us captive. The doctrine of justification, or any other doctrine, is irrelevant if it does not fit [address] the plea of the supplicant heart, the broken soul and the damaged life."[16] For example, if I were to look into the relevance of the two-kingdom doctrine for the twenty-first century, I could not but take the context into consideration. In India, my homeland, this doctrine does not work; instead, the people live out the theology of the cross. The freedom of a Christian is a genius of a doctrine, but a call to live it out will break the backbone of a caste-driven society like India; and much as I wish it to happen, that won't fly in India.

The focus of this book is a theology of the cross. The theology of the cross, simply put, is seeing the presence of the divine where one least expects to. It is about seeing possibilities where there seems to be none, especially when one takes the risk to transgress boundaries of traditional religious boundaries as well as disciplinary borders of academia. The two-kingdoms doctrine is problematic when viewed within the pedantic Western framework. But there are possibilities when one punches some holes in that frame so that another hue of light that peeks in, be it that of a different religious tradition like Hinduism or another academic discipline like biology, might add to the possibility the concept has to offer. Toward that end, I offer a re-reading of the two-kingdoms doctrine.

A RE-READING OF THE TWO-KINGDOM DOCTRINE AS A RESPONSE TO TWENTY-FIRST CENTURY IDOLS

Luther's doctrine is neither a curio nor a relic. Yet it has come to be the gauging stick for Lutheranism: a litmus test for Lutherans, as a sort of an ID. An ID gives me a label by which I will be tagged or referred to. But identity is much more than a label. It is how I live out my life as a Lutheran, and the label will not tell that. The question that needs to be posed is: How has the two-kingdoms doctrine been transformative or life-giving? *Has* it been transformative? If it has not, it is high time we asked, "why not?"

Luther's text "How People Should regard Moses"[17] is pertinent here. It is about how we understand the written texts, the scriptures, and their relevance or irrelevance for our times. The same goes for Luther. Or, as the late Brazilian theologian Vítor Westhelle said, Luther needs to be a *figura* that is repeatedly transformed.[18] If not, Luther becomes only a relic, and it is time to rethink or even cast out relics. But I love the old and the relic, and I am not ready to cast Luther or Luther's concepts out, at least not yet.

WHAT IS THE TWO-KINGDOM DOCTRINE?

To start with, how would I explain this doctrine to a seventh grader?

Spiritualia—You sit quietly in your room and say things for no one to listen to but God, and you know that this is okay and no one else needs to know.

Carnalia—You send a message to your friend for a happy hour, Google some information for a paper you need to write, do your homework, take care of the household chores, and on Sundays go to church, go to a play, knowing always that you will inevitably mess up something.

This is not only simple to understand but also makes perfect sense! The doctrine is of two-kingdoms, one of the Word (spirit) and the other of the flesh. But then, can it be that simple when the Word became flesh? I am reminded of C. S. Song's words here: The Word-become-flesh theology is a dangerous theology. He goes on to say, "It is dangerous because it asks questions that are not asked by conventional faith," not to mention conventional contexts. "It is dangerous because it ventures into areas that are out of bounds for traditional theology." So, how can this doctrine of two kingdoms be understood for our time and place? As Song implies, it opened my eyes to sights not found in theological textbooks. The doctrine, I say, is problematic for a number of reasons, but as a transformative, life-giving identifying label, it makes perfect sense. According to Luther,

> God has established two kinds of government among men. The one is spiritual; it has no sword, but it has the word, by means of which men are to become good and righteous, so that with this righteousness they may attain eternal life. He administers this righteousness through the word, which he has committed to the preachers. The other kind is worldly government, which works through the sword so that those who do not want to be good and righteous to eternal life may be forced to become good and righteous in the eyes of the world. He administers this righteousness through the sword. And although God will not reward this kind of righteousness with eternal life, nonetheless, he still wishes peace to be maintained among men and rewards them with temporal blessings. He gives rulers much more property, honor, and power than he gives to others so that they may serve him by administering this temporal righteousness. Thus God himself is the founder, lord, master, protector, and rewarder of both kinds of righteousness. There is no human ordinance or authority in either, but each is a divine thing entirely.[19]

So, God's activity in the world comes in a twofold way, in two "kingdoms"— the worldly or earthly or the *carnalia*, which is a place of conflict and coercion, and the spiritual or *spiritualia*, which is undergirded by the Word (spirit and grace).

This distinction runs the risk of culpable inaction in the face of grave injustice. This is especially true in the case of the many marginalized communities and peoples, especially of the global South. It is very true in the pandemic-ridden context we are in now, in which discrimination, disparities, and inequities, hitherto hidden, have come into view.

Growing up in India, I was looked after by an untouchable woman, Tharamma (the name is the untouchable/Dalit version of Sara). She may have been an illiterate untouchable, but she taught me more than someone with an advanced academic degree; she taught me the lessons of life. The Two-Kingdoms doctrine, this separation into the spiritual and earthly, does not do her and the millions of Dalits or the women of India any justice. The fact is that we not only have bodies, we *are* bodies.[20] And if the bodies are to be alive, they have to have the breath of life. One does not rule out the other; rather, one cannot be without the other. And, for Luther, the body, "matter," mattered to him, and so did the spirit. There is this perception that spirit is not matter. Is it really matter? Spirit is *ruah*, air that we inspire and expire. What is this spirit or the air we inspire or which inspires us? It is matter! The definition of matter is that it has to have mass and take up space. When you see trees swaying, you know the wind is blowing. The force of the wind, the pressure that it exerts, is what makes the tree swing. Pressure is force per unit area, so if there is pressure, you know the air must have mass. So you see, air, spirit, is matter! Furthermore, it is a form of matter than can change shape (just squeeze a balloon). And, this matter matters—that is one of the first things that I learned from Tharamma. Almost thirty years later, I have come to North America and my teacher tells me that Luther said the same.

AN UNTOUCHABLE'S INTERPRETATION OF THE DOCTRINE OF TWO KINGDOMS

Years ago, one late afternoon, I was lying on Tharamma's lap by the stream next to her hut—a hut made of coconut leaves for the roof and cow dung for the basic structure. She said to me:

"Kochu thambrati, a aruvi kando? kunju endha kanunne?" ("കൊച്ചു തമ്പ്രാട്ടി ആ അരുവി കണ്ടോ? കുഞ്ഞു എന്താ കാണുന്നെ?") Translated, it means, "Little princess, do you see that stream? What do you see when you look at it?" The little kid that I was and quite content on her lap, looked at the stream and said: "vellam ozhukunnu" ("വെള്ളം ഒഴുകുന്നു"), which means, "the water is flowing."

She nudged me and said, "sookshichu nokku" ("സൂക്ഷിച്ചു നോക്ക്"): "Look carefully." I looked again and said: "Tharaamma para gnan enna kananam" ("താറാ അമ്മ പറ ഞാൻ എന്നാ കാണണം"), "Why don't you tell me what you want me to see?" She then asked me if there was a difference on the sides of the stream as opposed to the middle. I said that the water was flowing in the center and it was stinky and sort of stagnant at the sides; in the center, the water was much clearer, though it was pulling the dirty water from the sides into it. And what Tharamma told me next stayed with me all these years. "Vellam ozhukunnidatha jivan; ennumparanju athu shudhavellam onum alla. nischala jalathu azhukku kooduthala; pakshe nallathum theeyathum koodiya nadukkathe ozhukku. Aathmavum shareeravum randa pakshe randalla" ("വെള്ളം ഒഴുകുന്നിടത്താ ജിവൻ; എന്നുംപറഞ്ഞു അത് ശുദ്ധവെള്ളം ഒന്നും അല്ല. നിശ്ചല ജലത്ത് അഴുക്കു കൂടുതലാ; പക്ഷെ നല്ലതും തീയതും കൂടിയാ നടുക്കത്തെ ഒഴുക്ക്. ആത്മാവും ശരീരവും രണ്ടാ പക്ഷെ രണ്ടല്ല"). Translation: "Still water quickly collects silt. It is where the water flows that life happens. It does not mean the water in the center is pure, but you can see things clearly; life happens when the good and the bad go together. Spirit and the body may be two, but not divided. They flow together." These are the words of a bent, illiterate woman who had not heard of Chalcedon or Luther or the doctrine of two kingdoms. But she lived out that doctrine, I believe, the way Luther intended it to be.

Just as the earth cannot be separated from the air, the body cannot be separated from the breath or the spirit. Just as earth without air is devoid of life, body without breath is dead. The two go together. The Sara, Martha, and Maria (or Mary) that we read about in the Bible were chosen ones, but the chosenness of Thara, presented here, is of a different kind. Her chosenness is because her life didn't matter! She was a no-person; she was disposable. She lived for her masters and mistresses; her life didn't actually belong to her. She was at the master's house at the crack of dawn and went home only after night had fallen. If she didn't come the next day, there would be much to pay—but it is not that she was indispensable. Her masters would find someone else!

The distinction of two kingdoms—*spiritualia* and *carnalia*—applied to Tharamma and so many like her is about the shirking of responsibility. This distinction gives *me* a way out. I can keep from having to see them, from being responsible for Tharamma or those like her. By saying that there is this kingdom where one can sit and talk to God and no one else, and another kingdom where one kills oneself to live and make ends meet, I am washing my hands of my responsibilities. "Love your neighbor as yourself" is gone with the wind! Tharamma cannot afford to make that distinction. For her, spirit and matter need to go together for life to happen, for life to flow from one moment to next. Everything is felt and done through the body!

Have you heard of Devadasis? They are women set apart as helpers in the temple. *Deva* means God and *dasi* means servant. But commonly, the Devadasi was the object of pleasure for the pujari, or the temple priest. While I do not want to generalize, to many outsiders she was a temple prostitute. What would the doctrine of two kingdoms mean to her? Every time she is violated, her body is screaming out to God; not silently talking to God, but crying out in silent submission. I am sure she would have loved to say things for no one but God to hear, and know that it is okay and that no one else needs to know. But she cannot afford that. Her body, the body that does the various chores and eats and pays the bills, those realities that belong to *carnalia*, that same body is the temple, the kingdom of *spiritualia*! It is embodiment par excellence!

Luther, I am sure, had good intentions when he came up with the doctrine of two kingdoms, but it is not applicable to Tharamma, to the Devadasis, and to many marginalized people. It is not possible to make that distinction, because everything that they feel is through the world where they toil. It is through the flesh, the body, that they experience and do everything. The spiritual realm and the carnal realm cannot be separated. They have to go together for life to happen. In that sense, this separation into *spiritualia* and *carnalia* is problematic.

But now we turn to why the so-called doctrine makes perfect sense.

HOMO SAPIENS □ SPIRITUALIA CARNALIA

The Canada jay is the national bird of Canada where I work and live currently (see figure 6.1). Its scientific name is *Perisoreus canadensis.* This type of classification is called binomial nomenclature, and it is part of modern taxonomy. It is the system of giving a scientific name to living things, thanks to Carolus Linnaeus. According to this system, any given animal or plant is given a scientific name consisting of two parts—genus and species. The typical rules are the following:

1. The first word refers to the name of the genus and the second word to the name of the species.
2. The name of the genus should start with a capital letter and the name of the species with a small letter.
3. Both the names should be written in italics.
4. The name of the scientist who first identified and described the species should be abbreviated and written after the species name, preferably in brackets. For example, the name of human beings is written as *Homo sapiens* (Linn). In the case of the Canada Jay, the scientist who first identified it was Mathurin Jacques Brisson, but it was Carl Linnaeus who gave the bird its binomial name, and so the scientific name is *Perisoreus canadensis* (Linn).

A species is a group of organisms that typically have similar anatomical characteristics and, in sexual reproducers, can successfully interbreed to produce

Figure 6.1. Canada jay, *Perisoreus canadensis.* **Illustration by Macdelln Samuel.**

fertile offspring. The species name is used to distinguish a particular species from others belonging to the same genus. *Genus* is a more general taxonomic category than is *species*. For example, the generic name *Perisoreus* includes the Siberian Jay, *Perisoreus infaustus*, the Sichuan Jay, *Perisoreus internigrans* and the Canada Jay, also called the Grey Jay or Whiskey Jack, *Perisoreus canadensis*. Together, the genus plus the specific epithet makes up the full scientific name for an organism. It is something that identifies the organism. Just one of the names does not give a full picture. Only when the two are put together does it work as an identifying mark. The identity is communicated only when the two are side by side. The two names constitute part of a communicating system.

What would be the comparable concept in theology? It is two natures, one person! Chalcedonian formula in life![21] Fully human and fully divine! What *communicatio idiomatum* is to the person of Jesus can be applied to the relationship between the two kingdoms—*spiritualia* and *carnalia*. It could be seen not as two separate kingdoms, but as one that has two natures or characters—spiritual and carnal. What can be said of the spiritual can be said of the carnal and what can be said of the carnal can be said of the spiritual. Just as Jesus' divinity was fully realized in his humanity, so it is in the case of the two-kingdoms doctrine: the spiritual kingdom manifests itself in the debased conditions of the carnal kingdom. The "inspirations" of the spiritual kingdom are made meaningful in the flesh. The spirituality is fully expressed in the carnality, and vice versa.

When I say I am hungry, I can say that of my body and my spirit as well. The food for each will differ, but hunger is there for both my body and spirit. It is equally true that when my body is fed, I am in better spirits, so to speak! When I am violated, it is not just my body that is violated, I can say that of my spirit, too. It goes without saying that we have bodies; but as mentioned earlier, what is more important to note is that we *are* bodies. In one of his lectures, Juan Luis Segundo (a Jesuit theologian born on Reformation Day) gives a helpful analogy to understand the Chalcedonian formula. He uses the analogy of map and territory.[22] I can know some things about the territory of India by looking at a map of Asia. But I have to be careful not to take the map for the territory;[23] I cannot "mix the qualities coming from the map with the qualities coming from the territory."[24] To quote Segundo again, "I cannot directly know from the size of the map the actual extension of the territory."[25] I can infer it from the scale. One allows us to interpret the other. So, if we were to apply this understanding of the two kingdoms to human beings, their scientific name could be renamed as *Spiritualia carnalia* (Luth):

Genus *spiritualia*—this is the more general taxonomic category. Therefore, the general characteristic I employed is that all of us have the breath of life, *ruah*, the spirit.

Species *carnalia*—the characteristics are more defined and specific. It is also the case that the species name can be in opposition to the genus name and does not have to agree in gender. So, in *carnalia,* it can be male, female, LGBTQIA2S+, Hindu, Buddhist, Roman Catholic, Indian, Brazilian, Danish, S. African—even Lutheran!

And to follow the rule, the abbreviated name of the person who first identified and described the species is added in brackets and so we have (Luth). And thus we are: *Spiritualia carnalia* (Luth). This would indeed be the litmus test or the identifying mark for Lutherans because that is what we are—spiritual and carnal beings—*Spiritualia carnalia* (Luth). Did Luther have this in mind when he came up with the doctrine of the two kingdoms? To affirm that may be a stretch, but this is certainly one of the ways that the doctrine can be understood today.

KAMA SUTRA

Another example that will further my argument also comes from my home-land, India—*Kama Sutra*! *Kama Sutra* and Two Kingdoms side by side! Crazy, scandalous, however one labels it, let's take a look, shall we? *Kama Sutra* is believed to have been written in the sixth century. So, it is quite possible that Luther was not only aware of its existence but also put it into practice! Vātsyāyana, the Hindu philosopher, is believed to be the author of *Kama Sutra*. Not much is known about him, though his treatises prove that he was well versed in the Vedic tradition. His premise was that human sexual behavior was the route to attaining spirituality. In other words, Kama Sutra is the coming together of the spiritual and the carnal. *Kama Sutra* falls under the tantric tradition. The spiritual concept and practices of *tantra* informs sexual behavior. However, *tantra* is not simply "spiritual sex," which seems to be the general perception. It is a spiritual practice and involves *gnana, yoga, kriya,* and *charya. Gnana* is knowledge that takes reality of the world as well as the transcendent seriously; *yoga* is not the yoga ball exercises in a gym, but contemplative practices as prescribed in *vedic* scriptures; *kriya* includes actions and deeds, both ritual and otherwise, and *charya* are both religious and secular commands. It is similar to the simple explanation of the Two Kingdoms doctrine, which involves the quiet conversations with God as well as the activities and chores in the mundane world. *Kama Sutra* covers it all.

Sexual activity guided by tantric principles brings about liberation of the consciousness into a unity with the divine. This happens not through any rigorous spiritual routines but through ordinary acts of eating, breathing, and making love.[26] Everything in creation is a form of the one divinity; it is an aspect, analogy, or expression of the One.[27] *Tantra* asserts that spirituality devoid of the physical is facile, and sex without the spiritual is shallow. So, lovemaking is a strong vehicle for spiritual formation and transformation.[28] The sexual act integrates the physical, emotional, mental, and spiritual, and provokes spiritual responses. It results in the transformation of the physical, carnal, sexual energy into spiritual energy. Athanasius' words, "For He was made [human] so that we might be made God"[29] express a similar idea. So, when I say that the sexual act of making love brings about transformation, it means that there is an organic, reciprocal, and palpable relationship between our sensual experience and our spiritual experience.[30] Succinctly put, "bodily experience can reveal the divine . . . "[31] Understood in this way, the principle of tantric *Kama Sutra* may be seen in various other theological precepts as well. *Theosis, anamnesis*, communion, prayer, and *shabbat* are just a few we might name.

The intention here is not to get into the details of *Kama Sutra* or tantric practices but to bring to the table that while Luther's doctrine, understood as describing two distinct kingdoms, one spiritual and the other carnal, is not a practicable doctrine for many contexts. However, when re-read as above, it is our identifying label, our scientific name as Lutherans—*Spiritualia carnalia* (Luth) and I add, for all human beings, minus "(Luth.)." We belong to genus *spiritualia* and species *carnalia*, each with its own characteristics, but communicating as one.

MODUS OPERANDI

So, how does all this come together? How is this a response to the chapters presented by Benjamin Taylor and Marit Trelstad?

Human beings are both spiritual and carnal beings, one not better than the other. We are both saints and sinners.[32] We are broken and beautiful at the same time! I do not always live out the image of God, but I also know that in my baptismal identity, I daily die to sin and rise to life. I will have idols that lock my gaze, and my theology will circle the drain. However, my identity, *Spiritualia carnalia,* will, I trust, help unlock my gaze, enabling me to see beyond the idol, and will embolden my theology to clear the drain.

Both Taylor and Trelstad talk of idols, one of white privilege, of whiteness, and the other of the colonial Lutheran theology. Both are tools of marginalization that were used to racially discriminate against some people, to promote apartheid. Taylor affirms the relevance of Luther's theology and employs it to critique the idols of our times—whiteness, greed, and environmental racism. Trelstad points to the importance of doing contextual theology. I am not contesting either but agreeing with both. Luther's *theologia crucis* is indeed a critique of power and a call to recognize the presence of God in creation, both human and nonhuman, and to be in solidarity with the poor.[33] All and any theology, if it is to be authentic, has to be contextual. The Lutheran understanding of orders of creation and the doctrine of two kingdoms are as problematic in the Namibian context as they are for the Indian context. And, of course, "responsible Lutheran theology is a non-universal process of interrogating Lutheran theological categories from within particular contexts and according to those most vulnerable."[34] The primary task of theology is, as Prosper of Aquitaine said in the fourth century, to listen to the plea of the supplicant.[35] But even that needs to be looked at from the perspective of who is holding the reins. It is always a question of power. This is what Chimamanda Adichie calls the "danger of a single story."[36] Who is telling whose story? If Lutheran theology is to be authentic, it needs to encounter other theologies, other traditions, other disciplines, so much so that it seeps into the other as spices do in cooking.[37] That is what makes it flavorful!

My invitation (or is it my challenge?), as exemplified in the pages above, is to look at Lutheran theology through different and variously colored lenses so that we can achieve "a balance of stories,"[38] to quote both Chinua Achebe and Chimamanda Adichie. Our identity as human beings created in the image of God and, by extension, our identity as Lutherans are all one needs to combat any idol. Just as the Christian story is one[39] but plural, this identity, *Spiritualia carnalia*, is one but plural. We are Lutherans, Methodists, Unitarians, Anglicans, Catholics, Pentecostals, Wiccans, Haudenosaunee, Ojibwe, Cree, Afro-Canadian, African American, Indian, Chinese, Palestinian, Israeli, Latinx, Mixed, Cis-gendered, LGBTQIA2S+, Liberals, Conservatives, Able-bodied, Disable-bodied, Poor, Disenfranchised, Rich, Powerful, Destitute, Incarcerated, Black, Indigenous, People of Color: the list can go on. And even embedded within these identities are several ecosystems. This identity is based on one of Luther's concepts, the Two-Kingdoms doctrine, but rubbed against non-Lutheran theologies, even non-Christian traditions, as I have explicated above. This identity in and of itself is sufficient to combat the idols of our times. These idols can be destroyed if one were to live out their identity as *Spiritualia carnalia*. Our gazes will no longer be locked onto the idol but will move beyond it to see the reality. If we were to live out our identity as *Spiritualia carnalia*, the Breonnas and Chantals and Georges would no longer be objects that can be discarded, but would have life in full. If we were to live out our identity as *Spiritualia carnalia*, there would be no more Alan Kurdis washing up on the beach fleeing from their homelands. If we were to live out our identity as *Spiritualia carnalia*, our planet would no longer groan in pain but would flourish.

Why? Because that which powers this identity is our freedom in Christ. It is the freedom to be who we are, created in the image of God. Luther's "Freedom of a Christian"[40] is a claim for unbounded freedom and radical commitment to the neighbor and to all of creation.

For Luther, freedom in faith and love in hope are the fundamental marks of Christian life. What does this mean in the context of responsibility to those that are bound (by others and/or idols) and denied justice? What does it mean in the context of climate change, the effects of which further discriminate and impoverish the marginalized in our societies? Where is our responsibility?

Our responsibility lies in living out this freedom as those whose identity is *Spiritualia carnalia*. It is freedom through faith in Christ to serve the neighbor. We are free in faith and bound in love to our neighbor. Our identity as *Spiritualia carnalia* frees us to love our neighbor in a way that we otherwise would not because this freedom in Christ opens us to know a different kind of justice. It is a compelling knowledge that impels us to raise our voices against injustices meted out to our fellow human beings and our planet earth. It is a knowing that propels us to take risks and call out injustice when and where it happens. It is a freedom that paves the way for the flourishing of black lives, indigenous lives, persons-of-color lives, even white lives! If we were to live out our identity as *Spiritualia carnalia,* where the question of liberation and Christian life are not relegated to two different spheres, but come together and communicate so that freedom is a reality, then there is still hope for Luther and Luther's theology in the midst of twenty-first-century idols.

The crucial question is what it means to be Lutheran in the contexts we are in. If it gets in the way of our living lives as those created in the image of God, of loving our neighbor, then being Lutheran has absolutely no relevance; nor does Luther's theology. But if Lutherans were to really live into the identity of *Spiritualia carnalia*, there is hope abundant!

The biblical passage often used to explicate the Two-Kingdoms doctrine is Mark 12:13–17, on the paying of taxes. Jesus' response, "Give to the emperor the things that are the emperor's, and to God the things that are God's," is said to be the most faithful rendition of that doctrine. Most faithful rendition or not, it is about the freedom to love and serve the neighbor. Paying taxes, much as it fills the coffers of the Caesars of our times, also goes into the care of my neighbor. That way, when I pay taxes, I am living out my identity as *Spiritualia carnalia*. The provincial and federal taxes I pay go into the treatment and care of my COVID-stricken neighbor; they go to housing and welfare programs for my poor and disenfranchised neighbor; they go to resettling my displaced neighbor; they go to children's education and child support services; they go to public transportation. By paying taxes to the government—the image on that coin—I am living out the image in which I am created—loving my neighbor and being a neighbor. So, Jesus' advice is to be followed as a mark of our identity of being created in the image of God.

Going back to where I started, to the question I asked myself—Do I even want to think about Luther or Luther's theology or Lutheran theologies amidst this pandemonium? Yes, I do, because I believe that it can bring about much needed change in our century as it did in the 16th century, and it need not be bloody; it can be beautiful.[41] However, it can and will be beautiful only if we use diverse lenses. I dare to say that we are called not only to entertain, engage, and critique Luther's theology, but also to pray and play with it. Lutheran theologies, if they are to be authentic and transforming, need to encounter other disciplines—the humanities, social sciences, natural and applied sciences, business—and other faith traditions as well, especially non-Christian traditions. Alternative perspectives from inside and outside of the Christian tradition are required to tell a wholesome and more inclusive theology.[42] "The search for more valid appropriations is . . . an attempt to recognize the complexity of the distinctive ways [Luther's theology] is understood."[43] Luther's theology, in this case, the Two-Kingdoms doctrine, when viewed through variegated lenses, is neither a curio nor a relic; it is not a mere doctrine; it is a practice that identifies us human beings—*Spiritualia carnalia.* It is something by which we live, and which aids us in combating the idols of the twenty-first century.

NOTES

1. Arundhati Roy, *The End of Imagination* (Chicago, IL: Haymarket Books, 2016), 104.

2. I pose this question as a response to the chapter by Ben Taylor, "Retrieving Luther's Critique of Idolatry for Our Fragmented World: Whiteness, Greed and the Environment" in this volume.

3. Debanjali Bose, "11 ways pandemics have changed the course of human history," *Business Insider*, March 18, 2020. https://www.businessinsider.nl/ways-pandemics-have-changed-the-world-from-feudalism-to-remote-work/.

4. Francesca Thornberry, "Using Human Rights to Leave No One Behind: COVID-19 Responses and Beyond," SDG Knowledge Hub, May 26, 2020, https://sdg.iisd.org/commentary/guest-articles/using-human-rights-to-leave-no-one-behind-covid-19-responses-and-beyond/.

5. Wangari Maathai, *Unbowed: A Memoir* (Toronto, ON: Random House, 2006), 114.

6. James Baldwin, "As Much Truth As One Can Bear," *The New York Times,* January 14, 1962, Section T, Page 11.

7. Taylor, "Retrieving Luther's Critique," 73–75.

8. Marit Trelstad, "A Non-Universal Lutheran Theology," 91–92.

9. Taylor, "Retrieving Luther's Critique," 76.

10. Ibid., 75.

11. Ibid., 80.

12. Trelstad, Non-Universal Lutheran Theology, 91–92.

13. Ibid., 92.

14. Ibid.

15. Richard Rohr, "God's Dream for Creation," Center for Action and Contemplation, Wednesday, August 26, 2020, https://cac.org/gods-dream-for-creation-2020-08-26/

16. Vítor Westhelle, "Transfiguring Lutheranism: Being Lutheran in New Contexts" in *Identity, Survival, Witness: Reconfiguring Theological Agendas*, ed. Karen L Bloomquist (Geneva: LWF/DTS, 2008), 11–23.

17. Martin Luther, "How Christians Should Regard Moses (1525)," in *Luther's Works, Volume 35, Word and Sacrament I*, ed. and trans. E. Theodore Bachmann (Philadelphia: Fortress Press, 1960), 161–74.

18. For an explication of this see Vítor Westhelle, *Transfiguring Luther: The Planetary Promise of Lutheran Theology* (Eugene, Oregon: Cascade Books, 2016).

19. Martin Luther "Whether Soldiers, Too, Can Be Saved," in *Luther's Works: Volume 46, The Christian in Society, III,* ed. Robert C. Schultz, trans. Charles M. Jacobs, rev. Robert C. Schultz (Philadelphia: Fortress Press, 1967), 99f. It needs to be acknowledged that the language is problematic due to its noninclusive nature but such was the context of the 16th century.

20. Allen Jorgenson, *Awe and Expectation* (Eugene, OR: Wipf and Stock, 2010), 72.

21. This is a metaphor. While metaphors facilitate comprehension, it does that only to a limit.

22. Juan Luis Segundo, "Is Chalcedon Out of Date?," first of the two lectures at Toronto School of Theology given on Monday, February 7, 1983.

23. Ibid.

24. Ibid.

25. Ibid.

26. Brad Lemley, "The Art of Sexual Magic," *New Age Journal*, March/April 1996, 74–79.

27. Philip Rawson, *The Art of Tantra* (New York: Thames and Hudson, 1978).

28. Ronald K. Bullis, "Biblical Tantra: Lessons in Sacred Sexuality," *Theology and Sexuality* 9 (September 1998): 103.

29. St. Athanasius, "On the Incarnation," New Advent, Chapter 54, accessed May 25, 2021, https://www.newadvent.org/fathers/2802.htm; see also "Why Did the Word Become Flesh?" Catechism of the Catholic Church, Paragraph 460, accessed February 18, 2021, https://www.vatican.va/archive/ENG0015/__P1J.HTM.

30. Bullis, *Biblical Tantra,* 109.

31. Christine Gudorf, *Body, Sex and Pleasure* (Cleveland, OH: Pilgrim Press, 1994), 217.

32. Luther identified us as *simul justus et peccator*.

33. Taylor, "Retrieving Luther's Critique," 83.

34. Trelstad, "A Non-Universal Lutheran Theology," 93.

35. Michael G. L. Church, "The Law of Begging: Prosper at the End of the Day," in *Worship* 73, no. 5 (September 1999): 442–53.

36. Chimamanda Ngozi Adichie, The Danger of a Single Story, TEDGlobal 2009, July 2009, https://www.ted.com/talks/ chimamanda_ngozi_adichie_the_danger_of_a_single_story?language=en.

37. Things—even people—have a way of leaking into each other. Salman Rushdie, *Midnight's Children* (New York: Random House, 2006), 37.

38. Chinua Achebe, "Today, the Balance of Stories," *Home and Exile* (New York: Oxford University Press, 2000), 92–93. Also cited by Adichie, "Danger of a Single Story."

39. In a recent conversation my colleague, Allen Jorgenson, a co-editor of this volume, contested this claim saying he was not sure if the Christian story is one story.

I maintain my stance. For me the Christian story is a story of love, love lived to its last consequence. However, it is told and read and experienced in various ways (and hence plural).

40. "A Christian is a perfectly free lord of all, subject to none; A Christian is a perfectly dutiful servant of all, subject to everyone." Martin Luther, "Treatise on Christian Liberty," in *Selected Writings of Martin Luther 1520–1523*, ed. Theodore G. Tappert (Minneapolis: Fortress Press, 2007), 19.

41. Referencing back to the epigraph by Arundhati Roy: "Either way change will come. It could be bloody, or, it could be beautiful. It depends on us." *The End of Imagination*, 104.

42. Michelle Voss Roberts, *Body Parts: A Theological Anthropology* (Minneapolis, MN: Fortress Press, 2017), xxxiii.

43. Nancy Pineda-Madrid, *Suffering and Salvation in Ciudad Juárez* (Minneapolis, MN: Fortress Press, 2011), 21.

BIBLIOGRAPHY

Achebe, Chinva. "Today, the Balance of Stories." In *Home and* Exile, 69–100. New York: Oxford University Press, 2000.

Adichie, Chimamanda Ngozi. "The Danger of a Single Story." TEDGlobal 2009. July 2009. https://www.ted.com/talks/ chimamanda_ngozi_adichie_the_danger_of_a_single_story?language=en.

Athanasius, Saint. "On the Incarnation." New Advent Chapter 54. Accessed May 25, 2021. https://www.newadvent.org/fathers/2802.htm.

Baldwin, James. "As Much Truth As One Can Bear." *The New York Times,* January 14, 1962, Section T, Page 11.

Bose, Debanjali. "11 ways pandemics have changed the course of human history." *Business Insider*, March 18, 2020. https://www.businessinsider.nl/ ways-pandemics-have-changed-the-world-from-feudalism-to-remote-work/.

Bullis, Ronald K. "Biblical Tantra: Lessons in Sacred Sexuality." *Theology and Sexuality* 9 (September 1998): 101–16.

Catechism of the Catholic Church. "Why Did the Word Become Flesh?" Paragraph 460. Accessed February 18, 2021. https://www.vatican.va/archive/ENG0015/__ P1J.HTM.

Church, Michael G. L. "The Law of Begging: Prosper at the End of the Day." *Worship* 73, no. 5 (September 1999) 442–53.

Gudorf, Christine. *Body, Sex and Pleasure*. Cleveland, OH: Pilgrim Press, 1994.

Jorgenson Allen. *Awe and Expectation*. Eugene, OR: Wipf and Stock, 2010.

Lemley, Brad. "The Art of Sexual Magic." *New Age Journal*, March/April, 1996.

Luther, Martin. "How Christians Should Regard Moses (1525)." In *Luther's Works, Volume 35, Word and Sacrament I*, edited and translated by E. Theodore Bachmann, 161–74. Philadelphia: Fortress Press, 1960.

———. "Treatise on Christian Liberty." In *Selected Writings of Martin Luther 1520– 1523*, edited by Theodore G. Tappert. Minneapolis: Fortress Press, 2007.

————. "Whether Soldiers, Too, Can Be Saved." In *Luther's Works: Volume 46, The Christian in Society, III,* edited by Robert C. Schultz, translated by Charles M. Jacobs, revised by Robert C. Schultz, 87–137. Philadelphia: Fortress Press, 1967.

Maathai, Wangari. *Unbowed: A Memoir.* Toronto, ON: Random House, 2006.

Pineda-Madrid, Nancy. Suffering and Salvation in Ciudad Juárez. Minneapolis, MN: Fortress Press, 2011.

Rawson, Philip. *The Art of Tantra.* New York: Thames and Hudson, 1978.

Roberts, Michelle Voss. *Body Parts: A Theological Anthropology.* Minneapolis, MN: Fortress Press, 2017.

Rohr, Richard. "God's Dream for Creation," Center for Action and Contemplation, Wednesday, August 26, 2020.

Roy, Arundhati. *The End of Imagination.* Chicago, IL: Haymarket Books. 2016.

Rushdie, Salman. *Midnight's Children.* New York: Random House. 2006.

Segundo, Juan Luis. "Is Chalcedon Out of Date?" First of the two lectures at Toronto School of Theology given on Monday, February 7, 1983.

Thornberry, Francesca. "Using Human Rights to Leave No One Behind: COVID-19 Responses and Beyond," SDG Knowledge Hub. May 26, 2020. https://sdg.iisd.org/commentary/guest-articles/using-human-rights-to-leave-no-one-behind-covid-19-responses-and-beyond/

Westhelle, Vítor. *Transfiguring Luther: The Planetary Promise of Lutheran Theology.* Eugene, Oregon: Cascade Books. 2016.

————. "Transfiguring Lutheranism: Being Lutheran in New Contexts." In *Identity, Survival, Witness: Reconfiguring Theological Agendas,* edited by Karen L Bloomquist, 11–23. Geneva: LWF/DTS, 2008.

Chapter 7

Retrieving Luther's Theology of Freedom for a Contemporary Ethic of Heteronomy

Robert Overy-Brown

Martin Luther is a thinker of distinction. A monumental figure of the Christian Reformation and the history of theology, his importance to Western philosophy, ecclesiology, and social ethics has been and continues to be relevant. But important to understanding him as a critical figure is to reread that description: Luther thinks distinction. Throughout his writings there is the intention to refine—a methodical practice of "not this, but that." This is no new way of approaching religious or philosophical discourse; instead, the point is that there is no easy Luther. This is seen frequently in misunderstandings of law and gospel, the theory of the two kingdoms, or in his opposition to freedom, when opponents and contemporary thinkers alike paint his work with a dismissive brushstroke. Rather, Luther is a vast thinker because of the distinctions. His breadth allows for continual reevaluations and stands as a crucial element to anyone considering the Christian tradition.

This chapter aims to examine the particular distinctions Luther makes concerning freedom, discussed specifically in theses 13–15 of *The Heidelberg Disputation* (1518) and further nuanced in later work. Especially important in this regard is his famous quotation: "A Christian is the most free lord of all, and subject to none; a Christian is the most dutiful servant of all, and subject to everyone."[1] While this oft-quoted pronouncement can be read in many ways—dialectically, paradoxically, and so on—this analysis will show that by looking specifically to Luther's distinctions, a particular account of freedom can be addressed. This necessitates examining Luther's account of freedom in general vis-à-vis this quotation in *The Freedom of a Christian*.

By looking to his own larger corpus on the theme and putting it into context within the tradition and later interpreters, the importance of Luther's view emerges. Luther's position appears to support not an autonomous notion of freedom but rather a heteronomous one. If it is the case that Luther in fact is in favor of this assessment, then this could be a significant part of a theological understanding of human activity and public participation that is counter to some prevailing strains of politics and economics. Such an understanding of Luther's interpretation of the Christian tradition would augment understandings of him as not merely a bridge to modernism but an important resource to recall in contemporary theory for the sake of public discourse on freedom.

LIMITING FREEDOM TOWARD THEOLOGICAL ANTHROPOLOGY IN LUTHER

To discuss freedom in Luther's writings must automatically introduce the notion of distinction. Two of his more famous writings at the surface sound on one hand affirmative toward the concept (*The Freedom of a Christian*) and on the other negative (*The Bondage of the Will*). Indeed, there are multiple angles from which to approach the topic within his thought and so it must be sorted out what Luther says about freedom and then what aspect of freedom it is that interests this exploration.

To begin, it must be clear what is meant by the term freedom. There is significant difference, for example, between free choice and free activity, the former located first and foremost in the mind and the latter in the corporeal substance, a body (which is why divine activity is typically figured through objects). Or in political discourse, there is a common split over *laissez faire* freedom from impositions and a freedom that emerges out of a governed, created context—the freedom to own a gun versus the freedom to live in a safe society without gun violence. In the *Critique of Pure Reason*, Immanuel Kant distinguishes between a transcendental and practical freedom, favoring the second as a basis for ethics over the first, which for him remains a speculative metaphysical ontology.[2] Though anachronistic readings must be avoided, these types of arguments that have been at the heart of philosophy through millennia must be the hermeneutic through which Luther is interpreted in order to strike at a translatable account of his position.

In reading Luther, it is not so clear that diversity of willing or choice and freedom are compatible at all. Luther himself implies in *The Bondage of the Will* that either there is freedom or not; a mediated or so-called compatibilist position is a limitation such that actual freedom of humanity is not possible.[3] Herein is the first distinction, between divine and human freedom. Philosophy of religion has schematized this through the problem of theodicy. If God is good, omnipotent, and absolutely free to act, how is the existence of evil to be explained? Or how would these qualities of the transcendent divine be true if humans were granted their own freedom? There have been many options for answering these questions. Luther's position is that God is free and humans are not.[4] In Luther's mind, any restraint on God limits divine sovereignty, which contradicts God's revelation known through scripture. Fundamentally, this alters the divine insofar as that thing no longer is actually something to be called "God." Humans, at the same time, are not divine and therefore not sovereign but in fact are slaves to the forces of good and evil—God and Satan.[5] Individuals then have no actual freedom to will on their own as they are compelled by these outside forces. Here, Luther is engaging in an argument of freedom and determinism: whether there are ultimately limitations to humans' ability to act, choose, or will.

That Luther supports divine freedom and not human freedom thus far remains a generalized statement. If juxtaposed with his famed quotation that is the pursuit of this analysis—the Christian as both lord and servant of all, subject to none and everyone—further parsing of the position is needed. The analytical point does not deal with the nature of divine freedom *per se* but rather that of the person, specifically the Christian. That is not to dispense with God. It will be shown that the activity of God is foundational to the point Luther is trying to make. Rather, the focus is less on theological problems of transcendence and theodicy as it is with theological anthropology. In this sense, the argument will be made in line with Kant's critical metaphysics. Whether or not a final determination on the ontological status of an individual to choose or act freely or is compelled by some force appears untenable by powers of reason. Luther argues this point as well, returning to Holy Scriptures and the witness of the Word of God through the Holy Spirit.[6] There are two distinctions he makes that support this move. The first is his insistence that "ought" does not imply "ability."[7] There is a fragmentation between the discourse of possibility and actualized decisions, or in the Kantian argument one's ability is speculative whereas the "ought," or the way one acts, is a basis for constructing ethics and responsibility.

Meanwhile, the division that exists between reason and theology[8] is replicated in a further distinction, which is that there is a fundamental difference between Luther's philosophical and pastoral texts. A glance at historical context would point to the obvious nature in the different audiences, academic and ecclesiological in the first but lay and public in the second. It is of course plausible to deny this distinction and claim that his writings have overarching coherence and repetitious themes; that the theology is consistent though stated in different terms and variant arguments, as though Luther intends always the same but crafts to a multiplicity of hearers. While that may be true, it may also not be helpful to understand what is at stake in the statement on Christian freedom. If it is the case that Luther is completely opposed to human freedom, his statement on a Christian as free either makes no sense or has a warped definition of terms. Instead, the proposal of a distinction between the scholarly and the pastoral writings allows a chance to see how the previous informs the latter and principally how the intention of Luther within these two forms varies greatly, and creates an alternate account of freedom that is located in theological anthropology.

For other theologians, it may be possible to separate anthropology and the discourse of freedom as discrete topics; for Luther it is not, as the descriptive nature of anthropology creates the framework to consider the possibility of human activity. This becomes evident when looking at the entirety of the text in which the focal quotation comes from *The Freedom of a Christian*, which is arguably a strictly pastoral writing. The first indication of this is the author's own words in the *Open Letter to Pope Leo X*, which was attached. There Luther describes the premise as "contain[ing] the whole of Christian life in a brief form, provided you grasp its meaning."[9] The most basic reading of this intention is that it is intended to be a short and simple statement, accessible certainly to the Pope but moreover to all who read it, as open letters are intended for mass consumption. Secondly, the language of *The Freedom of a Christian* is vernacular in a way: though written in Latin as it would have been naturally for the church hierarchy,[10] the method is not as rigorously structured as are his disputations, there are not as many direct quotations of ancient and traditional sources or even indirect appeals to schools of thought that are fleshed out in the text as compared to his other works. By making this claim, the emphatic point and logic of the text is not lost; to call the writing pastoral is not to diminish or demean it. The claim, however, reveals that here Luther moves the discourse of freedom from the metaphysical realm to the everyday experience, shifting from God to anthropology in order to explain how life ought to be lived. The relocation continues from his other works around human nature and ability to will, described in a formal structure of the inner and outer human.[11]

It has been stated above that Luther's position on human nature is that it is at the mercy of the powers of good or evil. More accurately, the natural position in which humans find themselves is a state of sin—the consequence of original sin—and as such are governed by the power of sin.[12] This is simply faithful to much of Christian theological tradition, dating back to Pauline writings (e.g., Romans 7). The individual actor does not choose to do good or evil; he or she simply exists in a state of sin and all actions are viewed through this, no matter any purposeful intention. Hence, a person does not have freedom in the strict sense that one could will good or bad. A person either wills sin, or is transformed by divinely-bestowed grace and can will good. Luther frequently frames this as the human who is dominated by either of two powers, God or Satan. The issue could also be seen as an operation of biological determinism—that individuals are predisposed to act out of necessity for interests of preservation, where what in traditional terms is called sin would correlate with self-interest. In that case, grace parallels a force that awakens an actor to move beyond purely selfish intention. The difference is significant, one naming a personal source of evil while the other does not. Luther's actual view is a theology from above, through the vocabulary of transcendence, metaphysics, and otherworldly forces; the latter biological view can be identified as what is contemporarily called a theology from below—theory that develops out of the human experience. In a move that does not disconnect God's freedom from humanity's but is more interested in the latter, thinking about anthropology from below alters the intention of what is at stake. Some may reject it as dismissing traditional Christianity or improper demythologizing. However, by reframing these concepts the analysis is not simply modernizing but throws Luther's framework into dialogue with other, more secular thinkers.

THE INNER AND OUTER HUMAN

To be able to properly compare, though, the way that the human in sin is transformed by grace in the inner and outer human in his language must be understood. The inner-outer distinction is not designed to substitute for the apparent contradiction of the free lord, subject to none versus the dutiful servant, subject to all, but the schema is how Luther elaborates the phrase in order to avoid logical conflict.[13] That is, the inner human does not simply correspond with the free lord and vice versa. Rather, the human "has a twofold nature, a spiritual and a bodily one."[14] The inner is the spiritual—the soul— and the outer the body. Again, Luther is not varying from Christian tradition in this duality yet this is not a static relationship either. It is not division full stop: Luther has in mind this process of transformation that exists in what has been said about theological anthropology. For him, it is the inner that affects the outer. Whatever the Christian is or does is viewed through this relationship; thus, whatever is to be said about human agency at all, which is to say the free/servant distinction, is located here.

The Inner Human

Then what does Luther mean by the inner human, and moreover, what is the nature and activity of this inner-ness? The answers have to do with three aspects of faith: where faith occurs, the powers of faith, and finally its effects. The first is the most simple of Luther's points, for it depends on a basic reading of the soul-body paradigm. Faith occurs in the soul and its freedom (or lack thereof) is unaffected by external circumstances.[15] Wealth, status, or possessions do not determine faith; nor is the soul affected by anything of the body. That is, believers (or nonbelievers) suffer and prosper alike and the actions of a person do not produce belief. Therefore, faith is wholly disconnected from and independent of any works good or bad. Belief is wholly internalized and any of the Christian language of transformation (justification, salvation) cannot be produced by the outer, bodily sense.[16] Instead, "[f]aith alone is the saving and efficacious use of the Word of God . . . ," which is to say that the change is produced by divine revelation, which is known through scripture in commandments and promises.[17] In this way, it is no tangible object and is not achievable. Faith is a gift to the soul. Not a disembodied soul, but to the inner sense of the human who is transformed from sinner to filled with grace.

After locating faith in the inner person, Luther goes on to describe three powers of faith. The first is a result of faith as an inner process: faith, which for him is the definition of Christian liberty, makes any outer activity "unnecessary for any man's righteousness and salvation."[18] Freedom for the Christian is being unbound from law and works. Again, Luther is restating Paul here and on this point parallels the "new Paul" studies that look to this uncoupling as a foundational practice for radical politics.[19] For contemporary theorists, the point is elevating the exception to the state in political liberalism; in Luther it serves to demonstrate that the inner moves toward the outer and not in reverse. The second power, Luther claims, is the production of trust in God, in whom faith has found God to be trustworthy.[20] Faith begets trust, which is ultimately to say that faith draws the inner nature of the individual into a deeper faith. This appears to be a circularity, yet is not surprising given what has been shown about Luther's view on human freedom already. If the person does not will outside of his or her given orientation to good or evil, then that individual cannot break that dependent status by his or her own power. Faith, once it breaks in and transforms the inner human, compels the will to move toward God because it comes from God and not any other source. Third, Luther describes another aspect of the power of faith as uniting the inner "soul" with Christ.[21] Using the biblical imagery of marriage (the bride is to bridegroom as is the church to Christ) the inner soul is saved and made right by Christ's sacrifice. The language of right, righteous, and righteousness is important here. Luther's position is that humans are predetermined to sin and are not righteous before God. Meanwhile, outward activity cannot produce or affect faith, and so there are no works to be done to be made right. Therefore, in traditional atonement theory, Christ who as incarnate God is righteous makes right the sin of humanity. Righteousness is obtained through the soul's unity with Christ and therefore is predicated on the inner person.

The righteousness that is given to the inner person through faith produces the same free lord of all that Luther refers to in his famous statement. This is the affective nature that faith produces in relation to the inner-ness. Here, it is significant that this righteousness is not of the individual's doing, but Christ's. Luther puts it this way in order to counter a theology that requires good works and at the same time create interesting perspective on the subjectivity of the person of faith. Or more to the point, the person with faith. That which gives the subject freedom (faith) is the same which does away with the necessity of externalized good works: God. Consequently, the inner human is never engaged as the I-who-acts or the I-who-chooses, but always in light of the Word made flesh: Christ. This point is crucial to be held on to as the analysis turns to later readers of Luther. In the interim, it is still quite evident here that even what Luther is calling "freedom" for a Christian is nothing of the sort, at least in contemporary terms. If freedom is only meant to be God's action to rupture the domination of sin, then yes, this is an account of freedom in the inner human. But if freedom has any meaning anthropologically other than what the divine has done on behalf of humanity, it must be located elsewhere. Luther also recognizes this problem, further compounded by biblical commands to do good works and acknowledgment that Christians live in a social setting. Therefore, he turns to the outer human.[22]

The Outer Human

As mentioned above, the outer refers to the embodied person and specifically for Luther what these bodies are doing. Where the inner focused on faith in three ways, the outer is concerned with works in three other functions: relation to the inner self, the positive value of good works, and love of neighbor. First, on the relation to the inner sense of self, Luther writes on the necessary discipline of the body.[23] This point draws from Pauline theology on the weakness of the flesh against sin. In order to make the point that if the inner soul is transformed in justification or salvation, it follows that the body of the same whole person goes through the process too. A person must not be lazy and ought to be careful to not fall back into lusts. Luther proposes that these instincts can be overcome through "fastings, watchings, labors, and other reasonable discipline . . . subject[ed] to the Spirit."[24] The body, then, is not synchronized with the soul and more importantly tends to revert more easily. The outer person needs to be disciplined through spiritual rituals, namely communion, confession, and hearing of the Word.[25] These, though, are all outward actions with an inward focus. Though there appears a split in the inner-outer relationship, they are not as far apart as one might think. The inner compels the outer to change, the outer acts in such a way that pulls the inner forward, as if the two areas of the self are in dialectical process together.

But beyond the rituals that take place within the life of the church, Luther also wants to retrieve a specific positive role for good works in the world at large.[26] This builds on previous points in both structures: that no work can produce faith in the inner self, whereas transformative faith pushes the believer to act and will for the good outside of him or herself. It is counter to the arguments that one could do good works and obtain salvation or faith, or that one need only be saved and no worldly activity beyond the inward soul is needed. On one hand, it is logical that a Christian perform good works. Having been transformed from sin, the actor instead is now aligned with the will of God, which chooses constantly for the good. On the other hand, the outer good must follow from the inner insofar as otherwise it would become a self-centered activity. If not, it would either render grace unnecessary or ignore the surrounding conditions. The Christian, or truly any person, is always a situated being. All aspects of Christianity preach this same message that the world is in want of good works, no matter whether oriented toward inner or outer eternal salvation of the soul or focused on social justice in the here and now. The difference between perspectives, then, concerns the end of works, yet both perspectives recognize the abundance of need.

To clarify what sort of good works he has in mind, Luther points to the figure of the neighbor as an archetypal case. He claims that life is for all others, or even further that one lives for others instead of for the self.[27] The argument certainly follows in the sense that activities, no matter how good or evil, are not to be done out of self-interest. If not for self, then for whom? One could answer God, but does God need to be acted on behalf of? Certainly not in Luther's theology, where God acts first so that the Christian may then follow. The neighbor, then, is a perfect object of activity for the Christian life because the faithful believer is called to act for the other without any regard or hesitation. At this moment, Luther breaks and rejects all distinctions—neither family nor friend nor enemy matter. This other-interested activity is then seen as work only if it is a burden, if it counters the nature of the inner self. Because the soul is first transformed by faith that comes from the grace of God, this carries over into activity in the outer realm. Luther, recognizing this shift within the person, similarly shifts the language of the text, referring to it later as love.[28] In this way, the radical change of the Christian is a breaking in of faith which produces love, not simply a state of sedentary being but praxis. This task, as this writing sees it, is to determine what constitutes an orthopraxis.

This relationship of faith moving to love remains problematic in terms of human activity on the surface. Subjectivity remains only mere appearance as God transforms the inner soul and the outer body works in love for others. Luther himself writes, " . . . a Christian lives not in himself, but in Christ and in his neighbor. Otherwise, he is not a Christian. He lives in Christ through faith, in his neighbor through love. By faith, he is caught up beyond himself into God. By love, he descends beneath himself into his neighbor."[29] This is all an active motion, not of the human by him or herself, but in actuality this is a motion of the divine—God to the individual to others. This is natural given that Luther's position that freedom belongs only in the divine realm and not to people. In a similar fashion to previous analysis, this position that Luther develops can be read differently if it is removed from transcendental categorization. Luther models in the inner-outer distinction how one ought to live if freedom is the case, particularly if aligned with the quotation that began the discussion. So, what position can be formulated if the inner is associated with, "A Christian is a perfectly free lord of all, subject to none," and similarly if the outer in conjunction with, "A Christian is a perfectly dutiful servant of all, subject to all?"

Freedom, Luther is clear, is the term associated with the transformed state of the soul from evil to good; the person is propelled by this freedom to love others through good actions and intentions beyond selfish, sinful purposes. Then the Christian is a perfectly free lord as far as the Christian is no longer enslaved by the snares of the Devil and sin, in Luther's parlance. But then what does it mean to be the free lord of all? Who is this all? If this freedom is the inner soul, Luther surely cannot intend for this to mean any sort of political power over others. Yet being subject to none clearly has a connotation in his context that the individual is not bound to any extra human requirements for justification. It is a spiritual matter with some interpersonal applications; Denis Janz proposes that this freedom in action is more appropriately labeled "vocation."[30] But in more stringent terms, it is an internal change of state that moves outward, yet resists domination by the other. In the second half of the statement, the assertion of the Christian as a perfectly dutiful servant implies that the Christian as such holds responsibility to and for others.[31] This reflects that there is actually some sort of possession by the other of this particular human, in being "subject to all." Nevertheless, being subject in love to a neighbor is far different than being a political subject, for example. This stands close to the aforementioned position of transcending sheer biological needs and desires to act for others even when it does not benefit the self. To divide the inner and outer as passive and active, even if it is faithful to Luther's commentaries on Romans and Galatians, diminishes each sense respectively and perhaps inverts Luther's thought here.[32] There is something to be gleaned on the nature of how a person relates to another. In other words, Luther's quotation offers multiple interpretations of intersubjectivity and the structure of action—autonomy or heteronomy—without becoming clear at present, chiefly because these are not categories that Luther himself employs. To probe further in this manner, two issues must be addressed: understanding

Luther within contextual frameworks that followed his work and direct interpretations of this text.

READERS OF LUTHER

It has not been unusual in the genealogy of philosophy and theology to trace
modernism's roots at least in part back to Luther. For instance, as Kierkegaard
had this structure of the outer person in mind in his *Works of Love*, it would be
easy to reduce the rest of his philosophy to a generalized proto-existentialism
and connect Luther to Kierkegaard's aphorism: "Truth is subjectivity."[33] This
would be a shallow reading of each, particularly as Luther's overall scheme
of freedom is far different than Kierkegaard's.[34] However, this is perhaps
a key example that demonstrates the problems that one faces reading the
quotation on Christian freedom against the backdrop of later interpreters.
How should the inner-outer distinction be read, and how does the problem of
freedom become resolved? Particularly, in what ways is Luther accused along
these lines of being a "modernist," and is that correct or not?

   On the question of modernism, the entire corpus of authors and scholars
who look back to Luther is too large to replicate here, yet a few major sources
demonstrate his significance. Marx, in a critique of Hegel, noted that while
German Idealism owed a debt to Luther in locating the primacy of freedom
in an inner transformation, but he nevertheless rejected Luther's work as too
transfixed on the duties of the outward bodies. Marx found this most notably
in Luther's actual politics that sought to stifle the outbreak of the Peasants'
War.[35] Mark C. Taylor identifies Luther as an inspiration for the modern notion
of the divided subject, especially in his reading of William James' phrase of
the individual in Luther as "homo duplex," or the justified sinner.[36] Taylor
recognizes that this subject is inseparable from what has been described as
the freedom rightly belonging to God and so is actually "inwardly heterony-
mous," but the distinction that Luther introduces leads directly to "the self-
legislating autonomous subject without which the political revolutions of the
modern era would have been impossible."[37] Reiner Schümann's analysis is
that Luther's turn to the Spirit over reason creates this modern singular subject, moreover pushing the critique further in claiming the subject's desire to
"be left alone."[38] While certainly the autonomous individual actor is a marker
for the modern period, from the analysis of Luther's *Freedom of a Christian*
it is clear that this is a step beyond what the reformer has in mind.[39] To clarify,
it must be described more closely what the inner-outer distinction looks like
from different modernist perspectives.

   One of the more well-known disputes of *Freedom of a Christian* was
instigated by thinkers like Max Scheler and Herbert Marcuse, who Eberhard

Jüngel takes to task in his own book on Luther's significance, titled *The Freedom of a Christian*.[40] Both of the former lean hard on Luther's distinction as too divisive a split between the inner and outer, particularly in the location of any sense of freedom in inward spirituality while the activity of the body is bound by duty to others. That is, this statement on Christian freedom of the soul while being captive to serve outwardly promotes the privatization of religion and impedes social organization in its outer unfreedom: the inner human resists democratic tendencies. Though Jüngel states that Scheler's critique has especially found little resonance in theological circles, this is actually similar to liberation theology's complaint against growing charismatic movements that focus too greatly on the individual's internalized relationship with the Spirit without much regard to praxis on the sociopolitical plane. Indeed, the claim points toward the rise and critique of the spiritual-but-not-religious. As the former and latter here can be interpreted as essentially inner and outer categories of relationality, this spirituality without religion is most possible in the contemporary age of narcissism, which may very well be Slavoj Žižek's most valid point on the alignment of Christianity and radical politics.[41] In total, though, this is a primary flaw of reading Luther as a contributor to modernity. The privatization of belief divorces the religiously constituted individual from public, collective practice in the secularized and secularizing state.

If the inner and outer human are truly discrete, then the modern dualism truly does begin here. Jüngel, however, disputes this notion as an accurate depiction of Luther's theology. First, he notes the dependence on Augustine.[42] Significantly, Luther as an Augustinian monk would have been versed in the ancient church father's theology and the dispute with the Manichees over this same type of dualism. Augustine's position was that unlike Mani and his followers, the soul was not in fact supremely good and the body purely evil, and therefore it was impossible to split the two because the whole person was created by God.[43] Therefore, Jüngel claims, Luther's position must be read differently as the person between (e.g., God-World, New-Old). This occurs in the exchange from the sinful state to the entry of Christ in justification, which Luther describes as the marriage of the soul to Christ creating righteousness, as was shown above.[44] Importantly, this exchange (of old for new, connecting the divine with the world) demonstrates Christ's offices of king and priest. Jüngel moves beyond Luther in his interpretation that this exchange is not only a matter of the soul and salvation, and the inability of others to impede one's relationship with the divine. Christ is now explicitly political and undoes the hierarchical distinctions that critics assume of the inner-outer divide.[45] Though Luther in his actual politics for practical reasons embraced some of the power structures of his time,[46] the transformative figure of Christ in the inner self is far more radical and always political in comparison to a reductive picture of a contemplative soul immune to the world at large.

If interpreters of Luther have discussed his thoughts on Christian liberty in such a way that it reflects the detrimental aspects of modernity, then how should the problem of freedom and human activity be approached? Does freedom exist as a possibility that is actualized in the relationship between another person with the same capability, nearing a Hegelian reading of inter-subjectivity?[47] Or does this action rest on the obligation to choose for the other who confronts the subject, a freedom that requires something of the individual, as in Levinas?[48] Perhaps it is the case of both for Luther. Freedom of the Christian indicates that this divine activity that imparts faith is some-thing that all Christians participate in and so there must be some element of symmetry between persons—particularly in Luther's reading that Christ's actions were for all humanity, and therefore it is not the theologian's place to qualify or quantify a soul.[49] Furthermore, within Hegel's unfolding of the Absolute Spirit in the world there is a parallel structure to Luther's insistence that absolute freedom of humanity would necessarily contradict divine activ-ity.[50] At the same time, Christians are always confronted with the need for good action, to impart love to their neighbors. This advent is an imperative within the other that addresses the self's own will and desire. Luther's posi-tion that one acts for others, but his ambivalence about theology translating to politics is another way in which this freedom resembles that of Levinas.[51] So, although many similarities exist through modern thought for negative or positive evaluation, it still remains undecided to what extent there is any meaningful human freedom and its implications within this theology.

RETRIEVING A PRACTICAL ETHIC

One of the underlying questions of the analysis thus far is just how useful Luther's philosophical and theological positions on freedom are in the con-temporary age. Though interesting points have arisen, to this moment a sin-gular determination has been deferred on account of difficulty in contextual translation no matter whether Luther's original intentions or through modern filters. To that end then, an alternative approach may be helpful. One option may be to follow the pattern of Jürgen Moltmann's *The Crucified God*, where he reclaims the Lutheran tradition of the theology of the cross to apply to his era's political needs.[52] Moltmann, for example, is dedicated to being faithful to the Christian tradition and highlights a particular branch of theology to serve his constructive political proposal. This is of course how current politi-cal theology operates, drawing from theology proper to move toward stances for the public at large. In other words, it is what may be called secularizing insofar as it reads the sociopolitical order—regardless of its religiosity—against various theological backdrops. It is possible to make a similar move with Luther's take on the freedom embedded within the Christian.

If the entire discourse of freedom is taken to be fraught with numerous problems, Kant's critical stance on the topic is appreciated. As mentioned earlier, he made his own distinction between transcendental and practical freedom. This is appealing because of its ethical impact, which was Kant's intention. To argue over whether God is the only absolutely free being or to what extent humans have free will may be a compelling discussion to some but without a definitive conclusion its significance eludes human grasping. There are certainly effects of taking a position one way or the other on metaphysical freedom, without a doubt. Luther recognizes that questioning God would make one rethink atonement theory.[53] However, to a great extent these arguments do not reach the vast majority of individuals in general. If not, then what benefit is there in debating human activity if human actors rarely consider even the possibility of these externalized choices? That is not to dismiss the argument on philosophical grounds as it is to justify a focus on a practical one. The common question that faces the self is not "Can I act?" but "How should I act?" This is why Kant turns to the second type of freedom to construct his ethics; Luther's statement on the Christian as both free lord and dutiful servant as one and the same is here read along the same track.

Besides the inward turn to the self, the modern period is similarly characterized by the prevailing view of the human subject as autonomous. This is due in part to the distancing of paradigms from the older theologies of God as the only free being and therefore absolute rule of predestination. It is also a result of the ascendency of Kantian ethics; the human becomes the one who chooses from ability and then acts according to desired will. There is, as a further modern movement, a tendency to view human activity through autonomy following the monumental shift in understanding anthropology. Luther's first clause on the Christian as free lord, subject to none reads in this fashion. On its own, this statement confirms the freedom of the individual, albeit internally. The second clause, however, cannot be described in support of autonomy by any stretch of the means. The Christian as dutiful servant, subject to all? At worst, here Luther describes slavery; more likely, this complicated phrasing finds itself in today's vocabulary as heteronomy.[54] Heteronomy, in its definition as different or alien rule—being ruled from outside—is slandered as opposed to freedom. Yet the concept does not limit the ability to act as much as it does the range of choice to act because these outside forces impose upon the individual. Is this not Luther's dialectical position? The Christian is free to act but acts always for the good of others because it is always faith in Christ that transforms the self in order to externalize love. That is, freedom in this sense chooses to act not for self-interest; rather, it is the person between God and neighbor that acts accordingly.

If Luther is truly thinking of what could be called heteronomy as a normative interpersonal ethic in describing Christian freedom, this pivots the perspective of understanding his significance. First, as modernity tends in the direction of autonomy, if Luther is suggesting an alternative, he is not merely a cog in the wheel toward the glorification of the human subject. Secondly, it aligns him with what is called postmodernity. When the postmodern project is actually defined as a move beyond the modern, it is composed of thinkers responding to the autonomous individual after some of the worst violence and brutality humanity has foisted upon itself in the twentieth century. As such, much postmodern thought illuminates skepticism regarding humanistic trends, rejecting absolute ethics in terms of relationalism.[55] Relationality here is intriguing as it is fundamentally the language of acting with and for the neighbor seen in Luther's externalized freedom. Postmodern theologian John Caputo is explicit about heteronomy as a retrieved notion existing within the Christian tradition as an imperative for the ethical action of hospitality.[56] Furthermore, where contemporary theology has turned to comparative studies, this depiction of heteronomy from within Luther's Christianity could have fruitful dialogue with Buddhism on the suffering state of humanity that requires an active search for alleviating.

Besides its significance for religion, identifying Luther's position as heteronomous can begin an investigation into political significance and implications. Autonomy in itself can hold positive value; to assert the ability to choose and act as one wills places great emphasis on that actor. Historically oppressed and marginalized peoples treasure autonomy, rightly. It is no stretch, though, to draw from Luther's ethical framework the free actor as subject to the responsibility to do good works for neighbors. The will is obligated to choose the good, not self-reflexively but outward to and on behalf of another. That person is not the individual consumer driven to the possession of things but the willing agent driven by service to others.[57] But can Luther's view be scaled to society at large? Although one could not say in an exact manner how Luther would preach to today's Christian, the breath of fresh air heteronomy offers might be able to cross contexts. Autonomy at the national level can become a troubling discourse, as is evident in a libertarianism that positively resists global war but negatively casts off promotion of the common good.[58] A realized heteronomy requires demonstrations of concretized political platforms and legal codification. However, it is clear that Luther's view of freedom may offer a necessary intervention to narrow politics and theologies that serve self-interest and cannot see a wider and greater good beyond the particular individual—the inner to the detriment of the outer. This establishes the power of retrieving an alternative formation: if it can be shown that autonomy is not the only option within Christianity or even further that it contradicts theological traditions, perhaps ways of countering dangerous politics while still embedded in religious language can emerge.

It has been made clear that reaching back five centuries to discover a programmatic theme within a thinker enormous in quality and quantity like Luther for today is difficult. Luther remains open to multiple positions because of clouded readings of terms like freedom, faith, and love. Appraising him at his word and in context, though, demonstrates a richness of possibilities and does not simply reduce him to a figure that bridges the medieval period to Enlightenment. Sorting meaning out of his contradictory statement in *The Freedom of a Christian* requires a broad synthesis of his own thought and sources as well as later interpreters. By discussing it in terms of human agency, the dialectic of the inner freedom and outer servant has been shown to have sympathies with postmodern thought and offers a chance for reorienting what theology can say in regards to contemporary politics. For the reformer, Christ transforms the person to be more than mere sinner. Political theology today reveals the person with the same value in declaring human actors to be irreducible; individuals are not mere economic numbers or biological processes. The freedom of a Christian in Luther ought to be read as a call for heteronomy as it moves to create a better society out of this reclaimed religious orientation.

NOTES

1. Martin Luther, "The Freedom of a Christian (1520)," in *Luther's Works, Volume 31, Career of the Reformer: I*, ed. by Harold J. Grimm, trans. W.A. Lambert, rev. Harold J. Grimm, 327–77. (Philadelphia: Fortress Press, 1957).

2. Immanuel Kant, *Critique of Pure Reason, 2nd Edition*, trans. Norman Kemp Smith (New York: Palgrave Macmillan, 2007), 634 [A 804/B 832].

3. Martin Luther, "The Bondage of the Will (1525)," in *Luther's Works, Volume 33, Career of the Reformer, III*, ed. and trans. Philip S. Watson (Philadelphia: Fortress Press, 1972), 116.

4. Ibid. 104, Cf. Denis R. Janz, *The Westminster Handbook to Martin Luther* (Louisville, KY: Westminster John Knox, 2010).

5. Ibid., 65–66. See also Martin Luther, "The Disputation Concerning Man (1536), in *Luther's Works, Volume 34, Career of the Reformer IVI*, ed. and trans. Lewis W. Spitz (Philadelphia: Muhlenberg Press, 1960), 138–39.

6. Ibid., 121–22.

7. LW 34, 143.

8. Theology is grounded for Luther in a certain collection of normative bases for knowledge, such as the Bible, theological traditions like Augustine, and church practice.

9. See Luther's, "Open Letter to Pope Leo X," found in "The Freedom of a Christian (1520)," LW 31, 343.

10. Roy A. Harrisville, III, "Introduction" in *The Freedom of a Christian*, trans. W. A. Lambert, rev. Harold J. Grimm (Minneapolis: Fortress, 2003), x.

11. The English translates human in all these texts as "man," which is unfortunately common for most German to English theological texts. Luther uses the German "mensch," which is not gender-specific, so here I choose egalitarianism despite its sense of generality over the gendered but specific "man." See Marin Luther, *"Von der freyheyt eynisz Christen menschen* (1520)" in *D. Martin Luthers Werke, Kritische Geßammtausgabe 7. Bande* (Weimar: Hermann Böhlaus Nachfolger, 1897), 12–38.

12. Martin Luther, "Disputation Against Scholastic Theology (1517)," in *Luther's Works, Volume 31, Career of the Reformer I*, ed. and trans. Harold J. Grimm (Philadelphia: Fortress Press, 1957), 9.

13. LW 31, 344.

14. Ibid.

15. Ibid., 345.

16. Ibid., 347.

17. Ibid., 346, 348.

18. Ibid., 350.

19. Cf. Slavoj Žižek, *The Fragile Absolute: Or, Why is the Christian Legacy Worth Fighting For?* (New York: Verso, 2008). See especially Ch. 12, "Christ's Uncoupling,"115.

20. LW 31, 350.

21. Ibid., 351.

22. Ibid., 358–59.

23. Ibid., 358.

24. Ibid.

25. Martin Luther, "Defense and Explanation of All the Articles (1521)," in *Luther's Works, Volume 32, Career of the Reformer III*, ed. George W. Forell, trans. Charles M. Jacobs, rev. George W. Forell (Philadelphia: Fortress Press, 1958), 16.

26. LW 31, 361.

27. Ibid., 364.

28. Ibid., 371.

29. Ibid., 371.

30. Janz, *The Westminster Handbook to Martin Luther*.

31. Paul L. Lehmann, *The Decalogue and a Human Future: The Meaning of the Commandments for Making and Keeping Human Life Human* (Eugene, OR: Wipf and Stock, 2002), 89.

32. Robert Kolb and Charles P. Arand, *The Genius of Luther's Theology: A Wittenberg Way of Thinking for the Contemporary Church* (Grand Rapids, MI: Baker, 2008), 77.

33. Cf. Søren Kierkegaard, *Works of Love*, ed. and trans. Howard V. Hong and Edna H. Hong (Princeton: Princeton U, 1995). Quotation from Søren Kierkegaard, *Concluding Unscientific Postscript to Philosophical Fragments*, ed. and trans. Howard V. Hong and Edna H. Hong (Princeton, NJ: Princeton University, 1992).

34. For a simple yet powerful account of the Christian theological movement culminating in the inward turn to self, see Michel Foucault, "A Preface to Transgression" in *Language, Counter-Memory, Practice: Selected Essays and Interviews*, ed. and trans. Donald F. Bouchard and Sherry Simon (Ithaca, NY: Cornell University, 2019), 29.

35. Karl Marx, "Contribution to the Critique of *Hegel's Philosophy of Right,*" quoted in Mark C. Taylor, *After God* (Chicago: University of Chicago, 2007), 85–86.

36. Taylor, *After God*, 62. Analysis of James is from William James, *The Varieties of Religious Experience* (Cambridge, MA: Harvard University Press, 1985).

37. Ibid., 64.

38. Reiner Schürmann, *Broken Hegemonies*, trans. Reginald Lilly (Indianapolis: Indiana University, 2003), 576.

39. Cf. Paul R. Hinlicky, *Luther and the Beloved Community: A Path for Christian Theology after Christendom* (Grand Rapids, MI: William B. Eerdmans, 2010), 25.

40. Eberhard Jüngel, *The Freedom of a Christian: Luther's Significance for Contemporary Theology*, trans. Roy A. Harrisville (Minneapolis: Augsburg, 1988). Cf. Herbert Marcuse, "A Study on Authority" in *Studies in Critical Philosophy*, trans. Joris de Bres (Boston: Beacon, 1973) and Max Scheler, "Von Zwei deutschen Krankheiten" (Reichl, 1919) as cited in Jüngel, 101n19, 101n29.

41. Žižek, *The Fragile Absolute, xxix*.

42. Jüngel, *The Freedom of a Christian*, 57. See also Martin Luther's treatment "Concerning the Letter and the Spirit" found in "Answer to the Hyperchristian, Hyperspiritual, and Hyperlearned Book by Goat Emser in Leipzig—Including Some Thoughts Regarding His Companion, The Fool Murner (1521)," in *Luther's Works, Volume 39, Church and Ministry I*, ed. Eric W. Gritsch, trans. Eric W. and Ruth C. Gritsch (Philadelphia: Fortress Press, 1970), 175–203.

43. Though it is curious that Luther only claims the inner person as created in God's image. See LW 31, 359.

44. Jüngel, *The Freedom of a Christian*, 62.

45. Ibid., 71–72.

46. Cf. Martin Luther, "To the Christian Nobility of the German Nation Concerning the Reform of the Christian Estate (1520)," in *Luther's Works, Volume 44 The Christian in Society I*, ed. James Atkinson, trans. Charles M. Jacobs, rev. James Atkinson (Philadelphia: Fortress Press, 1966), 115–217.

47. Slavoj Žižek, "Neighbors and Other Monsters: A Plea for Ethical Violence" in Slavoj Žižek, Eric C. Santner, and Kenneth Reinhard, *The Neighbor: Three Inquiries in Political Theology* (Chicago: U Chicago, 2005), 142. On the connection between Luther and German Idealism on freedom, see also Christian Lotz, "Faith, Freedom, Conscience: Luther, Fichte, and the Principle of Inwardness" in *The Devil's Whore: Reason and Philosophy in the Lutheran Tradition*, ed. Jennifer Hockenberry Dragseth (Minneapolis: Fortress, 2011), 95–96.

48. Emmanuel Levinas, *Totality and Infinity: An Essay on Exteriority*, trans. Alphonso Lingis (Pittsburgh: Duquesne University, 1969), 51.

49. Luther, LW 33, 293.

50. Ibid., 107.

51. Levinas, *Totality and Infinity,* 213.

52. Jürgen Moltmann, *The Crucified God: The Cross of Christ as the Foundation and Criticism of Christian Theology, 2nd Edition*, trans. R. A. Wilson and John Bowden (New York: Harper and Row, 1973).

53. Luther, LW 33, 81–82.

54. It would be interesting, however, to compare this religiously based heteronomy with what Paul Tillich calls "theonomous culture." Initially this is resisted along the lines of requiring further analysis of consciousness in Tillich's thought. Cf. Paul Tillich, *The Protestant Era*, trans. James Luther Adams (Chicago: University of Chicago, 1948), 43–44.

55. Cf. Mark C. Taylor, *Erring: A Postmodern A/Theology* (Chicago: University of Chicago, 1987).

56. John D. Caputo, *The Weakness of God: A Theology of the Event* (Indianapolis: Indiana University, 2006), 137–38.

57. The idea does not necessarily require stopping at human interaction merely because that is the language used by Luther. In fact, one might easily imagine a similar heteronomous ethical responsibility toward nonhuman animals and nature under the sign of divine creation that God has called good (Genesis 1:31).

58. It is unlikely that ignoring Holy Scripture on poverty and justice for the sake of reducing the federal deficit levels because of the expense of ensuring food for hungry children would ever be considered "good work." Neither could one justify a reading of Christian anthropology—that humans are created in God's image—alongside arguments opposing health care simply because bodies are poor at creating profit margins.

BIBLIOGRAPHY

Caputo, John D. *The Weakness of God: A Theology of the Event.* Indianapolis: Indiana University, 2006.

Foucault, Michel. "A Preface to Transgression." In *Language, Counter-Memory, Practice: Selected Essays and Interviews.* Edited and translated by Donald F. Bouchard and Sherry Simon, 29–52. Ithaca, NY: Cornell University, 2019.

Harrisville III, Roy A. "Introduction" in *The Freedom of a Christian.* Translated by W. A. Lambert. Revised by Harold J. Grimm. Minneapolis: Fortress, 2003.

Hinlicky, Paul R. *Luther and the Beloved Community: A Path for Christian Theology after Christendom.* Grand Rapids, MI: William B. Eerdmans, 2010.

James, William. *The Varieties of Religious Experience.* Cambridge, MI: Harvard University, 1985.

Janz. Denis R. *The Westminster Handbook to Martin Luther.* Louisville, KY: Westminster John Knox, 2010.

Jüngel, Eberhard. *The Freedom of a Christian: Luther's Significance for Contemporary Theology.* Translated by Roy A. Harrisville. Minneapolis: Augsburg, 1988.

Kant, Immanuel. *Critique of Pure Reason, 2nd Edition.* Translated by Norman Kemp Smith. New York: Palgrave Macmillan, 2007.

Kierkegaard, Søren. *Concluding Unscientific Postscript to Philosophical Fragments.* Edited and translated by Howard V. Hong and Edna H. Hong. Princeton, NJ: Princeton University, 1992.

———. *Works of Love.* Edited and translated by Howard V. Hong and Edna H. Hong. Princeton, NJ: Princeton University, 1995.

Kolb, Robert and Charles P. Arand. *The Genius of Luther's Theology: A Wittenberg Way of Thinking for the Contemporary Church.* Grand Rapids, MI: Baker, 2008.

Lehmann, Paul L. *The Decalogue and a Human Future: The Meaning of the Commandments for Making and Keeping Human Life Human.* Eugene, OR: Wipf and Stock, 2002.

Levinas, Emmanuel. *Totality and Infinity: An Essay on Exteriority.* Translated by Alphonso Lingis. Pittsburgh: Duquesne University, 1969.

Lotz, Christian. "Faith, Freedom, Conscience: Luther, Fichte, and the Principle of Inwardness" in *The Devil's Whore: Reason and Philosophy in the Lutheran Tradition.* Edited by Jennifer Hockenberry Dragseth. Minneapolis: Fortress, 2011.

Luther, Martin. "Answer to the Hyperchristian, Hyperspiritual, and Hyperlearned Book by Goat Emser in Leipzig—Including Some Thoughts Regarding His Companion, The Fool Murner (1521)." In *Luther's Works, Volume 39, Church and Ministry I*, edited by Eric W. Gritsch, translated by Eric W. and Ruth C. Gritsch, 137–224. Philadelphia: Fortress Press, 1970.

———. "The Bondage of the Will (1525)." In *Luther's Works, Volume 33, Career of the Reformer, III*, edited by Philip S. Watson, translated by Philip S. Watson, 3–294. Philadelphia: Fortress Press, 1972.

———. "Defense and Explanation of All the Articles (1521)." In *Luther's Works, Volume 32, Career of the Reformer III*, edited by George W. Forell, translated by Charles M. Jacobs and revised by George W. Forell, 3–99. Philadelphia: Fortress Press, 1958.

———. "Disputation Against Scholastic Theology (1517)." In *Luther's Works, Volume 31, Career of the Reformer I*, edited by Harold J. Grimm, translated by Harold J. Grimm, 3–16. Philadelphia: Fortress Press, 1957.

———. "The Disputation Concerning Man (1536)." In *Luther's Works, Volume 34, Career of the Reformer IV*, edited and translated by Lewis W. Spitz, 133–44. Philadelphia: Muhlenberg Press, 1960.

———. "The Freedom of a Christian (1520)." In *Luther's Works, Volume 31, Career of the Reformer I*, edited by Harold J. Grimm, translated by W.A. Lambert and revised by Harold J. Grimm, 35–70. Philadelphia: Fortress Press, 1957.

———. "To the Christian Nobility of the German Nation Concerning the Reform of the Christian Estate (1520)." In *Luther's Works, Volume 44, The Christian in Society I*, edited by James Atkinson, translated by Charles M. Jacobs, and revised by James Atkinson, 115–217. Philadelphia: Fortress Press, 1966.

———. "*Von der freyheyt eynisz Christen menschen* (1520)." In *D. Martin Luthers Werke, Kritische Geßammtausgabe, 7. Bande*, 12–38. Weimar: Hermann Böhlaus Nachfolger, 1897.

Marcuse, Herbert. "A Study on Authority" in *Studies in Critical Philosophy.* Translated by Joris de Bres. Boston: Beacon, 1973.

Moltmann, Jürgen. *The Crucified God: The Cross of Christ as the Foundation and Criticism of Christian Theology.* Translated by R. A. Wilson and John Bowden, 2nd ed. New York: Harper and Row, 1973.

Schürmann, Reiner. *Broken Hegemonies.* Translated by Reginald Lilly. Indianapolis: Indiana University, 2003.

Taylor, Mark C. *After God.* Chicago: University of Chicago, 2007.

———. *Erring: A Postmodern A/Theology.* Chicago: University of Chicago, 1987.

Tillich, Paul. *The Protestant Era.* Translated by James Luther Adams. Chicago: University of Chicago, 1948.

Žižek, Slavoj. *The Fragile Absolute: Or, Why is the Christian Legacy Worth Fighting For?* New York: Verso, 2008.

———. "Neighbors and Other Monsters: A Plea for Ethical Violence" in *The Neighbor: Three Inquiries in Political Theology.* Slavoj Žižek, Eric C. Santner, and Kenneth Reinhard. Chicago: University of Chicago, 2005.

Chapter 8

The Crux of Matter

Theology of the Cross and the Modern Extractive Imaginary

Terra Schwerin Rowe

Living at the intersection of a pandemic and climactic uncertainties, one readily experiences how sedimented systems of thought and ways of living can become unsettled, creating openings toward more or less just alternatives. That something similar was going on leading up to and during the Reformation gives one a profound sense of the possibilities and perils of living in such a time; a devastating pandemic was killing six out of every ten Europeans while the Little Ice Age made the regularity and reliability of the orders of nature seem unstable and less trustworthy.

Current theologians readily recognize that theology is always contextual. Yet the context considered often centers on human agencies, systems, and institutions. Theologians have frequently insisted, for example, on the influence of religious thought on economic systems, science, and technology. Considering the impact of such material changes on theological shifts, though, still meets resistance among many confessional theologians. The impact of *environmental* changes on patterns of thought about God and world is seriously considered more rarely still.

Like an effective trigger point treatment, this essay will place pressure on some of those often-unrecognized knots of theological and contextual entanglement in the hopes of releasing blocked flows of creativity and accountability. Specifically, this essay will focus on the shifts in theological perspective and creativity that can occur when we take seriously the historical context of the Reformation within the emergence of modern extraction—the Saxony mining boom. Separately, at least, these areas are not unexplored. The history of mining in Saxony has long been an important focus for mining historians, political ecologists, and literary ecocriticism. And there is, of course, an extensive history of Christian environmental ethical reflection on extraction as well as analysis of the environmental implications of Reformation theology among religion and ecology scholars. Yet, somehow, we have not attempted to think climate, extraction, and theology together. This essay will explore just that: what emerges when we attempt to think theologically about extraction and conversely examine climactic influences on and extractive impulses of theology.

Though, as mentioned, there is an extensive tradition of scholarship on the history of mining, this essay will be informed especially by the methodological shifts opened by the environmental humanities.[1] Pointing to the global inability to adequately address the climate crisis, these scholars insist that climate change is challenging the adequacy of traditional disciplinary bifurcation between science/technology and the humanities. Along these lines, environmental humanities scholars frequently evoke and analyze social and environmental imaginaries that can infuse science and technology as well as literature and religion.[2] Taking these cues, we will explore the modern extractive imaginary, analyzing the often unrecognized but profound entanglements of Reformation thought and extraction in the context of the Saxony mining boom and beyond.

Given colonial histories of justifying human for mineralogical extractions, all the while constructing race and a politics of domination,[3] it is tempting to read such sites of suffering, domination, and resistance as contexts where a theology of the cross must be brought to bear. Yet this particular theological lens proves more complicated and troubled that might be readily apparent. Given the theological and historical complexities of the modern extractive imaginary, a "scandalous" (Westhelle) theology of the cross—a cross against cross theology that emerges more as Holy Saturday Vigil—can be more attentive to the ways that these sites of human and mineralogical extraction remain traumas that do not stay in the past but continue to haunt the present in the form of environmental racism and socio-environmental injustice.

MINING THE REFORMATION, REFORMING MINING

We find roots of modern extraction firmly planted in Reformation soil. Economic historians, for example, have noted a significant increase in mining and metallurgy practices between the mid-fifteenth to mid-sixteenth centuries in central Europe.[4] Silver became especially important in central Europe. In the early to mid-fifteenth century, 20 tons was the average annual output of silver. Between 1470 and 1520, this jumped to 65 tons average annual output.[5] In Saxony's Ore Mountain region, Joachimsthal became an especially significant mining town. The mining boom began there in 1516, following a promising prospecting report initiated by a member of the local nobility. Soon after, a rush of miners commenced, at first from neighboring villages and then from more far reaching locales like Salzburg, Switzerland, and the Tyrolean region.[6] With 6,000–7,000 kilograms produced at its peak, this tiny town would have accounted for roughly 12 percent of central Europe's average yearly output. Dym confirms, in terms of economic impact, that "[b]etween 1545 and 1560 well over half of Germany's average yearly silver production came from the Ore Mountains, and sovereigns earned up to three-fourths of their total income from the mines."[7]

The more lasting impact, though, lay not in amassed wealth, but in the moral and scientific conceptual shifts emerging here that proved necessary for the rise of modern extraction. Georgius Agricola (born Georg Bauer, 1494–1555) played a leading role in both moral and scientific shifts that are often associated with a turn to modern mining. Frequently lauded as the "father of mineralogy," Agricola is most famous for his text *De Re Metallica*. Published a year after his death, in 1556, the tome is recognized as the first modern resource on mining methods, with an impact comparable to that of Copernicus' *De Revolutionibus Orbium Coelestium*.[8]

Working as town physician—first in Joachimsthal and then Chemnitz—and then serving terms as mayor of Chemnitz in the mid to late 1500's, Agricola was rooted in the heart of the Reformation upheaval and the Saxony mining boom. He took a keen interest in the mining endeavors of Joaschimsthal, visiting the mines at every chance, and credits most of the knowledge he reports in *De Re Metallica* from first-hand observations of mining efforts in this area.

While he remained a faithful Roman Catholic throughout his life—counting Erasmus of Rotterdam as a personal friend—he was also on friendly terms with Reformers like Philipp Melanchthon. Melanchthon and other Lutheran reformers seem to have taken a keen interest in Agricola's work. Christoph Entzelt (Christophorus Encelius, 1517–1586), a Lutheran pastor of Saalfield, Saxony, was inspired by Agricola's works to write his own *De Re Metallica*, published in 1557 with a forward by Melanchthon.[9]

Similarly, Lutheran pastor Johann Mathesius (1504–1565) knew Agricola personally and credited him with initially inspiring his interest in mining. Before becoming a pastor, Mathesius taught at the Latin school in Joachimsthal where he observed the rapid influx of miners and shifts in mining activity first-hand.[10] Following Agricola's advice proved enormously beneficial for Mathesius—and the Reformation. After a successful investment in a mining venture, Mathesius suddenly had a financial surplus which allowed him to leave his post at the Latin school and uproot to Wittenberg. There he continued his theological training, was among Luther's inner circle of friends and confidants,[11] presented a mining treatise to Luther and the Reformers (*Quaestio de rebus metallicis* [1540]), ordained by Luther himself, and then was sent back to Joachimsthal in 1545 to serve as pastor to the miners.[12] In Joachimsthal, Mathesius wrote *Sarepta oder Bergpostill,* containing sermons addressed to the miners. In his sermons he consistently framed the Protestant message in terms of mining knowledge and metaphors, providing a solid theological sense for the life of a miner as a glorified, religious, and providentially guided calling.[13]

In Mathesius' work, we begin to see the extent to which the context of modern mining and the message of the Reformation were entwined. Dym describes Mathesius' *Sarepta* as the "culmination of [his] life-long *fusion of mining and the spiritual life.*"[14] In fact, Mathesius portrays mining and the Reformation as wholly intertwined, key parts of God's providential aims for the world. Belief in the organic development of minerals was common at the time. Theorists believed minerals were generated and grew much like plants and animals, following a relatively short lifecycle overseen by a wise and caring creator. It was not uncommon, for example, for miners who had abandoned an unsuccessful mine to return and, upon finding significant mineral holdings, conclude that the minerals had previously been undeveloped but now had reached "a state of perfection or fruition in the form of silver-bearing ore or gold."[15]

Since minerals were constantly undergoing a process of perfection, timing was key for the miner. Finding a mineral too early, before it was properly perfected, was a common concern. Mathesius writes, "So raises the common occurrence among our miners that when they strike at bismuth, they say they came too early; by which they mean that if the ore had only sat longer in the mountain fire, it would have become silver."[16] Consequently, miners and their pastors like Johann Gottfried Rhese prayed that the timing of the miners and their minerals would correspond: "Let us come neither too early nor too late, but rather at the right time, when ore has reached its full power."[17]

While Agricola's work was well known to Mathesius, consistent with his Reformation theology, Mathesius differed from Agricola in insisting on the role of God's omnipotent will in the generation of minerals alongside natural processes. Consequently, Mathesius also emphasized a limit in human knowledge of the causes of mineral generation since, as Norris explains, "minerals are primarily the products of God's decree, and no amount of experience can further reveal [God's] methods to us."[18] Where mineral development was guided not just by natural causes but by divine providence, mining was a sacred calling in as much as miners were called to participate through their excavating activity in a divine, redemptive plan for creation.

For Mathesius, since minerals matured according to both natural causes and God's will, their development also corresponded with God's aims for the

Reformation. Just as undeveloped minerals sat in the earth, being perfected by time and heat, guided by God's will, so also the Gospel message had been proclaimed and then, after the time of the apostles, laid in wait, being perfected until brought again to the light of day, according to God's will, by the Reformers. Consequently, the correspondence of the Saxony mining boom and the Protestant Reformation was not coincidental, but revealed a providential plan. As Dym suggests, for Mathesius, "the Reformation inaugurated a second period of divine influence, which was most evident in Saxon mining."[19] God's providential guidance over the world was evident in the correspondence of the full development of modern mining and the full development of the gospel in the Reformation message. Clearly for Mathesius, evidence of the significance of the Reformation was not to be found solely in the souls of the faithful or ecclesial, political, and economic shifts—the gravity of the Protestant Reformation was also written in stone and inscribed in the sedimented layers of earth.

MODERN EXTRACTIVE IMAGINARY

Disciplinary divisions between the sciences and humanities, applied studies and theoretical pursuits, have thwarted attempts to reflect seriously about what might seem like an unremarkable insight: miners thought. Their thinking influenced their practice and their practice influenced their theologies.[20] As the example of Mathesius demonstrates, in Saxony during the Reformation miners were theologians and theologians were fully involved and invested (theologically, politically, and economically) in mining.

In Saxony and beyond, crucial shifts were taking place, not only in scientific knowledge of minerals and mining methods and technologies, but in concepts, theologies, and morality that would contribute to what could be identified as a modern extractive imaginary. An imaginary is an assumed, commonly shared, often unconscious or commonsensical understanding of a social community (such as the nation-state) or environment (as providentially given "resource," for example). Its commonsensical nature often obscures the historical constructedness of imaginaries, causing one to overlook, in the case of extraction, the extent to which extractive aims pervade economic systems, values, expectations, and logics in ways that would have been unrecognized in other times and contexts—or forget that extraction has not always had the same connotations and implications it does in a modern or even neo-liberal capitalist context.[21]

One of the key shifts we see in the imaginary of modern extraction is in the necessary presence of an external sovereign force acting on passive matter for the removal of a thing from its origin. Here we see reflected key shifts in ideals of power during the late Middle Ages. As with other imaginaries, concepts and ethics of extraction travel easily between mineral, human, and divine realms.

Divine Power and Extraction

A newly emergent sense of an exterior force is a crucial aspect of the modern extractive imaginary, and it is here in particular that theological changes need to be attended to. In the Middle Ages, key debates took place concerning the nature of divine power that had a profound effect on perceptions of the morality of mining and the emergence of a modern extractive imaginary. Political theologians have persuasively outlined these shifts in divine power, emphasizing that though belief in divine omnipotence is ancient, in the Middle Ages divine power gets uniquely consolidated and articulated as the ability to have force, to assert divine will in a way that is not conditioned or constrained by anything else. Such articulations of divine power bled into modern political concepts—sovereignty in particular.[22] I'm suggesting that beyond just political concepts, this transformation in the doctrine of God also infused and informed modern extraction, resulting in a new emphasis on the use of external force.

The dramatic transformation in ideals of divine power can be seen most potently by comparing Gregory of Nyssa's (335–395 CE) and later medieval doctrines of God. In "Address on Religious Instruction" Nyssa broaches a common question posed to Christians: why should a God who claims omnipotence have to trouble with the weakness of human flesh in an incarnation if it was possible to save humanity "by a mere command" or "by some sovereign and divine act of authority"?[23] Could such a God not have remained "free from weakness and suffering?"[24] Nyssa answers with what we might call his theology of the cross: the incarnation and cross were necessary because it is not within God's character to act by power alone as a sovereign will. Divinity is not just powerful "but also just and good and wise and everything else that suggests excellence."[25] More precisely, "not a single one of these sublime attributes by itself and separated from the others constitutes virtue. What is good is not truly such unless it is associated with justice, wisdom, and power. Power, too, if it is separated from justice and wisdom, cannot be classed as virtue. Rather, it is a brutal and tyrannical form of power."[26] For Nyssa, divine character is not constituted by the absolute of any single attribute (power/ will), but the mutual perfection or co-conditioning of multiple divine characteristics. Divine power may be perfect, but not absolute in as much as it is only truly divine power when bound or conditioned by divine justice, mercy, and wisdom. Consequently, divine power is not necessarily antithetical to divine suffering. Since the cross reveals the true nature of divine power—that it is not an assertion of force but conditioned by love, mercy, and compassion—Nyssa does not need to invoke paradox or irrationality when discussing the cross.

This sense of the proper binding of divine power was the norm at least until the eleventh century in Western Christianity. Francis Oakley has argued that the shift toward the unconditioned will of God is evident beginning with Peter Damian (Damiani) rejection of any conditioning or limitation on divine power.[27] Damian (1007–1072 CE) writes that God is "[i]ncapable in his omnipotence and in his eternal present of suffering any diminution or alteration of his creative power." Even those laws and orders set in place by God cannot interfere with divine freedom and power since, as Oakley writes, summarizing Damian "that natural order he could well replace, those laws at any moment change."[28]

Following Damian, in the context of an arms race of power and authority between Western popes and political rulers, objection to any theological limitation on divine power became increasingly vociferous and systematized. Resisting papal claims to absolute power in his own way, the Franciscan Brit, William of Ockham (1285–1347 CE), systematized this understanding of divine power by creating a new metaphysics where particulars (and not universals) were the only reality. This rejection of universals was eventually associated with the *via moderna*. Scholastic realism, on the other hand, had held to the ancient belief in the extra-mental existence of universals (the *via antiqua*). These universals (Platonic Forms or Aristotelian generals, common natures) were aspects of divine reason that humans could know at least in part (for Augustine and Aquinas, though, never apart from grace) through their capacities for reason. Universals ordered the created world such that nature, human reason, and divine reason reflected one another. Thus, theologians of the *via antiqua* "experienced the world as the instantiation of the categories of divine reason."[29] By contrast, theologians of the *via moderna* like Ockham rejected the reality of universals as they would necessarily constrain the power and freedom of God. Rather than the world emanating from a principle of divine reason (*logos*), they emphasized the ordering of the world by divine will (*voluntas*).[30] Consequently, although dominion and omnipotence were not new claims regarding divine nature, theologians of the *via moderna* were asserting in an unprecedented way that omnipotence was not, as Nyssa had claimed, one of several divine characteristics that co-constitute one another, but the "cardinal characteristic of God,"[31] conditioned by nothing. Divine power became a sovereign force, an unconditioned will to be reckoned with. Against the intention of medieval theologians, in modernity this ideal of divine power as unconditioned eventually slides into ideals of human political power.

Crucially, such shifts in divine power had a decisive impact on theologies of the cross. Whatever his complex relationship with Ockhamism (transmitted to Luther through Gabriel Biel) and the *via moderna*, these shifts in the medieval doctrine of God help account for significant differences between Nyssa's and Luther's theologies of the cross. Like Ockham, Luther rejected any correlation between divine reason and the orders of the world. He states this concisely in his Heidelberg Disputation: "That person does not deserve to be called a theologian who looks upon the invisible things of God as though they were clearly perceptible in those things which have actually happened (Rom: 1:20)" (Thesis 19). For Luther, unlike Nyssa, divine suffering and weakness cannot be rationally reconciled with divine power. This is the whole point of the cross from Luther's perspective. To claim that God, the all-powerful creator of the universe, is subject to human weakness and dies on a cross acts as an *aporia*, an irresolvable contradiction that utterly puts a halt to any access human reason might have to divine will and logic.[32] Luther thus insists on both the absolute form of divine power developed in the Middle Ages *and* divine suffering and death on the cross, precisely because it maintains a break between divine reason and the orders of the world.

Mining and Morality

Not only do these shifts in the medieval doctrine of God account for the distinctive characters both of Luther's theology of the cross and the emphasis in modern extraction on an active external force on passive matter, they also correspond with shifts in perceptions about the morality of mining. While Agricola is most well-known for introducing new methods of mining and knowledge of minerals that mark the beginnings of modern mining, his role in decisive shifts in the morality of mining is less commonly understood.

Numerous studies, including Agricola's text itself, demonstrate that while mining was practiced in ancient and medieval Western societies, its potential was constrained by moral objections. Ancient Western authorities seem to have agreed that while mining was at times necessary, it was not laudable and certainly not a moral good.[33] Arguments against mining depended on a logic consistent with the *via antiqua*. An ancient correspondence between divine rationality and the orders of creation implied a correspondence between the orders of creation and the will of God. Consequently, if something had been placed in the earth and covered over, this was part of the divinely ordained order of the world. Uncovering what God had covered plainly disregarded the providentially ordered *logos* of the world.

Georgius Agricola makes a forceful and influential argument against these moral objections, devoting the entire first book of *De Re Metallica* to summarizing and countering them. Assuming a humanistic version of the *via moderna* break between the divine *logos* and the orders of the world, Agricola argues that the morality of mining depends on human will (*voluntas*)—how humans decide to use it: "Now, the man who because they are abused denies that wine, strength, beauty, or genius are good things, is unjust and blasphemous towards the Most High God, Creator of the World."[34] By contrast, mining hurts "no mortal man"[35] and is useful to everyone from physicians who rely on minerals for treatments to artists to those in commerce. "In a word," he concludes, "man could not do without the mining industry, nor did Divine Providence will that he should."[36]

Michael Northcott illustrates the environmental effects of the voluntarist break between the orders of nature and the will of God in Great Britain. Monks holding vast tracts of land in the coal rich Tyne valley had known of the presence of coal on their land for centuries, but the ancient alignment between the will of God and the physical order of the world kept them from digging it up. Once an inherent connection between the *logos* of God and the *logos* of the created world was severed by the *via moderna*, moral restraints against uncovering what God had covered were dissolved. With moral impediments removed, when Britain's forests began running thin, the monks no longer had qualms about mining their Tyne valley coal in earnest.[37]

THEOLOGY AND EXTRACTION: THE CRUX

Agricola's text was remarkably persuasive. Just ten years after the publication of Agricola's text we find not just the Brits, but Italians and Spaniards also embracing Agricola's text, putting its knowledge to work for the project of colonization.[38] By Agricola's time (1560s), Spain was occupied with the project of colonizing South America through various techniques: not least of which was the extraction of mineral wealth. Potosí, in current-day Bolivia, was emerging as particularly efficient in this regard. Mineral extraction proved doubly efficient for the project of colonization—not only did it prove enormously lucrative, it also justified the enslavement of natives for work in the mines and then transatlantic slavery. Here, extractive logic of removal from origins through the use of force slides easily between the mineralogical and human: 4 million African slaves were brought over to replace native populations who were believed to be more prone to European diseases.[39] Working conditions were beyond brutal: the expected "working life" of enslaved miners was a mere six to eight years, and millions died in mining accidents or from lung disease and contamination from mercury used to process the silver.[40]

One of the mining engineers' most frequently referenced resources was Agricola's *De Re Metallica*. Indeed, given the extent to which mining operations in North America relied on this text and the kinds of rewards it made possible from these "new" lands, one wonders if the project of North American colonization would have been pursued with such vigor without it. This is demonstrated poignantly in Potosí where we have reports that priests literally chained Agricola's text to the eucharistic table as a way of continually reminding the miners of the sacredness of their work.[41]

Here, finally, we arrive at the crux of the matter: the intersecting point of theologies of divine-cum-political power, mineralogical and human extractions, and colonialism—all chained together on what could be either (or both) a sacrificial altar or communion table. Here various theo-philosophies and geo-sciences converge in a profound reimagining of the orders of the world, divine power, and human will. In the sedimented layers of extraction, colonialism, and common Reformation articulations of divine agency, we find a particular view of power idealized as the unconditioned, unconstrained ability to enact external force on passive objects. Far more than mere mining, layers of divine, human and mineral extraction intersect in Potosi and other sites in the Americas, resonating with and amplifying one another to construct a modern extractive imaginary.

What does a theology of the cross have to say in such a context? In light of Thesis 20, Luther's call to "comprehend the visible and manifest things of God seen through suffering and the cross" one might interpret in the profound human suffering and the abhorrent abuse of power, a sense of divine suffering or aporetic God against god divine abandonment. With Jürgen Moltmann's liberation influenced theology of the crucified god, or Douglas John Hall's existential theology of the cross protesting glorified power, or more recently and radically John Caputo's *destruktion/decónstruction* possibilities extended from Luther's theology of the cross to undercut the logic of the sovereign, one might comprehend in Potosí a God against god moment where the devices of one version of divine power are protested and undercut by an alternative claim to divine power only in weakness.[42]

Though these theologies of the cross protest triumphal Christendom and the kind of sovereign power that emerged in modernity, they do so by reiterating a rupture in logic complicit in the modern extractive imaginary. For Luther, the cross functioned as *aporia*—a stumbling block to all reason, baffling human logic. Here, the logic of "I give so that you may give (back)," or of getting what you are due that suggests a reasonable and orderly cosmos reflecting divine will and wisdom, breaks down. Here Luther affirms, with the *via moderna*, a wedge between any inherent link between the orders of creation, divine logos, and divine will. This same wedge between the logos of the world and the will of God makes possible, on the one hand, an articulation

of the foolishness of the cross as God's an-economic, unearned, unconditioned grace that can irrationally reckon righteousness to a sinner by act of
divine will, when in fact they remain a sinner and, on the other hand, the
assertion that justified the morality of modern mining: that just because the
earth is ordered in a certain way doesn't mean it is divine will that it remain
this way. In a curious sense, then, Agricola the faithful Roman Catholic and
Reformers like Mathesius were in profound agreement on this new modern
wedge between the *logos* of the world and the *voluntas* of God, thus rendering
Protestant enthusiasm for mining not merely a result of material, economic
benefits, but as a practice remarkably resonant with their theology of grace.

CONCLUSION: EXTRACTION VIGILANCE

From this perspective, we must not overlook the sense in which this particular
"foolishness of the cross" contributed to Potosí's conditions of possibility. So,
what would it mean at this juncture of fettered text and table to not "call evil
good and good evil" but "call the thing what it actually is" (Thesis 21)? Vítor
Westhelle points out that thesis 20 draws us back to some of the very earliest
formulations of the theology of the cross, influenced by Hebrew lament, and
lacking theologies of atonement, redemption, or triumph.[43] In the context of
fettered text and table in Potosí, conjoined mineralogical and theological ref-
ormations in Saxony, and climactic shifts of the Little Ice Age, lament draws
attention to the ways trauma is functioning here. I suggest that from this
perspective, the only appropriate "theology of the cross" for Potosí and other
sites of intersecting human, mineralogical, and divine materializations of
modern extraction is not a theology of Friday or Sunday, but Holy Saturday.

Frequently, Christian theology regulates clear distinctions between life and
death, suffering and resurrection, brokenness and wholeness, past and present. Yet, in the case of trauma, past and present, life and death do not stay
in their place. Rather than healing, these wounds continue to haunt, continually returning in the form of trauma passed from generation to generation of
enslaved and colonized peoples, or environmental racism repeating patterns
of colonization and enslavement in the form of black and brown bodies acting
as "buffer zones" between white neighborhoods and toxic sites of extraction,
or inscribed in Arctic ice cores as a "widespread anthropogenic signal."[44]
Theologian Shelly Rambo emphasizes that the challenge trauma poses to
traditional Christian theologies of redemption is that it "does not go away.
It persists in symptoms that live on in the body, in the intrusive fragments
of memories that return. It persists in symptoms that live on in communities, in the layers of past violence that constitute present ways of relating."[45]
Contemporary trauma theorists describe its "double structure": first, the

traumatic event; second, the reliving of aspects of that event that remain beyond comprehension. They are building here from Freud who first theorized that the signature of trauma was the confusion between these two—the originating event and the reliving of it, the past and the present. Just as trauma scrambles any sense of linear, progressive time or challenges any sense of a just and orderly logos of the world, it also disrupts carefully guarded psychic boundaries between life and death. As Rambo emphasizes, this, in particular, is a phenomena that Christian cross and resurrection-focused theologies have trouble adequately addressing. The reliving of a traumatic event delivers a strong sense of death as ever present, no longer a distant future event. Trauma philosopher Susan Brison describes the life after trauma as a "spectral existence" where, as Rambo adds, "death and life no longer stand in opposition. Instead, death haunts life."[46] Consequently, Rambo suggests that in upholding or protecting a binary between life and death most theologies of the cross and resurrection theologies cannot account for experiences of trauma. Instead, she calls for a theology of the middle, of Holy Saturday that attends—what Karen Bray, inspired by Rambo, calls "grave attending"—to those spaces between life and death, cross and resurrection, wounding and healing.[47]

Similar to a protesting theology of the cross as articulated by Westhelle, Moltmann, and Hall, or a deconstructing cross as articulated by Caputo, a theology of Holy Saturday is able to account for ruptures in an orderly sense of the world—for a sense that the world as it is could not possibly reflect the will of a loving and just god. It calls us to attend to those ruptures of clear and comforting space between life and death, between past and present. It accounts for the kinds of traumas that "shatter all that one knows about the world and all the familiar ways of operating within it."[48] Like a theology of the cross, it accounts for those moments in human history that defy reason and expectation, those times experienced as utterly god-forsaken.

Yet, like Nyssa's doctrine of God, a theology of Holy Saturday attends to these ruptures between the orders of the world and God's will without systematizing and indoctrinating them as did the *via moderna*. A theology of Holy Saturday, for example, would not need to affirm such ruptures as modes of assuring human passivity while protecting and consolidating the unconditioned power of God as a sovereign force. In place of theological assertions of divine power and moral justifications of extraction, it opens space in Christian theology to articulate a Spirit of witness and attending.

This Spirit addresses the ongoingness of the wounds of extraction. Rather than a spirit of life, progress, newness, and triumph, this is a Spirit of attending to life interrupted by death and haunted by continuing wounds. In Rambo's theology, Spirit calls not just for "the proclamation of what is new but the work of witness to what remains."[49] In the midst of what remains, there is no room for certainty, but ample capacity for confidence and determination "to imagine forms of life that are not clearly evidenced."[50]

The flux of a changing climate and a pandemic can profoundly challenge established systems, orders, and deeply rooted beliefs in divinity, the orders of nature, and morality.

For theologians of the late Middle Ages facing dramatic loss of human life and changing weather patterns, a rational ordering of the cosmos reflecting divine will began to seem untenable.[51] In 2020, we live in the wake of those shifts, while also experiencing some of the same conditions that inspired this opening for change. In living with the ongoing traumas of modern extraction, may we be guided by a Spirit of witnessing to what remains and inspired to reimagine modes of abiding with one another and the earth, wounds and all.

NOTES

1. See, for example, a key initiating text: Poul Holm et al., "Humanities for the Environment—A Manifesto for Research and Action," *humanities* 4, no. 4 (December 2015): 977–92.

2. For example, Lawrence Buell, *The Environmental Imagination* (Cambridge: Harvard, 1995) and Irene Klaver, "Accidental Wilderness on a Detention Pond," *antennae The Journal of Nature in Visual Culture* 33, (Autumn 2015): 45–58. Closely connected is Charles Taylor's *Modern Social Imaginaries* (Durham, NC: Duke University Press, 2004), though Taylor's focus is more on sociocultural agencies.

3. Cf. Kathryn Yusoff, *A Billion Black Anthropocenes or None* (Minneapolis: University of Minnesota Press, 2018); Macarena Gómez-Barris, *The Extractive Zone: Social Ecologies and Decolonial Perspectives* (Durham, NC: Duke University Press, 2017); and Willie James Jennings, *The Christian Imagination: Theology and the Origins of Race* (New Haven, CT: Yale University Press, 2010).

4. Dym, "Mineral Fumes and Mining Spirits: Popular Beliefs in the *Sarepta* of Johann Mathesius (1504–1565)," *Reformation and Renaissance Review* 8, no.2 (March 2006): 163.

5. Dym, "Mineral Fumes," 163.

6. John A. Norris, "The Providence of Mineral Generation in the Sermons of Johann Mathesius (1504–1565), in *Geology and Religion: A History of Harmony and Hostility*, ed. M. Kölbl-Ebert (London: The Geological Society, 2009), 37.

7. Dym, "Mineral Fumes," 163.

8. See Herbert Hoover and Lou Henry Hoover, "Introduction," in *De Re Metallica*, trans. Herbert Hoover and Lou Henry Hoover (New York: Dover Publications, 1950) and James Ruffner, "Agricola and Community" in *Religion, Science, and Worldview: Essays in Honor of Richard S. Westfall*, eds. Margaret J. Osler and Paul Lawrence Farber (Cambridge: Cambridge University Press, 1985): 297–324.

9. Christophorus Encelio, *De Re Metallica*, trans. Nellie E. Lutz, ed. Lloyd M. Swan (Canton, OH: Ohio Ferro-Alloys Corp, 1943).

10. Norris, "Providence of Mineral Generation," 37–38.

11. Mathesius is likely most famous for his role in transcribing some of Luther's sayings and then compiling them with others into Luther's *Table Talk*.

12. Henrike Haug, "In the Garden of Eden? Mineral Lore and Preaching in the Erzgebirge," *Renaissance Studies* 34, no. 1 (August 2019): 57–77.

13. As Norris explains, Mathesius' "profoundly providential attitude" provided mining a "positive perspective" by "glorifying minerals as evidence of God's generosity," ("Providence of Mineral Generation," 38).

14. Dym, "Mineral Fumes," 168.

15. Ibid., 180, citing Mathesius, *Sarepta*.

16. Mathesius, *Berg-Postilla oder Sarepta* (Freiberg, 12th edition, 1679,) 139, cited and translated in Dym, "Mineral Fumes," 180.

17. Johann Gottfried Rhese, *Der in Gott andächtige Bergmann* (Goslar, 1705), 367, cited and translated in Dym, "Mineral Fumes," 181.

18. Norris, "Providence of Mineral Generation," 39, referencing Mathesius, *Sarepta* 1571, xxxiii.

19. Dym, "Mineral Fumes, 175."

20. See Ernst Hamm, "Mining and History: People, Knowledge, Power" *Earth Sciences History,* 31, no. 2 (July 2012): 321–26 on miners and thought. See also Isabel Fay Barton, "Georgius Agricola's *De Re Metallica* in Early Modern Scholarship" *Earth Sciences History,* 35, no. 2 (December 2015): 265–82 on the influence of Agricola's work in bridging a commonplace practical/theoretical divide even in his context.

21. I have argued more fully elsewhere that modern extraction is distinct from ancient mining and here outline key lexical shifts in the usage and definition of extraction and its lexical variants. See Schwerin Rowe, *Of Modern Extraction: Gender, Energy, and Theology* (NY: Bloomsbury, forthcoming).

22. See Jean Bethke Elshtain, *Sovereignty: God, State, and Self* (Basic Books, 2012); Jürgen Moltmann, *Trinity and the Kingdom,* trans. Margaret Kohl (Minneapolis, MN: Fortress Press, 1993); Erik Peterson, "Monotheism as Political Problem," in *Theological Tractates,* ed. Michael J. Hollerich (Stanford, Stanford University Press, 2011); Francis Schussler Fiorenza. "Political Theology As Foundational Theology," *Proceedings of the Catholic Theological Society of America* 32, (2012). https://ejournals.bc.edu/index.php/ctsa/article/view/2881.

Controversial figure, Carl Schmitt coins the phrase political theology in his text *Political Theology: Four Chapters on the Concept of Sovereignty,* trans. George Schwab (Chicago: University of Chicago Press, 2005) making the argument that "all significant concepts of the modern theory of the state are secularized theological concepts" (36), emphasizing that modern political sovereignty in particular is a secularization of divine omnipotence.

23. Gregory of Nyssa "Address on Religious Instruction," trans. Cyril C. Richardson, in *Christology of the Later Fathers,* ed. Edward R. Hardy (Louisville, KY: Westminster John Knox Press, 1954), 296 and 291 respectively.

24. Ibid., 291. "Why did he take a tedious, circuitous route, submit to a bodily nature, enter life through birth, pass through the various stages of development, and

finally taste death, and so gain his end by the resurrection of his own body? Could he not have remained in his transcendent and divine glory, and saved man by a command, renouncing such circuitous routes?"

25. Ibid., 296.

26. Ibid.

27. Francis Oakley, *Omnipotence, Covenant and Order: An Excursion in the History of Ideas from Abelard to Leibniz* (Ithaca, NY: Cornell University Press, 1984).

28. Francis Oakley, *Politics and Eternity: Studies in the History of Medieval and Early-Modern Political Thought* (Leiden: Brill, 1999), 43–44.

29. Michael Allen Gillespie, *The Theological Origins of Modernity* (Chicago: University of Chicago Press, 2008), 14.

30. Most often, these debates are characterized by scholars today as a shift in the ancient primacy of *logos* to the modern primacy of *voluntas*—from intellectualism to voluntarism. Intellectualism gave philosophical and theological primacy to divine reason, while voluntarism gave primacy to the will. See Elshtain, Gillespie, and Oakley.

31. Gillespie, *Theological Origins of Modernity,* 21.

32. See especially Gerhard Forde, *On Being a Theologian of the Cross: Reflections on Luther's Heidelberg Disputation, 1518* (Grand Rapids, MI: Wm. B. Eerdmans, 1997) and Walter von Loewenich, *Luther's Theology of the Cross* (Augsburg Fortress, 1976) who emphasize this particular angle of Luther's theology of the cross.

33. See Carolyn Merchant, "Farm, Fen, and Forest: European Ecology in Transition," in *The Death of Nature: Women, Ecology and the Scientific Revolution* (New York: Harper Collins, 1980), 42–69; Barton, "Georgius Agricola's *De Re Metallica*"; and Dym, "Mineral Fumes," 165.

34. Agricola, *De Re Metallica,* 19.

35. Ibid., 20.

36. Ibid.

37. Michael S. Northcott, *A Political Theology of Climate Change* (Grand Rapids, MI: William B. Eerdmans, 2013), 53–55.

38. Jean Bodin, "the Italians and Spaniards enlist the services of German and English mining engineers on account of their supernatural skill in locating metallic veins and opening them up" (*Methodus ad facile historiarum cognitionem,* 1566, cited in Benjamin Farrington, *The Philosophy of Francis Bacon* (Liverpool, UK: Liverpool University Press, 1964), 34).

39. Kathryn Yusoff, *A Billion Black Anthropocenes or None* (Minneapolis: University of Minnesota Press, 2018), 49.

40. By comparison, a North American sugar plantation slave owner could expect 8–10 years from their slaves (Yusoff, *A Billion Black Anthropocenes or None*, 49).

41. Farrington citing Jean Bodin. See footnote 37.

42. Jürgen Moltmann, *The Crucified God* (Minneapolis: Fortress Press, 2015); Douglas John Hall, *The Cross in Our Context: Jesus and the Suffering World* (Minneapolis: Fortress Press, 2003); John D. Caputo, *Cross and Cosmos: A Theology of Difficult Glory* (Indiana University Press, 2019). Caputo in particular emphasizes the importance of deconstructing modes of sovereign power. Yet he continues to insist

on the unconditioned nature of different aspects of the divine gift—the call and the event in particular. He defends this insistence on the absolute and unconditioned, citing Derrida's affirmation of the "unconditional without sovereignty" ("The Exits*a*nce of God," *Cross and Cosmos*)—that is, something of unconditional worth without sovereign power. Given the importance Nyssa gives to the co-conditioning nature of all divine characteristics, particularly as a way of articulating divine power that is not tyrannical, I remain skeptical about just how much the unconditioned can extricate itself from sovereign power.

43. Vítor Westhelle, *Scandalous God: The Use and Abuse of the Cross* (Minneapolis: Fortress Press, 2006), 20.

44. A report in the 2015 *Proceedings of the National Academy of Sciences* found that the exponential expansion of mining in colonial America—focused mainly around Potosí—is legible in Arctic ice core records as a "widespread anthropogenic signal": 2015, *Proceedings of the National Academy of Sciences*, referenced in Jason Groves, "Petrofiction: Reimagining the Mine in German Romanticism," in *Readings in the Anthropocene: The Environmental Humanities, German Studies, and Beyond,* eds. Sabine Wilke and Japhet Johnstone (New York: Bloomsbury, 2017): 245–62.

45. Shelly Rambo, *Spirit and Trauma: A Theology of Remaining* (Louisville: Westminster John Knox Press, 2010), 2. See also Serene Jones *Trauma and Grace, Second Edition: Theology in a Ruptured World* (Lousiville, KY: Westminster John Knox Press, 2019)—her conversation with Kelly Brown Douglas on race and trauma especially.

46. Ibid., 3.

47. Karen Bray, *Grave Attending: A Political Theology for the Unredeemed* (New York: Fordham University Press, 2019).

48. Rambo, *Spirit and* Trauma, 5. Both Westhelle and Caputo resist any embrace of illogic or irrationality of the cross. Caputo, for example, cites Westhelle affirmatively in upholding a theology of the cross that "constantly transgresses the limits of accepted epistemes" looking for moments "when the conventional meaning breaks apart to open new possibilities" (Caputo, *Cross and Cosmos,* 5).

49. Rambo, *Spirit and Trauma,* 140.

50. Ibid.

51. Cf. Northcott, *Political Theology of Climate Change,* 42.

BIBLIOGRAPHY

Agricola, Georgius. *De Re Metallica.* Translated by Herbert Hoover and Lou Henry Hoover. New York: Dover Publications, 1950.

Barton, Isabel Fay. "Georgius Agricola's *De Re Metallica* in Early Modern Scholarship." *Earth Sciences History* 35, no. 2 (December 2015): 265–82.

Bethke Elshtain, Jean. *Sovereignty: God, State, and Self.* New York: Basic Books, 2012.

Bray, Karen. *Grave Attending: A Political Theology for the Unredeemed.* New York: Fordham University Press, 2019.

Buell, Lawrence. *The Environmental Imagination.* Cambridge, MA: Harvard University Press, 1995.

Caputo, John D. *Cross and Cosmos: A Theology of Difficult Glory.* Bloomington: Indiana University Press, 2019.

Dym, Warren Alexander. "Mineral Fumes and Mining Spirits: Popular Beliefs in the *Sarepta* of Johann Mathesius (1504–1565)," *Reformation and Renaissance Review* 8, no.2 (March 2006): 161–85.

Encelio, Christophorus. *De Re Metallica.* Translated by Nellie E. Lutz. Edited by Lloyd M. Swan. Canton, OH: Ohio Ferro-Alloys Corp, 1943.

Farrington, Benjamin. *The Philosophy of Francis Bacon.* Liverpool, UK: Liverpool University Press, 1964.

Forde, Gerhard. *On Being a Theologian of the Cross: Reflections on Luther's Heidelberg Disputation, 1518.* Grand Rapids, MI: Wm. B. Eerdmans, 1997.

Gillespie, Michael Allen. *The Theological Origins of Modernity.* Chicago: University of Chicago Press, 2008.

Gómez-Barris, Macarena. *The Extractive Zone: Social Ecologies and Decolonial Perspectives.* Durham, UK: Duke University Press, 2017.

Groves, Jason. "Petrofiction: Reimagining the Mine in German Romanticism." In *Readings in the Anthropocene: The Environmental Humanities, German Studies, and Beyond.,* edited by Sabine Wilke and Japhet Johnstone, 245–62. New York: Bloomsbury, 2017.

Hall, Douglas John. *The Cross in Our Context: Jesus and the Suffering World.* Minneapolis: Fortress Press, 2003.

Hamm, Ernst. "Mining and History: People, Knowledge, Power." *Earth Sciences History* 31, no. 2 (July 2012): 321–26.

Haug, Henrike. "In the Garden of Eden? Mineral Lore and Preaching in the Erzgebirge," *Renaissance Studies* 34, no. 1 (August 2019): 57–77.

Holm, Poul et al. "Humanities for the Environment—A Manifesto for Research and Action," *humanities* 4, no. 4 (December 2015): 977–92.

Jennings, Willie James. *The Christian Imagination: Theology and the Origins of Race.* New Haven, CT: Yale University Press, 2010.

Jones, Serene. *Trauma and Grace, Second Edition: Theology in a Ruptured World.* Louisville, KY: Westminster John Knox Press, 2019.

Klaver, Irene. "Accidental Wilderness on a Detention Pond," *antennae The Journal of Nature in Visual Culture* 33 (Autumn 2015): 45–58.

Merchant, Carolyn. *Death of Nature: Women, Ecology and the Scientific Revolution.* New York: Harper Collins, 1980.

Moltmann, Jürgen. *The Crucified God.* Minneapolis: Fortress Press, 2015.

———. *Trinity and the Kingdom.* Translated by Margaret Kohl. Minneapolis: Fortress Press, 1993.

Norris, John A. "The Providence of Mineral Generation in the Sermons of Johann Mathesius (1504–1565). In *Geology and Religion: A History of Harmony and Hostility,* edited by M. Kölbl-Ebert, 37–40. London: The Geological Society, 2009.

Northcott, Michael S. *A Political Theology of Climate Change.* Grand Rapids, MI: William B. Eerdmans, 2013.

Nyssa, Gregory. "Address on Religious Instruction," translated by Cyril C. Richardson. In *Christology of the Later Fathers,* edited by Edward R. Hardy, 268–326. Louisville, KY: Westminster John Knox Press, 1954.

Oakley, Francis. *Omnipotence, Covenant and Order: An Excursion in the History of Ideas from Abelard to Leibniz.* Ithaca, NY: Cornell University Press, 1984.

———. *Politics and Eternity: Studies in the History of Medieval and Early-Modern Political Thought.* Leiden: Brill, 1999.

Peterson, Erik. "Monotheism as Political Problem." In *Theological Tractates,* edited by Michael J. Hollerich. Stanford, CA: Stanford University Press, 2011.

Rowe, Terra Schwerin. *Of Modern Extraction: Gender, Energy, and Theology.* NY: Bloomsbury, forthcoming.

Rambo, Shelly. *Spirit and Trauma: A Theology of Remaining.* Louisville, KY: Westminster John Knox Press, 2010.

Ruffner, James. "Agricola and Community." In *Religion, Science, and Worldview: Essays in Honor of Richard S. Westfall,* edited by Margaret J. Osler and Paul Lawrence Farber, 297–324. Cambridge: Cambridge University Press, 1985.

Schmitt, Carl. *Political Theology: Four Chapters on the Concept of Sovereignty.* Translated by George Schwab. Chicago: University of Chicago Press, 2005.

Schussler Fiorenza, Francis. "Political Theology As Foundational Theology." *Proceedings of the Catholic Theological Society of America* 32 (2012): 142–177. https://ejournals.bc.edu/index.php/ctsa/article/view/2881.

Taylor, Charles. *Modern Social Imaginaries.* Durham, NC: Duke University Press, 2004.

von Loewenich, Walter. *Luther's Theology of the Cross.* Minneapolis: Augsburg Fortress, 1976.

Westhelle, Vítor. *Scandalous God: The Use and Abuse of the Cross.* Minneapolis: Fortress Press, 2006.

Yusoff, Kathryn. *A Billion Black Anthropocenes or None.* Minneapolis: University of Minnesota Press, 2018.

Chapter 9

Crux in the Balance

In Response to Rowe and Overy-Brown

Allen G. Jorgenson

"We live in unprecedented times." This description of our current age of eco-crisis and the novel Corona virus offers too much and too little. On the one hand, the world has gone through pandemics with higher mortality rates and the globe has seen seismic shifts that have obliterated unbelievably high percentages of species.[1] On the other hand, every era has its own quirky contours that give it unique purchase on how the cross looks in our present context. Moreover, the inordinate contribution of the human species to the environmental crisis in this Anthropocene adds a particular pathos to the morass in which we find ourselves. Additionally, our own construal of freedom has grounded the global capitalist greed that has so effectively conquered and divided humanity in a way manifestly evident in the current COVID-19 crisis.

In this chapter—shaped by this present age—I take leave from two of the various themes presented by Rowe and Overy-Brown (divine sovereignty and human freedom, respectively) and I then use their questions and insights as guides into a reading of *The Heidelberg Disputation*. My hope is that this reading will inform these questions raised in their papers: what is sovereignty and what does freedom look like? I will use the theme of balance to guide my explorations.

WHY BALANCE?

All theology is contextual, and our contexts shape the questions we ask and the answers we discern. This does not preclude universal themes that cut across contexts, but every context contributes to the process of theological reflection. My context as a Lutheran Canadian theologian includes the fact that I do theology on stolen land.[2] Indigenous people on Turtle Island (North America) have lived in a relationship of intimacy with this land, identified as their Mother. To live on this land with integrity means attending to the particular insights afforded Settlers who are willing to listen to Indigenous wisdom. George "Tink" Tinker, for instance, speaks of the importance of land, spatiality, community, and creation in the Indigenous imaginary.[3] These themes recur in the work of many Indigenous thinkers. Another theme of frequent importance is that of balance. This word speaks to the broader Indigenous attention to what Randy Woodley calls "the Harmony Way," which he connects to the biblical concept of shalom, which Jesus lived out and proclaimed in the Reign of God.[4] This way of being is evidenced in the Indigenous insistence on reciprocity and in the use of the phrase "all my relations," which recognizes the need for human beings to see all created reality as relations with which we live in communion with in an attitude of respect.[5] At first blush, this seems like a quaint or even nostalgic virtue to advance in our individual lives. However, an Indigenous understanding of balance infuses their ontology and epistemology to the end that it up-ends occidental preoccupations with progress. I note that balance is to be understood in a dynamic fashion. Balance is not about a static symmetry but reflects the ever-necessary dance of countering dynamic forces so that the whole holds. Balance is the *sine qua non* to the flourishing of creation, which speaks to us quite forcefully of the cost to be paid for imbalance. Both Overy-Brown and Rowe demonstrate this in their contributions to this volume.

Rowe's accounting of the pre-medieval construal of divine sovereignty notes the manner in which Gregory of Nyssa's account of sovereignty is conditioned by 'divine justice, mercy, and wisdom.'[6] The loss of this balance, with the ascendency of Christendom resulted in the coronation of a god whose image the emperor could aspire to mimic. She carefully traces how medieval sensibilities were informed by both nominalist philosophy (the *via moderna*) and a burgeoning capitalist purchase on reality that funded a worldview that makes possible the reduction of the earth to a resource. Rowe narrates a tale of a balance lost as the march of progress takes shape in the west.

Overy-Brown differently addresses the theme of balance, seeing it operative in the thought of Luther's accounting of freedom. He notes the dialectical accounting of the life of the Christian as simultaneously free and bound as evident in *The Freedom of a Christian*. This stands over against his accounting of freedom in *The Bondage of the Will*, where Luther precludes the possibility of a compatibilist position. Overy-Brown holds these two together in noting the differing modalities of discourse: vernacular/pastoral in the former and scholarly/philosophical in the latter. Keeping these two together in tension, or balance, allows one a fuller image of Luther's account of freedom, which can be held in contradistinction to that of Calvin, for instance, even if the logical consistency of Luther's positions is threatened. Overy-Brown points to the manner in which Luther is read—problematically in his estimation—as the founder of a theological anthropology from whom the human subject begins to be read as autonomous.[7] Here, the balance is broken and the conditioned and dialectically determined nature of human freedom is lost—a freedom that Overy-Brown wants to name as heteronomous.

Both Rowe and Overy-Brown, then, outline the loss of balance in narrating accounts of divine sovereignty and human freedom. Moreover, these losses fundamentally impair human relationships with land, humans, and the Creator, which are at the core of an Indigenous and biblical understanding of well-being.[8] In what follows, I will take this focus on balance and re-read *The Heidelberg Disputation* using this as a lens for seeing this beloved and perplexing text anew. After this, I will revisit Rowe's and Overy-Brown's themes of sovereignty and freedom in light of lessons learned, all the while informed by my context and accountable to where I am and the people of this land.

THEOLOGIANS OF THE CROSS

The Heidelberg Disputation famously distinguishes a theologian of the cross from a theologian of glory. The latter, for Luther, is identified against the backdrop of nominalist thought. Rowe has noted the importance of the sovereignty of God in this. Further to this, the nominalist affirmation of the univocity of being and the freedom of the human as located in the injunction *facere quod in se est* (do what is in you) are significant to the topics at hand.

The affirmation of the univocity of being in the nominalist paradigm, following Scotus, means that "being" is a term used of both the human and the divine even while the modality of each is utterly different. The "being" predicated of each subject is peculiar to that subject, including God. God's being is proper to God, and so the being of the human being is not participatory in the being of God to the end that God's transcendence is secured and not marred by human activity.[9] Humans and God are discrete instances of being, which is a piece of the voluntarist notion of God in nominalism—a corollary of its emphasis on sovereignty.

In an interesting counterpoint the human who stands before this sovereign God is commended by Gabriel Biel, after Ockham, to do what is in the self (*facere quod in se est*).[10] The human, then, exercises a kind of freedom over the self analogous to divine sovereignty, albeit limited and so in need of grace.[11] When humans do what is in the self, God will meet them in their free efforts to do what is right. The position advanced by Biel, for instance, would assert that the human is still saved by grace because doing what we are able is not yet enough. But the ball is clearly in the court of the human in this construal, and so Biel's proposition is thought to afford both the pastoral comfort of being able to say "I have done my best," as well as the theological assertion that God will provide the grace to bridge the crack between what I ought and can do, and what I really need to do.

Luther rejects this construal of a theological anthropology in that the former offers no pastoral comfort ("Have I really done my best?") and the latter offers a thin account of grace (grace as offer rather than intervention). *The Heidelberg Disputation (1520)* proposes a paradigm shift with theological paradoxes. The invitation to the disputation names this as follows:

> Distrusting completely our own wisdom, according to that counsel of the Holy Spirit, "Do not rely on your own insight" [Prov. 3:5], we humbly present these theological paradoxes to the judgment of all those who wish to attend, so that it may become clear whether they have been deduced well or poorly from St. Paul, the especially chosen vessel and instrument of Christ, and also from St. Augustine, his most trustworthy interpreter.[12]

The theses that follow were offered in response to the request of Luther by Johann von Staupitz, his supervisor in the Augustinian order, to address the topic of sin, free will, and grace for the good of his fellow Augustinians on April 26, 1518, in light of the theological development being advanced by the young Luther.[13] In what follows, Luther responds to this, but in so doing crafts a detour between the move from free will to grace in theses 19–24.

In the first 12 theses, he deprives the hearer of any confidence in their good works by first addressing our incapacity to fulfill the law and by dismissing any notion of a venial sin since the demand of the law is unconditional.[14] Moreover, our incapacity to ascertain our situation with respect to fulfilling the law leaves us in a precarious position wherein we existentially ascertain that things are not always as they appear. In the next six theses, he explores the theme of the will, outlining that while the human may freely decide how they will sin, they are really devoid of the capacity to decide if they will sin. Indeed, any good the human does is done in the mode of patient, through the working of God in Christ.

These first 18 theses then deprive the hearer of any confidence in their capacity to do good works and to will well. Instead of moving to the topic of grace, Luther shifts the conversation with the following two theses:

> 19. Hic ille non Theologus dicitur, qui invisibilia Dei per ea, quae facta sunt, intellecta conspicit,

20. Sed qui visibilia et posteriora Dei per passiones et crucem conspecta intelligit.[15]

The Annotated Luther: Roots of Reform has retranslated this, with a note indicating the significance of Luther's choice of the verbs *conspicit* and *intelligit*.[16] Unfortunately, the text is not consistent in translating these, and so I offer my own translation in an effort to mirror the careful framing of these theses by Luther:

19. That person is not to be called a theologian who perceives [*conspicit*] the invisible things of God as having been understood [*intellecta*] through those things which have been made.
20. But [the person who is to be called a theologian] understands [*intelligit*] the visible and more posterior things of God as having been perceived [*conspecta*] through the passion and cross.

A few comments on this translation are in order. First, as noted above, Luther very carefully contrasts the use of the verbs *conspicere* and *intellegere*. The verbs both admit a wide range of possible translations. *Conspicere* can mean to look at, get sight of, descry, contemplate, perceive, discern, etc.[17] *Intellegere* can mean to see into, perceive, understand, distinguish, observe, comprehend, judge, and so on.[18] There is a substantive amount of overlap between these two verbs and so the choice of "perceive" for *conspicere* and "understand" for *intellegere* is mostly heuristic. Both are verbs of apprehension and the semantic sense of these two verbs in these two theses is afforded by the object of their activity. So, what are these objects?

The person who is not to be called a theologian of the cross perceives (*conspicit*) the invisible things of God which are understood (*intellecta*) by means of those things which have been made (*quae facta sunt*). Dennis Bielfeldt notes that at the heart of Luther's work here is a refusal of "the ubiquitous human proclivity to grasp the infinite on the basis of the finite, to reach heaven by building a tower on the earth."[19] The theologian of glory, in contrast to a theologian of the cross, uses her understanding of the created (*quae facta sunt*) to perceive (*conspicit*) the invisible things of God, which are named in the explanation of thesis 19 as "virtue, godliness, wisdom, justice, goodness, and so forth." Most certainly "sovereignty" can be included in the *et cetera* of the Latin original.

By contrast, the person who is properly called a theologian of the cross understands (*intelligit*) the visible and more posterior things perceived (*conspecta*) by the passion and cross. Two points bear careful consideration. First, both verbs play in both theses. The conflict is found in the priority given and the object of the action of the verb. The theologian of the cross begins with the perceived (*conspecta*) passion and cross which allows her to understand (*intelligit*) the visible and more posterior things of God. The nesting of the verbs relates the two sets of objects, but in a way that the narrower verb with its objects gives purchase on the broader verb and its objects. That is, one first perceives the passion and cross to the end that one understands the visible and more posterior things of God. The passion and cross, then, are not to be equated with the visible and more posterior things of God but rather, numbered among them. However, they hold a kind of pride of place. What then, are these visible and more posterior things of God? This brings me to the second point.

As noted above, the first point to underscore is Luther's conviction that these visible and more posterior things can only be seen via the lens of cross and resurrection. The second is discerned by noting the editorial reference to the source text for the word *posteriora*, Exodus 33:23, where we read:

> And the LORD said, "See, there is a place near Me. Station yourself on the rock and, as My Presence passes by, I will put you in a cleft of the rock and shield you with My hand until I have passed by. Then I will take My hand away and you will see My back; but My face must not be seen.[20]

Luther's use of this verse is to underscore that just as Moses was only in a position for a renewed leadership by grace of God's moment of revelation, so the faithful still need a revelatory moment in their being shaped as theologians of the cross.[21] Luther's appeal to a biblical text here is continuous with its use *in situ*. Moses is put in a place where he sees the back of God, and the theologian of the cross is located in the cross where she can now see the *visiblia et posteriora Dei*.

This analogical use of the passage stands in marked contrast to the other biblical reference in these paired theses: Romans 1:20 in thesis 19 (*per ae, quae facta sunt*). In this passage, Paul appeals to the universal knowledge of created things by humans as the means by which he makes the claim that we all know God to outline that all fall short even while they have had access to knowledge of God via the things that are made. Luther's use of this verse is counterintuitive in that he advances knowing God via "the things made" as methodologically suspicious. Paul, by contrast, anticipates that "the things made" prove to all that God exists. Luther proposes that "the things made" cannot be the pathway to knowing the things "visible and more posterior." We might ask if "the things made" are ever and only to be understood in this way used by medieval theology, which is refused by Luther. Further insights are afforded in the explanation to the twentieth thesis.

God wished again to be recognized in suffering, and to condemn wisdom concerning invisible things by means of wisdom concerning visible things, so that those who did not honor God as manifested in his works should honor him as he is hidden in his suffering.[22]

The "again" in this passage is instructive. It indicates that God was once recognized and now needs to be recognized, again, but via suffering and cross rather than via the created things. But are these created things without any theological utility? Further to the above, the explanation to thesis 24 is instructive:

Indeed the law is holy [Rom. 7:12], every gift of God good [1 Tim. 4:4], and everything that is created exceedingly good, as in Gen. 1[:31]. But as stated above, the person who has not been brought low, reduced to nothing through cross and suffering, takes credit for works and wisdom and does not give credit to God. That person thus misuses and defiles the gifts of God.[23]

Without the experience of the cross, according to Luther, even creation can become for us a pathway to self-exultation rather than a reflection of the God who has left the divine witness everywhere. The human who has not experienced this "crossing" mistakes their good works and wisdom as their own. The experience of the cross, however, reorients us to the end that we are able to see the visible (*visiblia*), which necessarily includes the things that are made (*quae facta sunt*). The distinction is that these made things are no longer understood instrumentally—as per thesis 19 wherein they were dangerously used as a bridge to perceive the invisible things (including sovereignty). Instead, the things that are made, the visible things, are now understood by way of the perception of the cross. The things that have been made are brought into focus instead of being the lens for viewing invisible things. The visible things are no longer apprehended instrumentally, but via the instruments of suffering and cross they have become data[24] for our understanding of God. Via suffering and the cross we can look at the visible, created things as well as the more posterior things and learn something about God. The Rabbis imagine that the former includes the knots of the tefillin (metaphorically "worn" by both God and faithful Jews). Luther imagines that the posterior things includes the created order. We turn to Luther's reading now to explore a bit more about whom we discuss when we engage in God-talk, in theology.

CREATION UNDER THE CROSS: SOVEREIGNTY

Regin Prenter wrote *Creation and Redemption* in an effort to correct his perceived imbalance in Luther studies toward the topic of soteriology.[25] His work
was part of a broader movement called Scandinavian Creation Theology,
which included the work of Gustaf Wingren and Knut Løgstrup that had as its
goal an apprehension of Luther's rich theology of creation.[26] This correction
is especially apt in the context of North America where the created world in
understood, as per Rowe's analysis, as *resource*. This stands in marked contrast to the worldview of the Indigenous people in the Americas:

> First, when the word [creation] is used in a Christian sense, it seems to Indian
> peoples to connote a heavy dose of reification that is completely lacking in any
> Indian intellectual tradition, i.e., creation has been historically and continues to
> be objectified as a thing, something that is quite apart from human beings and
> to which humans relate from the outside. This objectification is strikingly dif-
> ferent from the traditional Indian sense that all of the created world—including
> every tree and rock—is just as alive and sentient as human beings are, and the
> further sense that Indian people have that we are related to all of these sentient
> persons in creation.[27]

Careful readers of Luther, however, note that the above description does not
fit Luther even though it might well describe the theological proclivities of a
good number of Lutherans. Luther had a decidedly more robust theology of
creation than many of his forebears. He is able, for instance, to affirm that the
sun and moon are words of God as surely as the apostle Paul and the person
who reads his or these words are words of God.[28] Indeed, the Word of God is
present in the very body of a hen.[29]

And yet, for Luther, the human holds a certain pride of place in the cosmos. The human alone is created for knowledge of God.[30] The human is
given dominion over the earth, now understood in terms of "industry and
skill,"[31] over an innocent earth that is burdened along with the curse of the
human.[32] This "dominion" is fractured because of sin and our stewardship of
the cosmos is broken and in need of healing.[33] Luther's theology, then, is far
removed from the theology of creation evident in the captains of industry who
do not see the earth as in need of care. Rowe invites us to ask how a theology
of the cross might provide leverage for disrupting an industrial imaginary—
especially against the backdrop of a sovereign God in whose image capitalists
are made to the end that they can do as they as they please. In a way, Rowe
is inviting us to ask how a theology of the cross can bring balance back to
our image of God's *potentia* to the end that creation and redemption really do
achieve some level of balance for the flourishing of creation. *The Heidelberg*

Disputation provides us some aid in abetting a theologian of the cross's counterpoint to capitalist common sense:

> In other words, the person who wishes to become wise does not seek wisdom by progressing toward it but becomes a fool by regressing into seeking folly. Likewise, one who wishes to have much power, honor, pleasure, satisfaction in all things must flee rather than seek power, honor, pleasure, and satisfaction in all things. This is the wisdom which is folly to the world.[34]

It is perhaps impossible to overstate the explosive potential of this passage which implies both the indicative and imperative moods. The indicative is implied in that the theologian of the cross has been given a lens by which they see God's doing precisely what this passage commends to the reader. God has divested sovereignty in order to be sovereign and because of this, we can now truly see. But the sovereignty that emerges is cross-shaped and therefore balanced (although perceived as imbalanced by theologians and economists of glory). Rowe's attention to Holy Saturday is helpful in this regard. God's sovereignty can be imagined as a Holy Saturday sovereignty where the divine does battle with forces in the halls of hell.[35] Balance always betrays a betweenness—even, or perhaps especially, with God. This is God's *modus operandi* and this way of being is also God's way of being human. This divinely self-imposed condition for God's way of being human obtains for God's relationship to being per se. In contradistinction to a nominalist ontology, Luther sees God implicated in being such that he can write in his explanation of the first part of the creed in the Large Catechism that

> This is knowledge of great significance, but an even great treasure. For here we see how the Father has given to us himself with all creation and has abundantly provided for us in this life, apart from the fact that he has also showered us with inexpressible eternal blessings through his Son and the Holy Spirit, as we shall hear.[36]

The first person of the Trinity is also available to us in the being of creation. But God is not only given in creation; God suffers in creation.[37] God is not only nailed to the cross but also pulsing in the veins of the earth being stripped in order that our cell phones keep us connected. God is not only battling Satan in hell, she is also pointing out the lies of climate changes deniers in the voice of Greta Thunberg. God is not only blowing out the Spirit of life from the cross in John 19:30,[38] she is also breathing hope in defiance of crosshairs searching still to silence Malala Yousafzai. God still speaks her truth from the tomb when Autumn Peltier from Wiikwemkoong First Nation reminds us that "we can't eat money or drink oil."[39] Sovereignty under the cross is unexpected; it is invested in divesting itself of worldly wisdom and success defined in terms of progress. Indigenous peoples in North America hold tenaciously to the theme of balance because they have experienced progress as rape: of their bodies, of their lives, their languages and their spiritualities.[40] The tonic for a sovereignty imbalanced is the image of God dead on the cross and God proclaimed in creation among the weakest and least. In pondering why God did not simply send the angels Michael, Gabriel, *et alia* in order to simply eradicate the forces of evil in show of sovereign strength, Luther writes:

> Precisely because the enemies boast of their power and might, God wants to destroy them with the mouths of babes and sucklings, as butter melts on the fire; or if they are not to be destroyed, in their great wisdom they should become children.[41]

In accord with his broader strategy of reading the bible from the vantage point of the cross, Luther here invites us to imagine that the cross and the cradle share a certain congruity in that weakness is where God is found. In a world that lauds and has always applauded independence and the myth of the self-made, the cross and cradle both preach because they slaughter this lie. In our being born and in our dying we are utterly dependent, our possibilities as actors thoroughly dependent on those willing to move our arms. Of course, this perplexes and vexes the strong-armed. Luther offers an alternate vision:

> In order to ordain this strength, He degrades Himself so profoundly and becomes a man, yes, even degrades Himself below all men, as it is written in Psalm 22:6: "I am a worm and no man; scorned by men, and despised by the people." Therefore he goes about in poverty . . . [42]

Luther invites us to ponder Christ as a worm, here described as being below the human, in order to speak of God's reversal of human expectations. But another complementary reading of the text might obtain if we are willing to take a lesson from our Indigenous friends. Indigenous folk on Turtle Island imagine a world where all beings are animated with a life force that makes us relatives. Human are not superior, and in fact are dependent on the benevolent care of the animals who give themselves up for our sustenance.[43] God in Christ as a worm from the vantage point of this more generous reading of creation might enable us to see Christ in another light: as one with "all of our relations."[44] Christ as worm—the crucial factor in the success of backyard compost bins—might be especially helpful in our current climate crisis, where images of recycling Jesus might need to supplant a Caesar-like Christ. Such would be a cross-shaped sovereignty, wherein the Sovereign becomes what the community needs for the sake of the well-being of all. This presumes a

God who is free over even her sovereignty. Can we imagine a human made and remade in such an image?[45]

CREATION AT THE CROSS: FREEDOM

Overy-Brown notes the importance of distinctions in the work of Luther. The use of distinction in service of clarifying concepts is, of course, formed by his training in the medieval tradition and a perdurable feature in Luther's work, as evident in his treatment of freedom in *The Heidelberg Disputation*:

> 13. Free will, after [the fall into] sin, exists in name only, and when "it does what is within it," it commits a mortal sin.[46]

Luther distinguishes the name "free will" from human activity and recognizes that the two do not cohere. While we can assert some choice in how we sin, our inability to prescind from sin precludes predicating "free will" to the human subject, a position iterated in *The Bondage of the Will* (1525), wherein Luther asserts that "Free Will" is a divine name.[47] As noted above, Overy-Brown delineates this use of freedom from that dialectical framing of it in the *Freedom of the Christian*, wherein the Christian is simultaneously a free lord and a bound servant. Together, he outlines how the images of freedom in these two documents constitutes a paradox and proposes the utility of understanding the freedom that can be accorded the Christian under "heteronomy," hopeful that this can open the possibility for freedom to have political utility.

Of course, readers of Luther are often also readers of Lutherans who struggled to make some sense of this paradox by distinguishing freedom in terms of spiritual and civil accounts of it in the Book of Concord.[48] This has a certain utility, although the distinction between these two is drawn by a very fine line that sometimes breaks, and reminds us that these are perilous waters.[49] Reframing freedom in light of the cross might allow some vantage points from which to tell the tale of freedom lightly: mindful that the divide between the inner and outer is porous, as is the divide between the spiritual and civil.

Luther's accounting of freedom in *The Heidelberg Disputation* only allows the possibility of doing good passively.[50] This "good" references doing right with respect to God, even while Luther sometimes allows the possibility that humans are able to will well in the civil and natural realm, insofar as we can discern good—such that Luther commends that the emperor who is an honest and competent Turk is to be preferred to one who is a dishonest and incompetent Christian. Spiritually deficient people can will well in the civil realm.

But herein lies the rub. Much harm has been done the world round with the best of intentions. Our intentions are ever mixed, and evidenced, for instance, in the role of the churches in state supported attempt to eradicate First Nations on Turtle Island. On the one hand, a few of the faithful involved in the running of residential schools, for instance, really desired to assist First Peoples, albeit so thoroughly mistaken in what aid looks like as to be tragic. On the other hand, too many of the faithful betrayed, in their actions in these schools *et alia*, a demonic grab for power in the colonial project and displayed a thorough disregard of basic human rights. The pessimistic edge of Luther's account of freedom seems well placed in light of this reality, and the manifold ways in which this story is told the world round. But there is more to Luther than first meets the eye.

Luther's account of the human in thesis 14 really does propose the capacity of doing some good, even while discounting an active role in the good achieved. Does that mean that the human acts in the mode of a robot, or such? It might but I don't think it needs to be seen as such.

First, it needs to be remembered that in this account of the passive Christian, God is at work. The nature of God's working is such that "God's love does not find, but creates, that which is pleasing to it."[51] The pastoral significance of this begins in the recognition that we are the loveable object that God creates by loving us. He further identifies this as "the love born of the cross, which turns in the direction where it does not find good, which it may enjoy, but where it may confer good upon the evil and needy person."[52] This love not only claims us but also names us as beloved and so worthy of love both in terms of being loved and having the capacity to love.

Luther famously distinguishes between the human "activities" of faith and love. Faith itself is already a work being worked in us as evidenced in Luther's assertion *"in ipsa fide Christus adest"* (in faith itself Christ is present). Faith as trust arrives when Christ encounters us. Faith is the shape of Christ between me and God. Love in like manner is the shape Christ takes between me and my neighbor, human and not. This love is mediated by Christ insofar as my relationship with Christ involves me in this those one whom Christ loves. This love of Christ (in both the objective and subjective genitive) could be seen as the *heteros* of Overy-Brown's heteronormativity. Of course, it might be objected, that a freedom that is normed by anything other than the *autos* is no freedom. But freedom is not located, for Luther, in the self but in the God who alone has the name and the claim of freedom. Our freedom, then, is participatory. We are free only—but wholly—in God. We are free as we participate in the love of God. And just as God's love is aimed at the other, so our love for God finds its home in the other. Who is this other? Luther names the neighbour as other, but more needs to be said in countering the hubris of the Anthropocene.

The Johannine claim that God so loved the world (*kosmos*) is a cosmological claim (John 3:16). In an era of the Anthropocene a heteronormative freedom lives out a participatory love in attention to the delicate ecological balance in which we find ourselves. There is, of course, an anthropologically centred approach to the question of environmentalism, asking what we can do to ensure the continuation of *homo sapiens*—sometimes framed in such a way that the fate of the world is on the shoulders of our species. The cosmos will, of course, have a future with or without us. An indigenous understanding of the human as the least and weakest of all of Creator's creations serves as an important balance to this valuation of the human and might assist us in reading Luther beyond Luther. Indeed, Luther provides us with some resources for doing this in his rich appreciation for creation. This is evident in his assertion that "Christians hold converse with the trees and all else that grows on earth" and pointing out that the fields are full of sermons.[53] Luther's rich theology of creation allows us to see all of created reality as our relations, but also as our neighbours whom we love. But love without reciprocity is no longer love. Love of the neighbour is not unidirectional, and so in caring for creation we commit ourselves—if we enter into this task with integrity—to being cared for by creation. This is manifestly evident in an Indigenous imaginary, but patently obfuscated in a colonial and global capitalists worldviews. Being free to love the world means being bound to receiving care from this same cosmos. Such is our freedom, such is God's sovereignty that balances creation and redemption; freedom and service; and love and faith.

SOME CONCLUDING COMMENTS

Freedom and sovereignty both gain meaningful purchase when theologians of the cross attend to the congruity of creation and redemption in grace and promise. Reframing freedom and sovereignty is desperately needed in a world in which eco-justice calls forth a new way of being human and accounting for humanity in the circle of creation rather than at the top of a hierarchical pyramid.

Terra Rowe has called us to subject the notion of sovereignty to the crucible of the cross and Robert Overy-Brown has bid us to subject freedom to a canon other than the self. These are both singularly important contribution which I have explored under the Indigenous call to attend to balance, or harmony in all things. The crux of the matter, then is that there is no freedom without justice and peace. This holds true for Luther's accounting of the Christian life in his Heidelberg Disputation and beyond. Some 430 years after the writing of *The Heidelberg Disputation*, the Declaration of Human Rights by the United Nations was penned in support of justice for all. However, COVID-19 has made manifestly evident that this remains an aspiration rather than an achievement, and the climate regularly reminds us that freedom for humans without justice for the cosmos is a freedom in name alone. Now, as much as ever, Christians, along with all people of faiths and people of good conscience, are called to bind freedom to justice and peace, for all, including the cosmos.

NOTES

1. Elizabeth Kolbert, *The Sixth Extinction: An Unnatural History* (New York: Picador, 2015), 103. Kolbert notes that the end-Permian era resulted in the loss of "something like ninety percent of all species on earth."

2. Allen Jorgenson, "Empire, Eschatology and Stolen Land," *Dialog* 49, no. 2 (2010): 115–22.

3. George E. Tinker, *American Indian Liberation: A Theology of Sovereignty* (Maryknoll, NY: Orbis Books, 2008), 7.

4. Randy S. Woodley, *Shalom and the Community of Creation: An Indigenous "VIsion"* (Grand Rapids, MI: Eerdmans, 2012), 18, 32. For the importance of the theme of balance, see also Clara Sue Kidwell, Homer Noley, and George Tinker E, *A Native American Theology* (New York: Orbis Books, 2002), 23; Alfred, *Peace, Power, Righteousness*, 12.

5. Woodley, *Shalom and the Community of Creation*, 81: "The idea that all people and things are related to each other includes all of humanity. This idea opens us up to the possibility of once again becoming the family we already are. . . . A worldview based on reciprocity and familial relatedness also has tremendous ecological implications. In humanity's dependence upon the earth, we allow ourselves renewed opportunities for sustaining our planet and for finding fresh prospects for developing food, water, and renewable energy."

6. See above, p. 158.

7. See above, p. 144.

8. With thanks to Matthew Anderson for his insights on this, and for other helpful comments regarding this chapter.

9. Louis Dupré, *Passage to Modernity: An Essay in the Hermeneutics of Nature and Culture* (New Haven, CT: Yale University Press, 1993), 123: "Scotus was the last great theologian to attempt to reconcile the Greek idea of divine sufficiency with the existence of a contingent world order dependent on a divine decision. He presented the entire order with all it implied as the effect of a single divine decision made in the beginning, thus dispensing God from ever having to react to creaturely actions as they developed in time since such a reaction would have rendered God dependent upon his creation."

10. Heiko A. Oberman, *The Harvest of Medieval Theology* (Grand Rapids, MI: Baker Academic, 2000), 152.

11. See Dupré, *Passage to Modernity*, 124: "Nor do the voluntarist theologies account for the outburst of creative activity in the early modern age, although more than any other factor this awareness of creative power contributed to the new perception of freedom. Freedom henceforth became a self-choice, more than a choice that selects among given alternatives. It refused to be restricted by the given."

12. Martin Luther, "The Heidelberg Disputation (1520)," in *The Annotated Luther, Volume 1, The Roots of Reform*, ed. Timothy J. Wengert, trans. Harold J. Grimm (Minneapolis, MN: Fortress Press, 2015), 81.

13. See Harold J. Grimm's "Introduction," to Martin Luther, "The Heidelberg Disputation (1520)." In *Luther's Works, Volume 31, Career of the Reformer: I*, ed. Harold J. Grimm, trans. Harold J. Grimm (Philadelphia: Fortress Press, 1957), 37, 38.

14. Venial sins are understood to be sins, which while serious, do not merit damnation. Mortal sins, by contrast, do.

15. Martin Luther, *Dr. Martin Luthers Werke, 1. Bande* (Weimar: Böhlau, 1883), 360, 17–20.

16. TAL 1, 83 n. 22.

17. "Conspicio," Latinitium, accessed January 5, 2020, https://www.latinitium.com/latin-dictionaries?t=lsn10586,lsn10587,do541.

18. "Intellego," Latinitium, accessed January 5, 2020,. https://www.latinitium.com/latin-dictionaries?t=lsn24114,do260.

19. TAL 1, 78.

20. *Tanakh, The Holy Scriptures: The New JPS Translation According to the Traditional Hebrew Text* (New York: Jewish Publication Society, 1985). Exodus 33:21–23. The word "back" here translates *achrei*, which is in the singular. The rabbis understood this noun to reference the Tephillin-knot found at the back of the head of G-d. See Rashi's comment on this point: "Exodus 33," Sefaris, accessed December 11, 2020, https://www.sefaria.org/Exodus.33.23?lang=bi&with=Rashi&lang2=bi. The Vulgate, which Luther quotes, has *posteriora*, which is plural and comparative. That the head Tephillin-knot was connected to the arm Tephillin-knot could be the basis for rendering this in the plural in the Septuagint translation, as per email conversation with Daniel Maoz, December 11, 2020. Further, the use of *achry* with verbs of motion imply a position of discipleship and so an overtone of this might resonate for certain readings of this text. See Dennis Stoutenburg, "'Out Of My Sight!,' 'Get Behind Me!,' Or 'Follow After Me!': There is No Choice in God's Kingdom," *Journal of the Evangelical Theological Society* 36, no. 1 (March 1993): 175.

21. Cf. John D Caputo, *Cross and Cosmos: A Theology of Difficult Glory* (Bloomington, IN: Indiana University Press, 2019), 274, 275. Caputo suggests rendering this as the "backside" of God and asserts that "*[p]osteriora dei* means a concealed and radically absconded God, vulnerable and mortal, contingent and non-sovereign . . . . The *posterior dei* refers to a God of the gaps, not one who fills gaps but one who opens them, exposing abyss within abyss." This is helpful but not yet enough in that Luther also affirms that the theologian of the cross understands (*intelligit*) not only the *posterior dei* but also the *visibilia*. Moreover, both of these are viewed via suffering and the cross. It is not only a gap that is opened, but a gap through which we see God and God's doings anew.

22. TAL 1, 99.

23. TAL 1, 101.

24. *Data* in Latin is the perfect passive for what have been given.

25. Regin Prenter, *Creation and Redemption*, trans. Theodor I. Jensen (Philadelphia: Fortess Press, 1967).

26. See also Gustaf Wingren, *Creation and Law* (Eugene, OR: Wipf and Stock, 2003); Knud E. Løgstrup, *Metaphysics Volume I*, trans. Russel L. Dees (Milwaukee, WI: Marquette University Press, 1995); Knud E. Løgstrup, *Metaphysics Volume II* (Milwaukee, WI: Marquette University Press, 1995); Gustaf Wingren, *Creation and Gospel* (Toronto, ON: Edwin Mellen Press, 1979). For recent developments in this see Niels Henrik Gregersen, Bengt Kristensson Uggla, and Trygve Wyller, *Reformation Theology for a Post-Secular Age: Løgstrup, Prenter, Wingren, and the Future of Scandinavian Creation Theology* (Göttingen: Vandenhoeck & Ruprecht, 2017).

27. Kidwell, Noley, and Tinker, *A Native American Theology*, 34–35.

28. Martin Luther, *Luther's Works, Volume 1, Lectures on Genesis, Chapters 1–5*, ed. Jaroslav Pelikan, trans. George V. Schick (St. Louis, MO: Concordia Publishing House, 1963), 21.

29. LW 1, 53.

30. LW 1, 80: "Then it is shown here that man was especially created for the knowledge and worship of God; for the Sabbath was not ordained for sheep and cows but for men, that in them the knowledge of God might be developed and might increase."

31. LW 1, 67.

32. LW 1, 204.

33. LW 1, 133.

34. TAL 1, 101.

35. Of course, how we construe God on Holy Saturday is not unrelated to how we see ourselves in the same. Helpful in this regard is the invitation to consider that "through the eschatological and mystical act of baptism that followers of Jesus participate in the curious [Holy Saturday] voyage of Christ" See Matthew R. Anderson, "The Curious Voyage of Christ: *Katábasis, Anábasis*, and the New Testament," *Les Études Classiques* 83 (2015): 394.

36. Timothy J. Wengert and Robert Kolb, eds., *The Book of Concord: The Confessions of the Evangelical Lutheran Church* (Minneapolis, MN: Fortress Press, 2000), 433.

37. Jaqueline A. Bussie, in exploring Luther's words to women suffering miscarriage notes his appeal to the presence of God in suffering. She writes: "According to Luther in this passage, hope is not found in eschatological postponement of justice but instead in our very own heartache, tears, and groans, signifying an implicit hope that God is imminent and present with eyes and ears wide open to see and hear them. "Luther's Hope for the World," in *The Global Luther: A Theologian for Modern Times*, ed. Christine Helmer (Minneapolois: Fortress Press, 2009), 120.

38. The Greek has Jesus hand over the Spirit: *paradōken to pneuma*.

39. The Canadian Press, "'We Can't Eat Money or Drink Oil,' Autumn Peltier Tells UN | CBC News," CBC, September 28, 2019, https://www.cbc.ca/news/world/canadian-indigenous-water-activist-autumn-peltier-addresses-un-on-clean-water-1.5301559.

40. Barbara Rossing notes the way in which iconography of empires makes use of rape: "Women's bodies represent enslaved nations; spectacular marble sculptures personify conquered lands as feminine bodies, showing graphic scenes of brutal rape and torture." "Reimagining Eschatology Toward Healing and Hope," in *Planetary Solidarity: Global Women's Voices on Christian Doctrine and Climate Justice*, eds. Grace Ji-Sun Kim and Hilda P. Koster (Minneapolis, MN: Fortress Press, 2017), 339.

41. Martin Luther, "Psalm 8," in *Luther's Works, Volume 12, Selected Psalms I*, ed. Jaroslav Pelikan, trans. Jaroslav Pelikan (St. Louis, MO: Concordia Publishing House, 1955), 115.

42. Luther, LW 12, 110.

43. See Basil Johnston, *Ojibway Heritage* (Toronto, ON: McClelland and Stewart, 2008), 49–50.

44. See footnote 5 above.

45. This is a question asked by Mary Solberg when her epistemology of the cross illumines us as interdependent and made for the end of "mutual moral accountability." See her chapter "All That Matters: What An Epistemology of the Cross is Good For," in *Cross Examinations: Readings on the Meaning of the Cross Today,"* ed. Marit Trelstad (Minneapolis: Fortress Press, 2006), 143.

46. TAL 1, 95.

47. Martin Luther, "The Bondage of the Will (1525)," in *Luther's Works, Volume 33, Career of the Reformer, III*, ed. Philip S. Watson, trans. Philip S. Watson (Philadelphia: Fortress Press, 1972), 68.

48. Timothy J. Wengert and Robert Kolb, *The Book of Concord: The Confessions of the Evangelical Lutheran Church*, 517–20.

49. Schleiermacher argues quite cogently that the spiritual life of people emerges out of material processes and so the sharp distinction sometimes drawn between spiritual and civil is blurred. See Friedrich Schleiermacher, *On the Doctrine of Election, with Special Reference to the Aphorisms of Dr. Bretschneider*, trans. Iain G. Nicol and Allen Jorgenson (Louisville, KY: Westminster John Knox Press, 2012), 62–63.

50. See Matin Luther, *Dr. Martin Luthers Werke, 1. Bande* (Weimar: Böhlau, 1883), 354, 7–8: *"Liberum arbitrium post peccatum potest in bonum potential subiectiva, in malum vero active semper."*

51. TAL 1, 104.

52. TAL 1, 104, 105.

53. LW 28, 180 and LW 1, 209.

BIBLIOGRAPHY

Alfred, Taiaiake. *Peace, Power, Righteousness: An Indigenous Manifesto*. Second Edition. Oxford: Oxford University Press, 2009.

Anderson, Matthew R. "The Curious Voyage of Christ: Katábasis, Anábasis, and the New Testament." *Les Études Classiques* 83 (2015): 385–96.

Busie, Jaqueline A. "Luther's Hope for the World: Responsible Christian Discourse Today." In *The Global Luther: A Theologian for Modern Times*, edited by Christine Helmer. Minneapolis: Fortress Press, 2009, 113–28.

The Canadian Press. "'We Can't Eat Money or Drink Oil,' Autumn Peltier Tells UN | CBC News." CBC, September 28, 2019. https://www.cbc.ca/news/world/canadian-indigenous-water-activist-autumn-peltier-addresses-un-on-clean-water-1.5301559.

Caputo, John D. *Cross and Cosmos: A Theology of Difficult Glory*. Bloomington, IN: Indiana University Press, 2019.

Dupré, Louis. *Passage to Modernity: An Essay in the Hermeneutics of Nature and Culture*. New Haven, CT: Yale University Press, 1993.

"Exodus 33." Sefaris. Accessed December 11, 2020. https://www.sefaria.org/Exodus .33.23?lang=bi&with=Rashi&lang2=bi.

Gregersen, Niels Henrik, Bengt Kristensson Uggla, and Trygve Wyller. *Reformation Theology for a Post-Secular Age: Løgstrup, Prenter, Wingren, and the Future of Scandinavian Creation Theology*. Göttingen: Vandenhoeck & Ruprecht, 2017.

Johnston, Basil. *Ojibway Heritage*. Toronto, ON: McClelland and Stewart, 2008.

Jorgenson, Allen. "Empire, Eschatology and Stolen Land." *Dialog* 49, no. 2 (2010): 115–22.

Kidwell, Clara Sue, Homer Noley, and George Tinker E. *A Native American Theology*. New York: Orbis Books, 2002.

Kolbert, Elizabeth. *The Sixth Extinction: An Unnatural History*. New York: Picador, 2015.

Latinium. Accessed January 6, 2021. https://www.latinitium.com/index/.

Løgstrup, Knud E. *Metaphysics Volume I*. Translated by Russel L. Dees. Milwaukee, WI: Marquette University Press, 1995.

———. *Metaphysics Volume II*. Milwaukee, WI: Marquette University Press, 1995.

Luther, Martin. "The Bondage of the Will (1525)." In *Luther's Works, Volume 33, Career of the Reformer, III*, edited by Philip S. Watson, translated by Philip S. Watson, 3–294. Philadelphia: Fortress Press, 1972.

———. *Dr. Martin Luthers Werke, 1. Bande*. Weimar: Böhlau, 1883.

———. "The Heidelberg Disputation (1520)." In *Luther's Works, Volume 31, Career of the Reformer:I*, edited by Harold J. Grimm, translated by Harold J. Grimm, 327–77. Philadelphia: Fortress Press, 1957.

———. "The Heidelberg Disputation. " In *The Annotated Luther, Volume 1, The Roots of Reform*, edited by Timothy J. Wengert, translated by Harold J. Grimm, 67–120. Minneapolis, MN: Fortress Press, 2015.

———. *Luther's Works, Volume 1, Lectures on Genesis, Chapters 1–5*, edited by Jaroslav Pelikan, translated by George V. Schick. St. Louis: Concordia Publishing House, 1963.

———. "Psalm 8." In *Luther's Works, Volume 12, Selected Psalms I*, edited by Jaroslav Pelikan, translated by Jaroslav Pelikan, 97–138. St. Louis: Concordia Publishing House, 1955.

Oberman, Heiko A. *The Harvest of Medieval Theology*. Grand Rapids, MI: Baker Academic, 2000.

Prenter, Regin. *Creation and Redemption*. Translated by Theodor I. Jensen. Philadelphia: Fortress Press, 1967.

Rossing, Barbara. "Reimagining Eschatology Toward Healing and Hope." In *Planetary Solidarity: Global Women's Voices on Christian Doctrine and Climate Justice,* edited by Grace Ji-Sun Kim and Hilda P. Koster, 325–47. Minneapolis, MN: Fortress Press, 2017.

Schleiermacher, Friedrich. *On the Doctrine of Election, with Special Reference to the Aphorisms of Dr. Bretschneider*. Translated by Iain G. Nicol and Allen Jorgenson. Louisville, KY: Westminster John Knox Press, 2012.

Solberg, Mary. "All That Matters: What An Epistemology of the Cross is Good For." In *Cross Examinations: Readings on the Meaning of the Cross Today,"* edited by Marit Trelstad, 139–53. Minneapolis: Fortress Press, 2006.

Stoutenburg, Dennis. '"Out Of My Sight!" "Get Behind Me!" or "Follow After Me!": There Is No Choice in God's Kingdom," *Journal of the Evangelical Theological Society* 36, no. 1 (March 1993): 173–78.

Tanakh, The Holy Scriptures: The New JPS Translation According to the Traditional Hebrew Text. New York: Jewish Publication Society, 1985.

Tinker, George E. *American Indian Liberation: A Theology of Sovereignty*. Maryknoll, NY: Orbis Books, 2008.

Wengert, Timothy J. and Robert Kolb, eds. *The Book of Concord: The Confessions of the Evangelical Lutheran Church*. Minneapolis, MN: Fortress Press, 2000.

Wingren, Gustaf. *Creation and Gospel*. Toronto, ON: Edwin Mellen Press, 1979.

———. *Creation and Law*. Eugene, OR: Wipf and Stock, 2003.

Woodley, Randy S. *Shalom and the Community of Creation: An Indigenous Vision*. Grand Rapids, MI: Eerdmans, 2012.

Chapter 10

Luther, Politics, and the Production of Theological Knowledge

Christine Helmer

Frustrations with inheritances of Lutheran theology are being articulated by Lutheran theologians concerned with human rights. These theologians, represented in this volume, have become "woke" to problematic aspects of the Lutheran theological tradition that they see to be complicit in the abuse of human rights and freedoms. Theological ideas derived from Martin Luther, such as the orders of creation and the doctrine of the two kingdoms, are criticized for their legitimation of oppressive political regimes such as National Socialism, as Bonhoeffer pointed out in the 1940s; the 1960s establishing of apartheid in Namibia, as Marit Trelstad shows in her chapter "A Non-Universal Lutheran Theology: Contextual Theological Practice in Namibia"; and white Christian privilege in contemporary American society, as Caryn Riswold argues in "Already Freed, Christians Should Serve (Cake): Religious Freedom Claims and Christian Privilege." As Mary Lowe claims in "A Lutheran View of Conscience: Bound and Free, Constrained and Embodied," even a Lutheran church noted for its progressive stance on same-sex marriages and gay clergy, such as the Evangelical Lutheran Church in America (ELCA), is not immune to the deleterious effects of the appropriation of Luther's idea of conscience. LGBTQIA+ people continue to be vulnerable to harm in the ELCA as well as in American society. Theologians thus working from within the Lutheran tradition call out the ways in which doctrines have functioned to establish racial, gender, and cis-heteronormative hierarchies and thereby falsify other theological ideas concerning the divine pronouncement of goodness on the wonderful diversity of creatures God has made.

While some doctrines prop up mechanisms of oppression, others are oriented to justice. The Lutheran theologians named above advance new possibilities of Lutheran resources with the aim of establishing a doctrinal basis for justice-creating practices. Luther's epistemology of two theologians that he articulated in the 1518 Heidelberg Disputation is a powerful critical tool. The theologian of glory is one who misuses God's name to legitimate the oppression of marginalized populations, while the theologian of the cross discerns the reality of divine grace in human suffering and seeks to liberate victims from injustices that perpetuate their suffering. Another important text is the second part of Luther's 1520 treatise *On the Freedom of the Christian*. Luther dedicates this section to the topic of love of neighbor as the "external" reality of the self who has been freed by Christ as her "inner" reality. Faith that frees the inner aspect of the self from its selfish desires inevitably and necessarily orients the self's interests to the neighbor's needs. Robert Overy-Brown uses Luther's notion of neighborly love in his "Retrieving Luther's Theology of Freedom for a Contemporary Ethic of Heteronomy" to argue that the Christian working in the world must be concerned with care for the other. Like Lowe, Overy-Brown suggests that a political discourse of justice can be absorbed into the Lutheran ethic of love of neighbor in order to concretely prescribe how a neighbor's needs are to be taken on as one's own. Luther's "formal" ethic of love of neighbor can be concretized by contemporary justice norms. The "external" freedom of the Christian is exercised as advocacy on behalf of the needs of others who are diminished by contemporary social, political, and ecclesial deployments of power.

This book's aim is to show that contemporary Lutheran theologians are indeed concerned with justice, particularly in view of the 1948 Universal Declaration of Human Rights. This document was created after a time that had witnessed depraved humanity effecting the ruthless genocide of European Jews and the torture and murder of political dissidents, the disabled, and the queer. In a context in which war had displaced millions, the document uplifted "the inherent dignity and the equal and inalienable rights of all members of the human family [as] the foundation of freedom, justice and peace." It attested to a powerful and hopeful vision of humanity that hate and evil could not annihilate.

The function of this statement is not to point to the world as it is. In 1948 as today, social, ecclesial, and political reality is characterized by the inequalities of white privilege, the patriarchy, heteronormativity, wealth, and empire. The statement is entitled a "declaration." It declares an ideal view of humanity that, while not empirically real, is no less real. As an ideal, it is a reality in the language that picks out an alternative to the empirical degradation of humanity. It spells out a view of the world in which every member of the human race is endowed with "inherent dignity." A global society of peaceful co-existence can be imagined on this ideal foundation. It is an ideal orienting both thought and politics. A new possibility of thinking about every member of the human race as inherently worthy of equal rights and freedoms assists the work of communities and churches, societies and politics. Reality as it "ought" to be is the goal that should orient political practice.

It is fitting that theologians commemorate the sixtieth anniversary of the Universal Declaration on Human Rights. Theologians (like philosophers) are trained to work with universals, concepts that have to do with features common to all members of a group. According to the Declaration, a universal feature of all humans is the endowment of every individual, irrespective of any difference, with dignity. Theologians also do their work by conceptually distinguishing between features that on the surface look similar across a number of members of a group, but from another perspective, exhibit differences between them. Distinguishing features among humans can be race, gender, sexual orientation, and mental and physical ability. Yet these differences, according to the logic of the Universal Declaration, are insignificant in view of the equality of dignity assigned to every human person.

Theologians also have a distinctive vocabulary they deploy to identify reality. They use terms such as systemic sin in order expose the degrading mechanisms in contemporary culture and politics directed at women, African Americans, Latinx, and LGBTQIA+ persons. Theologians use the language of redemption to point to reality as it ought to be. They deploy the term, "love of neighbor" to prescribe behaviors that facilitate the neighbor's justice and flourishing. Theologians can thus take a historic statement, such as the Universal Declaration, and examine its truth from theological perspective: God endows each created human being with the grace of goodness and love and God works together with persons to establish justice for those whose humanity—whose *imago dei*—has been effaced by sin and evil.

This volume's contributors are primarily Lutheran theologians who identify with a progressive political agenda. The intellectual legacy of these theologians is particularly well suited to articulating the theological truth at stake in the Universal Declaration. These theologians are specifically attuned to how critical reason can and must be mustered to pay attention to how Christian doctrines have been misused to perpetuate injustices. They adapt critical reason to work out the theological perspective from which the reality of injustice is named. The question I consider in my response to these contributions has to do with the métier of theology as the production of knowledge. How can the theological privileging of critical reason—its diagnostic and political aspects—be complemented by a recovery of theology's contemplative dimension? Or in other words, how can contemporary progressive Lutheran theology with its focus on the *vita activa* benefit from the *vita contemplativa*?

THEOLOGY AND POLITICS

Mainline Protestant theologians have recently become interested in connecting their work to politics. Various publishing venues have become available for dissemination of this scholarship. The journal *Political Theology*, founded in 1999[1]; a website devoted to the emerging and ongoing discussions in political theology[2]; and new opportunities for funding have all garnered attention for this growing field.[3] In some respects, this development can be seen as the liberal Protestant complement to what has been a longer effort on the part of evangelical theologians to connect theology to a political agenda. The "culture wars" as played out in Protestant circles over the past three decades has significantly shaped the landscape of American religious politics as well as configurations of mainline Protestant denominations, many of them splitting into two churches of the same denomination with respect to opposing views on queer persons. The 2009 churchwide decision of the Evangelical Lutheran Church in America (ELCA), for example, to permit same-sex unions and the ordination of gay clergy led to the exit of parishes and pastors who disagreed with the vote and their creation of new Lutheran synods and even a (nonaccredited) seminary.[4] While there is a theoretical difference between the scholarly field of political theology and the application of theology to a political agenda, it is evident that Protestant theologians have become more and more attuned to the social, cultural, and political context in which they do their work and to which they speak. Even Lutheran theologians, who for a long time have been cautioned to keep law and gospel, politics and Christ, absolutely distinct, are embarked on in constructive endeavors to imbue their theological commitments with a political dimension.

The recent Lutheran theological interest in politics is to be noted, given the aversion in late twentieth-century Lutheran theology to confusing theology and ethics. This caveat was itself a reaction to the disturbing legacy of German Lutheran theologians who supported German nationalism before and during World War II. Emanuel Hirsch, for example, identified the area demarcated theologically by "law" as subject to divine ordinance. Political obedience to the Führer was required because God, as creator of the political realm, is hidden behind its human operatives. Hirsch appealed to Luther's interpretation of Romans 13, whereby citizens are required to obey the government without any criteria as to whether that government is oriented to justice or to fascism.[5] Thus, Hirsch legitimated Nazi rule by creating a political theology on the basis of Luther's theological theory of the two empires of church and state. Canadian historian James Stayer and American scholar Susannah Heschel have furthermore recently shown how some influential German Lutheran theologians were politically affiliated with National Socialism. For example, Paul Althaus, who allied himself publicly with National Socialism, signed the "Ansbach Memorandum" from June 1934, which was a response to the Barmen Declaration (May 31, 1934). The Ansbach Memorandum, Stayer writes, staked out "an orthodox Lutheran tradition that was pro-Nazi, although distinct from that of the German Christians and their Luther Renaissance advisers."[6] These theologians also made use of particularly theological categories attributed to Luther, for example Karl Holl's idea of the paradox of sacrifice, in order to argue for sacrifice in military terms.[7] Some of them further inscribed Luther's own anti-Judaism into a political-theological antisemitism. Heschel, for example, shows in her work that Lutheran theologians associated with the Jena Institute for the Study and Eradication of Jewish Influence on German Christian Church Life were active in eliminating any references to Hebrew and Judaism in Lutheran song books and to militarize Lutheran piety with images.[8]

If the German Lutheran theologians of the war decades reciprocally related law and gospel for political ends, then the Lutheran theologians of the post-war years sought to completely separate law and gospel. Many theologians in Germany and in North America, some of whom had gone to Germany in order to study with Werner Elert, took up his theological positioning of a sharp distinction between law and gospel as critical to hermeneutics, homiletics, and even ontology. As American Lutheran theologian David Yeago has aptly demonstrated, Elert amplified what Luther understood to be the *in situ* distinction between law and gospel for the purpose of justification into an overarching ontological distinction between church and world, God and human, theology and ethics.[9] For this postwar generation of Lutheran theologians, justification was considered the article by which the church stands and falls, and any attempts to include works, even works contributing to a person's sanctification, were assigned to the rubric of "world" or "ethics," in other words, the realm of God's law and judgment. A strict line was drawn between God and the human, between divine freedom and human captivity, between God as sole agent and human as mere passive recipient of grace. The divine work of justifying the sinner was to be kept theologically distinct from any human work. The accusation of works righteousness was launched against any theological position that assigned merit to human good works prior to justification. The criticism of "third use of the law" was used to deny any salvific dimension to works performed after justification. Any concession to the Calvinist third use of the law tainted the purity of Lutheran doctrine.

The peculiar development in postwar German Lutheran theology and its American counterparts was indeed a hostility to works as either meriting divine judgment in the prohibition required by justification that any work was inconsequential for divine merit, or that any work after justification was inconsequential for justification. A stark distinction between law and gospel served both as the hallmark of the Lutheran contribution to a contemporary American culture in which ethics and theology were already blurred because of Calvinist and evangelical proclivities on the one hand, and Catholic moral teaching on the other hand. The social gospel, a theological position that advocated political action on the basis of moral responsibility to the society of which one was a part, was rejected by Lutheran theologians who insisted on their peculiar identity in American culture in terms of a doctrine of jus-tification without works. While some American Lutheran communities have inherited Pietist tendencies from Norwegian or German origins that empha-size works of goodness for the justified, the dominant Lutheran "doctrine" remained the law/gospel dialectic.

Lutheranism's stubborn and unapologetic stand on grace is especially unique in an American Protestant context in which Reformed, Calvinist, and Wesleyan traditions to varying degrees advocate introspection and action, holiness and perfection, good works and political reform. Lutherans have been the theological holdout for a peculiar position on grace without works, even grace that neglects looking at works. The motto "by grace alone" is sig-nificant in a landscape that tends to merge providence with human action.[10] The Lutheran position is thus inherently critical on this landscape, insisting on divine agency against a dominant theology of grace with works.

Lutheran theologians, however, could not keep silent during the "culture wars" that began in the 1990s. They learned from the grave evils of German Lutherans during the Nazi era. They seized the tools of American democ-racy. Protest and change became central to a new theological formation. Theologians, many of them historically marginalized from church power, identified injustice in church and society as inconsistent with God's plan. As they became more familiar with gender and sexuality studies, with critical race theory and liberation theology, these Lutherans focused the doctrine of sin onto the many injustices experienced by particular persons and communi-ties in America. They became attuned to contemporary American realities in which a decadent capitalism sustains hierarchies that guarantee the value of some over others.

The integration of new areas of critical theory into Lutheran theology and ethics meant that the traditional German theological inheritances required revision. American theologians turned to Nordic Lutheran theologians as interlocutors. The Nordic approach emphasizes created goodness, rather than a world under law.[11] By starting theology with God's pronouncement of good-ness rather than judgment, Nordic theologians draw theological implications for ethics and for a politics of social welfare. As Finnish Luther scholar Antti

Raunio has pointed out, the appropriation of Luther's social theory is productive for the modern welfare state exemplified by the Scandinavian countries.[12] The direction taken by Scandinavian and Finnish theologians is helpful to North American Lutherans looking to fit theology and ethics, doctrine and praxis, into a more coherent frame.

Contemporary Lutheran theologians, particularly those attuned to naming oppression and marginalization, have used their theological platform to prescribe a political agenda, even within the church. Politics do not stop at the entrance to sacred space. The church, by virtue of its existence as a cultural institution within a particular political landscape, participates in the dissemination of common values. Theologians represented in this volume deploy theological critical reason to explain how specific doctrines have exacerbated cultural and political oppressions in the church. Their work is to retrieve the potential of Luther's ethical commitments in his theology of vocation and love of neighbor. A revision orients church and world to God's plan for human and created flourishing.

POLITICS OR CHURCH?

Progressive Lutheran theologians are deeply concerned with justice, and rightly so in a contemporary context in which injustice thrives in lived human experience. These theologians challenge a dominant Lutheran theological model that separates theology from ethics, gospel from law, justification from justice. They insist on new constructions in theology that bring experience into closer proximity to theological claims, and thereby situate the gospel more closely with the reality of healing that is promised. Justification tracks the arc of history bent toward justice.

The question I am interested in pursuing concerns the aim and task of theology. How do Lutheran theologians with their new approach understand the task of theology? Or in other words, *What is theology for?* Until recently, Lutheran theologians have identified their task in Luther's own terms: to reflect on the justifying God and the human sinner in a particular relation of grace that is given as gift to the human recipient. The particular Lutheran inflection of the theological task was to insist on the *vita passiva* as the way in which humans exist as objects of divine grace. Yet the image of the passive human, as these theologians concur, is not an accurate representation of the reality of human living in the world. Human freedom "below" salvation indeed occupies the entire span of personal and corporate life. Contemporary Lutheran theologians are now interested in the many aspects of human existence submerged by the former preoccupation with the *vita passiva*, namely the *vita activa*.

Emphasis on the *vita activa* facilitates a constructive theological direction that includes reflection on the political reality of justice articulated in the Universal Declaration of Human Rights. The Lutheran theologians in this volume agree that a key text by Luther for embarking on this path is the second part of the 1520 Freedom treatise. Overy-Brown, for example, takes up this text—the section on the "outer" dimension of the Christian—and works out a theological theory of Christian agency. Faith is necessarily connected to love, just as inner is to outer, theory to praxis. The justified Christian is oriented toward a world in which moral agency embodies freedom in neighborly love. The Christian lives in the world of concrete social and political relations; the gospel is made real through the enactment of agency. The object of divine agency is a political agent in the world.

The question I want to raise at this point is one of emphasis. Has the critical take on the pernicious inheritances of German Lutheran theology resulted in too much of a correction? Has the contemporary emphasis on orienting Luther's theology of grace to political theology missed a significant dimension of *theology*? Theology's classical task, articulated by Schleiermacher in the early nineteenth century, is constructed through its aim in prescribing outcomes for an institution existing outside the academy, namely the church. The discipline of theology is identified by its task in equipping church leaders with the knowledge and theory of practical knowledge to administer to the church for the purpose of its flourishing. According to Schleiermacher, the specific disciplines learned in an academic setting have a combined purpose of garnering knowledge of the church through past and present critical analysis. Theology is not exclusively theoretical, nor solely practical, but a "positive science" attuned to the church's reality.[13]

The question concerns the way in which progressive Lutheran theologians deploy the second half of the treatise on Christian Freedom. Is this section on the "outer Christian" to be understood in view of the Christian in the church or the Christian in the world? How are the two spheres of agency to be negotiated? The question of the reality of the Christian agent is at stake, and specifically the way in which theology must give an account of that reality.

Luther's theological reforms entailed ethics. This is the significant constructive-theological contribution of the Lutheran theologians represented in this volume. The Christian life, originally freed by Christ, consists of the vocation lived out in service to the other. Christian freedom endows the self with a selflessness that orients the self to respond wholeheartedly to the needs of the other. The externalization of Christian freedom occurs in church and world. But does this externalization in church and world imply different ways of realizing Christian freedom? Is there a distinction to be made in terms of agency in the church and agency in the world? Further, if the theological preoccupation is solely with politics, then what happens to a theology that, at some level, must address human failing in the political realm? When does theology get real with the gospel?

The political direction proposed by progressive Lutheran theologians is important for both church and world. Yet the danger of collapsing theology into political theology needs to be addressed. Can theology retain a contemplative moment that has its own integrity? Theology as a critical discipline has a mandate to identify sin and evil and point to hope that is available as a free gift through distinctive ritual. As a constructive discipline, theology explains how new insights into personhood and system, critical theory and cognitive science can be integrated into theological theory of sin and grace, immanence and transcendence, freedom and justice. My concern, however, is to retain a contemplative dimension to theology. Can theology identify places of resistance, transcendence, and redemption without immediate absorption into a political modality? Does a theological theory of redemption have its own contemplative integrity apart from political prescription? At the very least, I think it important that theologians reserve a contemplative moment for Jesus' witness to the imminent kingdom of God without too quickly moving to action in bringing it about. Theology has a task of deploying critical reason on the basis of disengagement between subject and object. Critical reason is thus free to imagine possibilities for human existence, and to construct modes of engagement. From this contemplative distance from politics, theologians can then also reflect on the distinction between church and world, and the difference in theological prescription that each area entails. Even if church has become optional for some theologians—and indeed it has, particularly for theologians depressed by what they see as the abdication of any intellectual accountability in proclaiming the gospel—it still has historically functioned as the institution in relation to which theology has developed as a discipline. Any premature foreclosing of the church in favor of politics in the world— even in the name of a theologian who has been disappointed over and over again by the mediocrity reigning in the church—does not do full justice to theology's historical task of speaking about God to the church.

PERNICIOUS DOCTRINES?

One of theology's tasks is the production of doctrine, in both a critical and a constructive register. As the contributors to this volume agree, the critical aspect is significant in Lutheran theology because of particular German inheritances that have historically been paired with abusive tendencies. Work has begun in unearthing and analyzing this past. Yet theological work must continue to identify aspects of doctrines that have the propensity for pernicious application. Knowledge of where Luther's doctrines have come from, why they have been deemed significant, and how they have historically been deployed are important issues when considering which doctrines are helpful in guiding contemporary Christian belief and praxis.

A recent insight into the function of Luther's person for the history of the West is key. Much Lutheran theology has been vested in a Luther who inaugurated modernity with his ideas of freedom, individual courage, and a common priesthood. Yet, on closer examination, these key ideas are seen to be the products of particular early twentieth-century German Lutheran theologians.[14] For thinkers such as Karl Holl and Reinhold Seeberg, Luther was not the late medieval Catholic working out church reforms with trepidation. Luther was the bold male figure whose reforms made him the first hero of modernity. Much rests on promoting this myth of the modern Luther. Protestant identity, theories of the modern self, freedom from authority, and even democracy and human rights have all in some ways been tied to the modern narrative with Luther at the origins. According to this interpretation, Luther is not a reformer of the church, but of religion *per se*. Luther's particular mysticism, his terrifying experience of God, and his paradoxical experience of divine love under this terror inform Luther's religion that bypassed Catholicism and place him in the pantheon of religious innovators, among them Jesus and Paul. The German Lutherans made religious-cultural use of this particular Luther. As Bismarck unified the German states under the Prussian flag and as academic colleagues made arguments on behalf of Germany as a modern nation, Lutheran theologians saw Luther as symbol of modern religion.

Particularly pernicious was the implication of Luther's religion for ethics that Holl advanced. Holl was concerned with the distinct kind of modernity that the German Luther represented. He qualified modernity as freedom from the law. Taking seriously the ethical idea from Luther's Freedom treatise that love spontaneously flows from inner freedom, Holl oriented a Lutheran ethic to a love that knows no law. An ethic of love cannot be prescribed; love knows no laws. It can only be lived under the conditions of society, culture, and politics. As such, it does not add a prescriptive dimension, but infuses society, culture, and politics with a distinctive ethos. The modern ethos as Holl envisioned it could also be mustered in a state of exception. Love as the "teleological suspension of the ethical" could be exploited in a fascist context in which love as sacrifice could be taken in a military sense.[15] Because there was no criterion for determining the concrete content in the Lutheran ethic of love, merely freedom as inner motivation for external expression of love of an abstract neighbor, the idea was prone to the nationalist interpretation that Holl assigned to it. It was after all Holl, the father of the Luther Renaissance, who joined the *Deutsche Vaterlandspartei* in 1917 and influenced a generation of

Lutheran theologians who allied themselves to varying degrees with National Socialist interests.[16]

We know that the "German Luther" was on the wrong side of history. But in contemporary corrections of this Luther, what orienting principles can be used? If the Luther who is coopted for generating ethics and politics that serve a justice-oriented agenda is precisely the Luther who was created by the Germans in the first place—the progenitor of modernity—then a more careful analysis of how particular themes in Luther, even love, were used during the Third Reich for purposes very different from what contemporary theologians mean by them.

CONSTRUCTIVE LUTHERAN THEOLOGY

Luther at the origin of modernity is a fiction created by particular early twentieth-century German Lutheran theologians. It is time to put this Luther to rest. As scholars carefully study Luther through historical-critical lens, they are creating new possibilities for theology and ethics with potential for constructive theology today. The current approach entails a twofold task. On the one hand, Lutheran theologians must take seriously the research carved out by proponents of the "medieval Luther" in order to better understand the theological categories Luther used, such as vocation, love, and the cross, as products of his own struggles to articulate his understanding in relation to inherited medieval meanings.[17] On the other hand, Lutheran theologians must continue to acknowledge and study categories in which German Lutherans received Luther for their particular theological and political programs in the first decades of the twentieth century. Both tasks must be critical, figuring out the theological tendencies that have the potential for being used for abusive ends; both tasks must be constructive, working out possibilities for seeing God's good will for created reality. This important historical and constructive theological effort is the task of the *vita contemplativa*. Without serious contemplation, the possibilities for justice-creating visions and policies run the risk of forgetting the theological dimensions at stake.

Crucial for going forward is to take seriously Luther's reforms for the church that differ from his prescriptions for the world. Luther was a late medieval Catholic priest whose most exigent concerns were with the church's falsification of the gospel through its affiliation with "worldliness."[18] He directed his reforms primarily to the church. Even his theory about economic justice was first and foremost a theological theory to be practiced in the church.[19] Justice within the church, according to Luther, is predicated on specific theological criteria having to do with the church's essential mission in communicating and distributing the gospel. An ethics of the church for the world is based on a kind of justice that is distinctly political, and operates through political mechanisms. A contemporary assessment of the generativity of Luther for contemporary justice-seeking initiatives—and this fruitfulness is truly explored in this volume's essays—cannot be done at the expense of foreclosing dimensions of Luther's thinking that are intently focused on Christ and the church. A premature jump to consider political justice elides the important theological difference between church and world. The effect exposes progressive Christianity to a weak ecclesiology and theological arguments that are reducible to political prescription. The *vita contemplativa* must be preserved as some moment in the theological process. It holds open the theological task of historical and analytic rigor and the theoretical imagination in proposing new words and models for orienting faith and morals, thinking and praxis. Considering this *vita*, at the very least, invites contemporary constructive Lutheran theologians to remember that the church/world distinction is theologically significant.

Theological commitment is directed to the church, in which priesthood and laity embody the spirit of Christ in personal and communal ways. The church is after all the place in which Christians are called to speak the reality of Christ-created wholeness and peace. Theologians must keep the church focused on its mission, and ensure that Christ's supernatural benefits are communicated to and experienced in ordinary lives.

Taking Luther's Catholic perspective into account is a desideratum given the scholarly direction that distances the modern German Luther from his late medieval Catholic template. It behooves contemporary Lutheran theologians to remind their readers that the Catholic Luther is the one who is, in fact, appropriated for modern purposes. When Riswold points to "Christian experience," does she include Catholic experience? When Overy-Brown writes about politics, does this include a Catholic dimension? Lutheran theologians today cannot pretend that the 1999 Joint Declaration on the Doctrine of Justification was never signed. As the most significant ecumenical dialogue in contemporary times, its theological and political implications must be integrated, at some level, into contemporary Lutheran thinking. The western schism is in some way irrevocably associated with Martin Luther. Contemporary Lutheran theologians thus must recognize in their writing that Roman Catholics have continued to exist since the sixteenth century and have contributed to the making of the modern West in ways that are significant. For too long, Luther has been coopted as a progenitor of modernity along a supercessionist historiography that has conceptually left Catholics in the Middle Ages. As thinkers have come up with accounts of modernity, they have tended to do so with a forgetfulness that negotiations of Protestant-Catholic relations are a contemporary reality. Concepts considered exclusively Protestant, such the priesthood of all believers, vocation, and community, are actually on closer look embedded deep within medieval Catholic thinking. Theologians working constructively with these themes should at some level acknowledge their indebtedness to the Catholic tradition.

The exciting development in Lutheran theology is precisely its constructive orientation. For too long, Lutheran theologians have been hampered by the historical method that their predecessors in Germany had championed. Yet theologians are freeing themselves from this methodological restriction, while tailoring its critical intention for constructive purposes, both theological and political. Contemporary politics is important to theological work. Particularly today, the political climate requires urgent acknowledgment by theologians. Yet even as politically attuned, they are *theologians*. When politics fails abysmally at its task to achieve justice—as it inevitably will because humans are involved—theologians will still have a message about the just God. When politics is unable to make real the ideals articulated by the Universal Human Declaration of Human Rights, theologians will still have their task to witness to the reality in the living God who is the guarantee of success. God's plan for justice will not fail. It is this hope that contemporary Lutheran theologians interested in political theology must keep alive.

NOTES

1. *Political Theology* (1999 to present), accessed January 5, 2020, https://www.tandfonline.com/loi/ypot20.

2. *Political Theology Network*, accessed January 5, 2020, https://politicaltheology.com/.

3. Recently, for example, the "Emerging Scholars in Political Theology," *Political Theology* Network, accessed January 5, 2020, https://politicaltheology.com/call-for-participants-emerging-scholars-in-political-theology-2020-2021/.

4. Such as The North American Lutheran Church (NALC), accessed January 5, 2020, https://thenalc.org/; and its seminary, The North American Lutheran Seminary, accessed January 5, 2020, https://www.thenals.org/; Lutheran Coalition for Renewal (CORE), accessed January 5, 2020, http://lutherancore.website/.

5. For a detailed account of Hirsch's position, see James M. Stayer, *Martin Luther, German Saviour: German Evangelical Theological Factions and the Interpretation of Luther, 1917–1933*, McGill-Queen's Studies in the History of Religion (Montreal/Kingston: McGill/Queen's University Press, 2000); Susannah Heschel, *The Aryan Jesus: Christian Theologians and the Bible in Nazi Germany* (Princeton, NJ: Princeton University Press, 2010).

6. Stayer, *German Saviour*, 131.

7. See my *How Luther Became the Reformer* (Louisville, KY: Westminster John Knox, 2019), 80–81.

8. Heschel, *Aryan Jesus*, 106–65 (ch. 3).

9. David S. Yeago, "Gnosticism, Antinomianism, and Reformation Theology: Reflections on the Costs of a Construal," *Pro Ecclesia* 2, no.1 (Winter 1993): 37–49.

10. For a detailed argument see my "Providence: A Deflationary Mandate," in *Divine Action and Providence: Explorations in Constructive Dogmatics*, ed. Fred Sanders and Oliver Crisp (Grand Rapids, MI: Zondervan, 2019), 76–97.

11. For a recent edited volume outlining "Scandinavian Creation Theology," see Niels Henrik Gregersen, Bengt Kristensson Uggla, and Trygve Wyller, eds., *Reformation Theology for a Post-Secular Age: Logstrup, Prenter, Wingren, and the Future of Scandinavian Creation Theology*, Research in Contemporary Religion 24 (Göttingen: Vandenhoeck & Ruprecht, 2017).

12. Antti Raunio, "Searching for the Neighbor's Good: Luther's Social Theory in the Contemporary World," in *The Global Luther: A Theologian for Modern Times*, ed. Christine Helmer (Minneapolis, MN: Fortress Press, 2009), 210–27.

13. For more on Friedrich Schleiermacher's definition of theology as a positive science, see his *Brief Outline of Theology As a Field of Study*, 3rd ed., essays and notes by Terrance N. Tice (Louisville, KY: Westminster John Knox Press, 2011).

14. See my *How Luther Became the Reformer*.

15. For a treatment of the "teleological suspension of the ethical" see Søren Kierkegaard, *Fear and Trembling*, trans. Alistair Hannay (New York: Penguin Books, 1985), 83–95.

16. For a detailed account, see ch. 4 of my *How Luther Became the Reformer*.

17. See Christine Helmer, ed., *The Medieval Luther*, Spätmittelalter, Humanismus, Reformation/Studies in Late Middle Ages, Humanism, and the Reformation 113 (Tübingen: Mohr Siebeck, 2020).

18. For a detailed analysis of Luther's criticism of priestly worldliness, see my essay "The Priesthood and Its Critics," ch. 15 in *The Medieval Luther*.

19. See lectures 28 and 29 of my free massive open online course (MOOC), "Luther and the West"; Coursera, accessed February 27, 2021, www.coursera.org/learn/luther-and-the-west.

BIBLIOGRAPHY

"Emerging Scholars in Political Theology." *Political Theology Network*. Accessed January 5, 2020. https://politicaltheology.com/call-for-participants-emerging-scholars-in-political-theology-2020-2021/.

Gregersen, Niels Henrik, Bengt Kristensson Uggla and Trygve Wyller, eds. *Reformation Theology for a Post-Secular Age: Logstrup, Prenter, Wingren, and the Future of Scandinavian Creation Theology*, Research in Contemporary Religion 24. Göttingen: Vandenhoeck & Ruprecht, 2017.

Helmer, Christine. *How Luther Became the Reformer*. Louisville, KY: Westminster John Knox Press, 2019.

———. "Luther and the West"; Coursera, accessed February 27, 2021, www.coursera.org/learn/luther-and-the-west.

————. "Providence: A Deflationary Mandate." In *Divine Action and Providence: Explorations in Constructive Dogmatics*, edited by Fred Sanders and Oliver Crisp, 76–97. Grand Rapids, MI: Zondervan, 2019.

————, ed. *The Medieval Luther*, Spätmittelalter, Humanismus, Reformation/Studies in Late Middle Ages, Humanism, and the Reformation 113 (Tübingen: Mohr Siebeck, 2020).

Heschel, Susannah. *The Aryan Jesus: Christian Theologians and the Bible in Nazi Germany.* Princeton, NJ: Princeton University Press, 2010.

Kierkegaard, Søren. *Fear and Trembling*, translated by Alistair Hannay. New York: Penguin Books, 1985.

Lutheran Coalition for Renewal (CORE). Accessed January 5, 2020. http://lutherancore.website/.

The North American Lutheran Church (NALC). Accessed January 5, 2020. https://thenalc.org/.

The North American Lutheran Seminary. Accessed January 5, 2020. https://www.thenals.org/.

Political Theology (1999 to present). Accessed January 5, 2020. https://www.tandfonline.com/loi/ypot20.

Political Theology Network. Accessed January 5, 2020. https://politicaltheology.com/.

Raunio, Antti. "Searching for the Neighbor's Good: Luther's Social Theory in the Contemporary World." In *The Global Luther: A Theologian for Modern Times*, edited by Christine Helmer, 210–27. Minneapolis, MN: Fortress Press, 2009.

Schleiermacher, Friedrich, *Brief Outline of Theology As a Field of Study*, 3rd ed., essays and notes by Terrance N. Tice. Louisville, KY: Westminster John Knox Press, 2011.

Stayer, James M. *Martin Luther, German Saviour: German Evangelical Theological Factions and the Interpretation of Luther, 1917–1933*, McGill-Queen's Studies in the History of Religion. Montreal/Kingston: McGill/Queen's University Press, 2000.

Yeago, David S. "Gnosticism, Antinomianism, and Reformation Theology: Reflections on the Costs of a Construal." *Pro Ecclesia* 2, no.1 (Winter 1993): 37–49.

Index

About the Editors and Contributors

Anthony Bateza is an associate professor of religion at St. Olaf College in Northfield, Minnesota, and an ordained minister in the Evangelical Lutheran Church in America. A specialist in Martin Luther, moral theology, and Christian ethics, Dr. Bateza examines Luther's understanding of human agency and his relationship with the virtue tradition in his research. His other scholarly interests include the broader Augustinian tradition; the impact of Luther's thought on nineteenth-century philosophy; and questions of race, identity, and social justice.

Christine Helmer holds the Peter B. Ritzma Chair of Humanities and is professor of German and religious studies at Northwestern University in Evanston, Illinois. She was awarded an honorary doctorate in theology from the University of Helsinki in 2017. She is the editor of *The Medieval Luther*, published in 2020, and the author of *The Trinity and Martin Luther* (2nd edition, 2017), *Theology and the End of Doctrine* (2014), and *How Luther Became the Reformer* (2019). Her massive open online course (MOOC) "Luther and the West" is free online at coursera.org/learn/luther-and-the-west. Her current book project is on theology in the contemporary research university.

Allen G. Jorgenson is assistant dean and holds the William D. Huras Chair in Ecclesiology and Church History at Martin Luther University College at Wilfrid Laurier University in Waterloo, Ontario. He is the author of *Indigenous and Christian Perspectives in Dialogue: Kairotic Place and Borders* (Lexington, 2021), coeditor (with Hussam S. Timani and Alexander Y. Hwang) of *Strangers in This World: Multireligious Reflections on Immigration* (Fortress, 2015), and cotranslator (with Iain G. Nicol) of *Jesus' Life in Dying: Friedrich Schleiermacher's Pre-Easter Reflections to the Community of the Redeemer* (2020). He is especially interested in comparative theology and the insights that indigenous traditions afford Christian theology.

Kristen E. Kvam is professor of theology at Saint Paul School of Theology in Greater Kansas City and Oklahoma City, where she teaches courses in the fields of constructive Christian theology; engaging world religions; and women, society, and church studies. Christian doctrine, scriptural interpretation, and Luther studies form primary concerns of her scholarship. Coeditor of *Eve and Adam: An Anthology of Jewish, Christian, and Muslim Readings on Genesis and Gender,* Kris recently wrote commentaries on Luther's text addressed to women who knew tragedy in childbearing and in his preface to the psalms for the Annotated Luther series. She is currently working with Don Saliers on a theological commentary on the psalms for the Belief Series by Westminster John Knox Press.

Mary Elise Lowe is professor of religion at Augsburg University in Minneapolis, Minnesota. Her teaching and research focus on contemporary, LGBTQIA+, Martin Luther's, and disability theologies. Her most recent chapters and articles include "The Queer Body-Mind in Martin Luther's Theology: From Subaltern Sodomite to Embodied *Imago Dei*" in *The Alternative Luther: Lutheran Theology from the Subaltern* (Lexington/Fortress Academic, 2019) and "From the Same Spirit: Receiving the Gifts of Transgender Christians," which was published in *Dialogue: A Journal of Theology.* In her work and teaching, Lowe generates scholarship that is both accessible and academic.

Robert Overy-Brown is a doctoral candidate in philosophy of religion and theology at Claremont Graduate University. His research interests are in expanding the scope of political theologies toward methodological and practical pluralism. He teaches theology, philosophy, and ethics with special emphasis in contemporary thought in Los Angeles, California.

Mary Philip (a.k.a. Joy) is associate professor of Lutheran Global Theologies and Mission at Martin Luther University College at Wilfrid Laurier University in Waterloo, Ontario, and the director of the Center for Earth Consciousness and Gender Justice. A native of India, she taught zoology there prior to obtaining her doctorate in theology. She is passionate about contextual theology and ecojustice, brings together ecology and theology in her vocation, and is dedicated to promoting ecologically informed theological education. Editor in chief of *Consensus: A Canadian Journal of Public Theology*, her writings and involvements are evidence of her commitment to decolonization and racial justice, where doing theology is not only an intellectual exercise but also a practice. Her most recent work is a coedited volume with Chad Rimmer and Tom S. Tomren, *Religion, Sustainability and Education: Pedagogy, Perspectives and Praxis towards Ecological Sustainability.*

Caryn D. Riswold, PhD, is professor of religion and the Mike and Marge McCoy Family Distinguished Chair in Lutheran Heritage and Mission at Wartburg College in Waverly, Iowa. She is the author of many essays and articles as well as three books, including *Feminism and Christianity: Questions and Answers in the Third Wave* (2009).

Terra Schwerin Rowe is assistant professor in the Philosophy and Religion Department at the University of North Texas. Her work has focused on critical analyses of and constructive proposals for Protestant thought from the perspective of environmental and feminist concerns. Her book *Toward a Better Worldliness: Economy, Ecology and the Protestant Tradition* was published with Fortress in 2017. Her current project on extraction, gender, and theology will be published in 2022.

Benjamin Taylor is a PhD candidate in systematic theology at the Lutheran School of Theology at Chicago. His dissertation aims to develop the political and cultural significance of the idol in Luther's theology.

Marit A. Trelstad is the university chair of Lutheran studies and professor of constructive and Lutheran theologies at Pacific Lutheran University in Tacoma, Washington. Her scholarly work combines feminist, process, and Lutheran theologies. She wrote *Cross Examinations: Readings on the Meaning of the Cross Today* (Fortress, 2006) and contributed chapters to *Luther from the SubAltern: The Alternative Luther* (Lexington/Fortress Academic, 2019), *Theological and Ethical Perspectives on Climate Engineering* (Rowman & Littlefield, 2016), *Transformative Lutheran Theologies* (Fortress, 2010), *Lutherrenaissance: Past and Present* (2014), *Theologies of Creation: Creatio Ex Nihilo and Its New Rivals* (2014), and *Creating Women's Theology: A Movement Engaging Process Thought* (2011).

www.ingramcontent.com/pod-product-compliance
Lightning Source LLC
Chambersburg PA
CBHW022312280326
41932CB00010B/1077